P9-BXY-977

بسم الله الرحمن الرحيم

Baghdad Bound:

An Interpreter's Chronicles of the Iraq War

Mohammed Fadel Fahmy

Order this book online at www.trafford.com
or email orders@trafford.com

Most Trafford titles are also available at major online book retailers.

Print information available on the last page.

ISBN: 978-1-4120-1911-8 (sc)

Trafford rev. 01/15/2020

www.trafford.com

North America & international
toll-free: 1 888 232 4444 (USA & Canada)
fax: 812 355 4082

Dedication

To my parents with love
To Adel & Sherif

To the Sons of Al-Rafidin

Table of Contents

This is not a Preface, actually, it's more of a pre*chapter* where I will explain how I ended up working as an interpreter in a war zone not long after arriving in Kuwait from Canada. I want the reader to know first and foremost that this book is told with an accurate notion of respect to every single person I encountered in Iraq. In Iraq I extracted quotes and feelings from the simple Iraqi Bedouin and the most sophisticated coalition members and their associates. There are no exaggerations or alterations to the facts. I feel it is my duty to entertain you with the following true story I stumbled upon during the pre-war days in Kuwait. I like to write in my spare time, I am not a professional but I think that what I witnessed during those four chaotic months in Kuwait and Iraq is a story that hasn't been told, one that's worth telling.

Two months into my new marketing job at Kuwait University, I was already wondering how to refresh what had become a monotonous daily routine. I decided to make use of a TESOL certificate I got in Canada and teach English to teenage students at night school. I also joined a local gym to stay in shape, but I was still restless. At that time everyone sensed that the war was looming and Kuwait was probably the most exciting and terrifying place to be during the build-up. My Iraqi girlfriend, a graduate of media studies, was looking for work in the field of journalism and was eager to be at the frontlines of what was happening. During my free time I took it upon myself to fish out some leads for her and quickly found myself rubbing shoulders with big names from high-profile news agencies like CNN and the BBC.

Of course the search for the invisible weapons of mass destruction and the possibility of war in Iraq were prime topics for discussion. Small talk at the gym I went to mostly revolved around the rising political tension in the region. Between sets and in the locker rooms names of *war heroes* like Collin Powell, George Bush, and *villains* like Saddam rang through my ears as I tried to listen to the average Kuwaiti interpret the daily news. Like Saddam Hussein, I did not think this war would materialize. Expecting things would remain relatively calm, I insisted on finding a media job for my girlfriend.

One day I found this ad in the classified section of the Al Seyassah Kuwaiti daily newspaper:

Fluent English speakers required for a new business company
Please call 688-XXXX.

The ad did not move me but it sure did excite an unemployed friend of mine. He immediately called me at work with news that the job pays anything from $1500 to $5000 per month, depending on work experience. He also informed me that the employer's accent sounded American and for me, that was a sign that this would be a professional well-organized company. I decided to call the number out of curiosity. It sounded easy, as all it required was a good command of the English language. Upon making the initial phone call the man on the receiving end identified himself as 'Isaac'. He simply recorded my name, citizenship, mobile number, and then briefly asked me about my current salary and position. His answer to my only question was as vague as the placement ad: "We are a business advising company. Someone will contact you soon to set up an interview."

During the next three days I landed a job with the Los Angles Times through the wife of a CNN producer working with me in Kuwait University. The Times needed someone immediately as a translator-fixer for their reporting in Kuwait and the job paid well, so I decided to take it.

This took place in February and in Kuwait February is a month of jubilation. It hosts the country's Independence and Liberation days on the 25th and the 26th. Along with the thousands of troops filing into Kuwait, the country was gripped by a sort of mild hysteria with the arrival of hundreds of journalists, chemical weapons experts, and crisis management teams from Europe and the U.S. Word that Saddam was expected to use his weapons of mass destruction in the case of war ignited a new form of unity among the residents of the country. People were frantically sharing information on how to combat biological and chemical weapons. Back at the University, a shelter was set up and students were bombarded with flyers with detailed facts on different chemical agents, how to use the gas mask and canisters, and the fastest route to take towards the shelter should there be an attack. The major dilemma on everyone's minds was weather to stay in Kuwait or just take off.

While working on a Times story about entrepreneurs in Kuwait affected by the possible war, my cell phone rang and the name "Isaac *Shady*" (as I had saved it) flashed on my caller id. The interview was set for the next day in the Hashimi Hall of the SAS Hotel at 10:00 am, and I was told there would be a translation exam. After I hung up with Isaac, I continued our Times interview with "King Hummer," a Kuwaiti businessman profiting from his unprecedented sales of used Hummers to media broadcasting stations. Before the war King Hummer was selling an average of four vehicles a month, mainly to members of the Al-Sabah Kuwaiti royal family. This month in particular he had already sold thirty Hummers. I was not surprised to learn that CNN had purchased four of these heavy-duty and expensive vehicles.

That morning outside the SAS, I had never seen such extensive security checks in my life. I was hoping this mysterious business firm had posted signs with a company name, but there was nothing available. Upon reaching the examination hall, I waited with a diverse crowd of twenty-six people: Bankers, college students, retired men and women eager to pass this translation exam. The friend who had told me about the position registered for the later examination session, noon that day, in hopes that he could get tips from me.

Sure enough, the shady Isaac showed up and invited everyone to enter the lavishly red-carpeted Hashimi conference room. I watched the small built man carefully adjust his glasses as he led us in following his two female assistants. I appreciated the importance of confidentiality involved with recruitment, but the company did not even present their name on the application form everyone was filling. Once again, Isaac proved his shiftiness as he responded to our questions with ultimate ambiguity. A few minutes later, his African-American assistant walked in quietly with a stern headmistress look on her face as she collected our applications and passport photocopies. There seemed to be a lack of organization as I saw Isaac argue with his other European assistant about where to put the resumes she had collected from all the candidates.

As one of the ladies handed out the short English exam sheets, Isaac's cell phone rang interrupting the silence in the room. My eyes were perched on him when he walked over to the corner of the room. His hush-hush responses sounded scripted:

"I am at location *A* now. Just stay there with my boys at location *C*...Tell me their first names only. "

We had twenty minutes to translate eight sentences from Arabic to English and everyone in the room was noticeably nervous. The overtly political nature of the statements caught everyone off guard. Here is a glimpse at some of the sentences:

1) North Koreans may be well on their way to building additional nuclear weapons.
2) Tony Blair yesterday acknowledged that Arabs believe the West is indifferent to the Palestinian issue.
3) Globalization has been sped up by technology and its traditional notions of sovereign nation-state powers.

Upon completing the short multiple choice English exam, Isaac approached me and shook my hand. My Lebanese friend had established a warmer relationship with him and had informed him that we were buddies. Not only was Isaac excited about my American accent and education, but he also knew my nickname: Moody. He came closer and whispered in my ears: *I have a feeling you will be one of our stars*. Indeed, I was weirded out. I had no clue what he was talking about.

I waited outside with the rest of the candidates for the oral test. I watched Isaac conduct his quick interviews, typing notes about each applicant on to his lap-top. An older man approached me with the same question I couldn't get out of my head: "Why is a business company using terms like nuclear and Saddam Hussein in their exam?"

When my turn came for the oral test, Isaac looked at me and said, "I don't need to test your skills."

"So what is your last name," I asked him.

"It's irrelevant...so where'd you get the nickname Moody?"

"I got in high school as an athlete. I used to get fired up on the basket ball court and performed better when I got *moody*."

"You have a dual citizenship, right?" Isaac asked.

"Yes. I am Egyptian-Canadian."

"We'll call you sometime this week for a second interview."

By now, the stress in Kuwait was at its maximum. Expatriates were flooding back to their countries in fear of Saddam Hussein. Most companies had contingency plans and the ones that did not, just preferred to close down until further notice. Many citizens and residents still scarred from the Iraqi invasion in '91 preferred to leave rather than get stuck behind for months like in the first Gulf War. The situation at home was also extremely tense. My mother would not leave without my father, while my kid brother insisted on heading out to Egypt. When we received an alarming email from the Canadian Embassy, my mother purchased plane tickets for her, my brothers, and the maid. The Ambassador's message was clear:

Dear Sir, Madam,

February 15, 2003

Further to my message of January 31st, I am writing to you today to inform you that the Department of Foreign Affairs and International Trade has revised its advice to Canadians regarding Kuwait. It now recommends that Canadians should not travel to Kuwait. Canadians in Kuwait should consider departing if their presence is not essential. In light of our concerns over the security situation, I have authorized the departure of dependants of Canadian staff at the Embassy. I suggest that you seriously consider departing if you and your family's presence in Kuwait are not essential. I would be grateful if you would inform the Embassy or your district Warden of your decision as soon as possible.

While the decision to leave the area is your own, you should be aware that the longer you delay the more difficult it might be to leave through commercial means. The security situation in Kuwait could change rapidly without notice, and could affect services, including the reduction or suspension, of commercial air transport. The Embassy can not provide special transport for you or your family and, should conditions worsen, we may not be able to provide assistance to you and your family. The cost of your departure is your personal responsibility. Heightened tensions as a result of the Iraq situation, together with increased threats globally from terrorism, including the possible use of non-conventional weapons, put Canadians at risk. In the event of a conflict in Iraq, the threat will increase significantly and Canadians in Kuwait and elsewhere in the region will be subject to more stringent security measures. Recent criminal and terrorist incidents have also raised the possibility of increased dangers. Canadians who choose to remain in Kuwait despite this advice should maintain a high level of personal security awareness at all times as the security situation could deteriorate rapidly without notice. Exercise extreme caution, particularly in commercial, public, and tourist areas frequented by foreigners. Canadians should monitor local developments, avoid crowds and demonstrations, as well as register and remain in regular contact with the Canadian Embassy in Kuwait.

I ask you to provide a copy of this letter to any Canadian citizen that you know.

Richard Mann
Ambassador

The following days were full of action and anxiety. I juggled work at the University and set up interviews for the Times. I had also established a very intimate paranoia with my cell phone.

As I was trying to track down some female activists in Kuwait for a Times story on women's rights, I realized that it could well be "impossible" to ever see women voting in Kuwait. On the same story, I was able to reach a member of the Al Shaiji family who happened to be a leader in the Islamic Salfi movement in Kuwait. He was outspokenly anti-Western and looked like any American's worst nightmare with his Bin Ladinesque beard. When we reached his luxurious home for the interview, the man refused to communicate with the Times reporters in English but let me translate his well-fumed words against allowing women to vote in Kuwait. At one point Tony Perry, the Times Staff writer excused himself to use the bathroom and returned with a huge grin. He later told us that he had spotted posters of Madonna and Michael Jackson on the walls of his daughter's room.

Later on that week, "Isaac Shady" flashed on my Nokia's screen while I was giving an English lesson at 9:00 pm. He informed me in his serious tone that I was one of the fifty candidates who passed the test.

"You still don't want to reveal the company's name?" I asked.

"International Business Advisors"

"Ok. Isaac what is the nature of the job exactly?"

"You will accompany business men across the Gulf and translate for them. We have two interview sessions tomorrow at the Sheraton, at noon or 6:00 pm."

"I will be there at 6:00 pm," I confirmed.

After I hung up I stared at my students replaying the conversation in my head, still not convinced of this man's reasoning or tone of voice. His pitch was unsettling. If this was a business company then why was the test filled with political statements?

The next day, I walked into the reception of the Sheraton on time and followed the sign stating "International Business Advisors." This time our mysterious hosts provided a light dessert buffet accompanied by the usual coffee and tea. Isaac sat conducting oral interviews in the corner of the room while his assistants roamed the room silently. My Lebanese-Canadian friend and I sat scanning the scene with total skepticism. When my turn came, Isaac shook my hand then led me to his lap-top. His questions were very normal; a bit on my work experience, one or two questions about my education. Then he asked me a question that caught me way off guard.

"Have you ever been arrested in the United States of America?" I had never gotten into any sort of legal trouble in the U.S. I answered no.

On our drive back home my friend and I shared our information on this short interview.

"What did you say when he asked about the arrest?" I asked.

"I lied and said no. How would he find out anyway?"

"I don't know man. These guys seem really sketchy."

"Have you ever been arrested in the *U.S.*?"

"Maybe they need translators for the U.S. army"

"Could be, but, I read in the paper that the U.S. army hired only Kuwaiti translators with prior military experience," I added.

We stopped at another police barricade in a city preparing for an inevitable war.

As he dropped me home he looked back and yelled, "I hope they are the U.S. army! They pay six hundred dollars a day! We could be rich very soon!"

A week later, Isaac's phone call disrupted my sleep. He apologized for waking me up so early in the morning on a Friday, my cherished weekend.

"Could you come to the Marriott tomorrow for the last interview?"

"What time?"

"Just be at the reception at 10:00 am. It will be a long interview. Someone will find you when you arrive," Isaac added, with more elusiveness.

"Does this job include traveling to Iraq?" I asked sleepily.

"Why do you say that?" he asked, with a chuckle in his voice.

"Just wondering, considering the situation now and all."

"Tomorrow we will have a long talk. Bring your passport with you please."

The next morning at the Marriott I was calm, wearing my favorite shirt and tie in anticipation for the final interview. Still, there was no sign to follow or any indication of this business company. I quickly scanned the faces of the few people sitting in the reception, but could not find Isaac among them. However, my gaze fell on a tall bulky man, who at first glance looked like he was simply sitting down and reading his newspaper. Upon closer inspection it seemed more like he was pretending to read the newspaper; a front for a stakeout operation. Again, the scene was all too reminiscent of a spy movie. My instinct was right. The man stood up, folded the paper, and approached me with a smile saying,

"Are you Mohamed Fahmy?"

"Yes."

"I am Mike. Isaac and the team are waiting for you upstairs."

I almost burst out laughing at the man's cool attitude as men called Mike usually didn't tend to have his heavy Arabic accent and dark features.

He looked more like an Ahmed or Hassan. I had to ask him during the walk to the elevator:

"So where are you from Mike?"

"I am French."

"*Tu parles Francais*?"

"No. I am not French. I am German," he replied, with a smile.

"*Sprachen zie Deutch*?" I asked in German.

As we arrived to the fifth floor, the man smiled and surprisingly confessed that he wasn't German either. "I will tell you where I am from when you *join us*," he added, as I walked away from him. Isaac was sitting on a leather couch waiting for me.

"Hi Moody, the team will be ready for you shortly," he said, leading Mike and I to a waiting room filled with a couple of other *lucky* candidates. I have to admit I did not know what to think anymore about this so-called business company. I have never seen or heard of such a bizarre hiring system. Mike sat in the room reading his paper calmly. Trying to keep my cool, I started a light conversation with him.

"Ok, Mike. So how long have you been in Kuwait?" I asked in Arabic.

"I don't speak Arabic man," he replied, with his silly bad acting.

"C'mon man. You say you are French, German, you say *join us*... You look Iraqi," I teased, in a friendly manner.

Indeed, Mike's tongue slipped when he replied in Arabic then quickly switched back to English. "Once an *Arab* always an Arab," I whispered, smiling at the man as I left the room.

Isaac appeared and called me over saying, "The team is ready for you, follow me." When we reached the last room in the long hallway, Isaac tapped the door. When it opened he looked at me, turned his back and said, "Good luck Moody, be very calm."

Any suspense or questions building in my mind during the past weeks were doubled when I saw the set-up of this hotel room. A blond woman with an American accent welcomed me then led me into a smaller room within the quarters. As soon as I set foot inside the carpeted well-lit room, she disappeared and left me standing with two middle-aged American men. By now, I was used to the "no name" or "first name only" manner of this *business company,* so I was not surprised when the two interviewers did not share their identity. The two men wore jeans and casual t-shirts along with Nike sneakers to go with their perfect American accents. The blond man standing closer to me informed me that they would need my photo. Without a pause, I posed with a serious gesture drawn on my face for the man's digital camera, which immediately transformed the image on to the other man's laptop. They directed me to sit on the chair facing the couch they both occupied. On the coffee table between us lay a paper displaying a list of countries. Next to it was a laser-fingerprinting gadget connected to their laptop, which was also unusually sitting connected to another electronic gadget (probably a lie detector of some sort, or a voice recorder).

I did not know what to think anymore but I wanted to see how far this was all going to go. I followed their instructions and placed my thumb four times on the laser-fingerprinting machine. Seconds later, a quick chain of beeps confirmed that my fingerprints were recorded successfully along with my photo on to their unconventional hi-tech laptop.

"Which countries on this list have you visited?" the blond man asked. I stared quietly at the list, which consisted mostly of Middle Eastern and Gulf countries in addition to hot spots like Afghanistan, Libya, Israel, and Iraq. "Bahrain, Qatar, Egypt, U.A.E," I answered, as the other man sat in front of me typing every word I said on to his lap-top.

Without a warning the man bombarded me with a series of detailed questions about the names of my parents, grandparents, aunts, uncles, brothers, their jobs, countries of residence, ages, occupations, and addresses.

Then came the unexpected inquiries about what assets my family or I own in Egypt, Canada, or elsewhere and their approximate value. The man really stunned me with the next question:

"Who are the women you dated in the past five years and in which countries did they reside?"

"Are you serious?" I demanded.

"Ok. What is your girlfriend's name and where does she live?"

I paused for a few seconds then gave them her first name only. In hindsight, I'm not even sure why.

"Could you give us your previous addresses in Kuwait, Egypt, and Canada?"

"All of them?" I asked.

"Yes Please…"

After that, I listened to the man shower me with even more personal questions: Have you ever been addicted to any drugs? Did you ever enter a drug-rehabilitation program? Are you a violent person? Have you sexually assaulted anyone before? Do you drink? If yes, are you an alcoholic? Have you been arrested before? If yes what were the charges and the outcome of the case?

The next set of questions were very tricky, yet I still held my composure and answered them calmly.

"What will you do if the war starts and your family decides to travel? Will you leave with them?"

"My family is strong and I have two brothers supporting my parents. They have been through the first Gulf War and only left months after the invasion. No, I would not leave."

"Why do you want to work with us?"

"I am not sure what kind of company you are exactly, but I wouldn't mind working with Americans because of my education.... and judging from this whole process you seem like a well to do company to work for," I answered, scanning the blond man's blue eyes for any clues.

"I like that. You have loyalty," he added, looking into the questionnaire.

The Yes/No questions: "Do you have any association with the following terrorists or organizations?"

Al Qaeeda, *No*

Osama Bin Laden, *No*

Saddam Hussein, *No*

Egyptian Jamaha Islamia, *No*

Hezbollah, *No*

Hamas, *No*

Abu Sayaf, *No*

The list went on with names of terrorist organizations I did not even recognize. Needless to say, by now I was sure this job had nothing to do with business or translation. However, I had no time to think or even try to guess who these people really were. I cautiously listened to the interviewer's opinionated questions with a subtle tension in my answers: "What do you think about the Palestinian-Israeli conflict? What are your views on the Iraq predicament? What do you think of bin-Laden and Al Qaeeda?"

I felt butterflies in my stomach as I loosened my tie's knot. I answered with honest diplomacy. Subconsciously, I was weighing the events and questions of the past hour and a half:

"I think bin-Laden is definitely responsible for the events of 9/11. I also think he is a sick man. His beliefs and actions do not represent the purity of the Islamic religion. He has put Muslims across the world in a very critical position."

The following question fell on my soul like a bomb, eliminating any of my emotional restrictions: "Would you operate for us in Egypt, if we needed your services there?"

The man's tone resonated in my head like a bell. I felt goose bumps raise on my arms, my lower back tensed up, and I sensed a subtle formation of sweat under my arm pits. Replaying the question's grammatical construction I felt insulted and stood up shouting,

"Are you guys looking for a spy? Is this what this whole so-called business is all about?"

The two men fell silent at my outrage. At that exact moment Isaac burst into the room with his silly undercover-agent-calmness and said:

"Moody calm down, I assure you this is not espionage."

I went silent and got more paranoid. Isaac had conveniently stepped in at the appropriate moment, that is as soon as I lost my temper. This meant I was either being monitored through that stupid painting hanging on the wall or through some sort of audio recording device. I clenched my fists in anger:

"You play me around for weeks and insult my intelligence with your business company stories! I have *no* idea who you guys are or *why* you are paying such high wages for a translator! *And* to top it all off you bring me into this room and *drill* me with questions about my mom and my girlfriend, and you want me to be *calm!*" Before Isaac could answer, I added: "I think I have the right to know at this stage what you guys are exactly and why you're asking me if I would *operate* in Egypt, my mother country."

"We are with the U.S. Intelligence…" he said, in a low voice.

"CIA?!"

"Are you going to continue this interview, we have just a couple of more questions?"

I glared at Isaac's bespectacled blue eyes. The cards were face-up now, and I felt calm to this new reality, sarcastically silent. As I sat down, the three men went through my passport very thoroughly. I was expected to justify my numerous visits to the U.S. through out the past fifteen years. The vibe remained dry with no space for any more secrets.

"Would you go to Iraq in the case of a war?"

"I can't answer this right now…until I think about this whole fiasco carefully at home."

I drank my orange juice in the lobby of the hotel waiting for the *team* to take a decision, very angry at the style of the interview. My Lebanese buddy kept me company, smoking his anxiety away.

"Mr. Mohamed. Sorry, we can not *use* you," Isaac said, as he shook my hand.

"I would like to know the reason, please," I replied.

"I am not authorized to give you any reasons. The decision is out of my hands."

"What? You give me the runaround for weeks, and all you can say is we can't *use* you. I 'm going to expose you to the Kuwaiti government! *And* I'll inform my embassy!"

Isaac apologized and walked away from my seemingly delusional threats. Here I was standing fuming in the lobby threatening the most intelligent agency in the world. It was all very surreal.

My Lebanese friend made the cut and left with Isaac exchanging very puzzled looks with me. That same night, my friend had already been affected by the ways and wonders of the CIA. He hesitated many times before telling me some details about his new life as an *operative* or whatever they will call him. I had calmed down after what had happened in the hotel, but I got pissed off again with the new set of information he revealed.

The names Isaac and Mike were just cover identities of course. The men disappeared from Kuwait after supervising blood tests and recruiting new operatives. The contract my friend signed contained a confidentiality clause that left his lips shaking as he revealed bits of top-secret information.

Days later, I learned more news from his confused mother. Apparently, they had shaved his head and provided him with a military outfit and she seemed unhappy about this newly acquired lifestyle. Before being shipped to Iraq, my *operative 'friend'* called me from a satellite phone and asked my opinion on a top-secret proposition: He had the choice to enter Iraq under the cover of a *military police man*, a *field engineer, or maybe a journalist.* I advised him to enter poised as a military man since he always loved guns when he trained with Hezbollah in his youth back in Southern Lebanon.

It was good to know some of the intelligence community in Iraq. During my short visit to Baghdad airport four months later; guess who I bumped into: My *operative friend!*

I

UNILATERAL BREAKTHROUGH

Chapter 1: A local Iraqi woman hit by shrapnel after a U.S. Apache Helicopter bombed her farm in Safwan village. Photo by Brian Walski.

SUNDAY MARCH 23, 2003

The heroic journalists of this war are divided into two teams, yet collaborated to bring the simplest details to our TV sets and our morning papers. The Pentagon had invented the "embed," describing journalists accompanying the soldiers in this war, in an effort to portray a new, 24-hour coverage of an historical war. Embedded journalists were literally sharing cots with the army and more or less under the same stress as they roamed the battlefields with the tanks, humvees, and infantry. The revolution of the media in this war and live stunning scenes of Baghdad bombarded at night is a product of such dedication to bring out the truth. The teams of journalists better known as Unilateral, on the other hand, were the free man's daring eye on the ground. Free to roam the country at personal curfew, we established our own rules, signs, and survival techniques in order to reach the ultimate goal of duplicating the live truth onto paper. Embeds were naturally exposing more coverage about the military, the fighting, strategies, and the specific weapons used by the army. However, unilateral journalists were free to cover such army stories plus humanitarian aid to Iraq, status of civilians, and many other events that were all based on actual interviews with Iraqi people on the ground. Los Angeles Times writer, Mark Magnier best described the position of Unilaterals as the "Special Forces" of the media. Indeed, it did look like a special-forces operation on the night we actually decided to hit the Kuwaiti border for a run through to Southern-Iraq.

The Times already had six reporters and two photographers embedded with American forces in Iraq. Our crew consisted of writer Sam Verhovic and me in one SUV, along side Mark Magnier and staff photographer, Brian Walski in another. Armed with gas masks, chemical suits, food, water, gasoline, a generator, and an arsenal of telecommunication equipment we finally decided to meet up with a couple of other media teams at the Hilton-Kuwait as a starting point for the beginning of our mission. Leaving suite 672 in Sheraton- Kuwait towards our meeting point at 4:00 am, I could not get my mind off the unprecedented scenes of the bombing of Baghdad live on television. Minutes ago, I had been flicking back and forth through FOX, CNN, NBC, and Arabic news channels. I could just imagine the American population back in the U.S. watching this war live and coming together around pop-corn and beers just like they do during the SuperBowl season. Watching my cab glide through the haunted streets of Kuwait City, I again had no clear idea of what my job in Iraq as a translator with the Los Angeles times had in store. Just on time, outside the Hilton, I loaded our SUV with my huge bag and chemical kit. I had visited the Hilton only once to set up my CFLCC media credential required by the U.S. army for any reporter entering Iraq. With my name, Mohamed Fahmy boldly printed on my CFLCC media pass along with the two other local Kuwaiti credentials issued by the Ministry of Information and the Ministry of Defense. I was legal, calm, and ready to go. The Hilton was the operations castle for the Coalition Forces Land Component Command. A top-of the-line beach resort, the reception of the hotel stood rich in architecture and technology with walls alternating into different shades of colors. Many journalists and top army personnel had stayed in this hotel, including some of our crew in efforts to picking up secret information leaks from high-ranked army commanders and other tips that had proven useful throughout our reporting from Kuwait. Now standing with my crew and other teams like Newsweek, Wall Street Journal, and Newsday, we all reviewed our paperwork, credentials, and made sure to mark our SUVs with the visible letters "TV" or the word **[Press]**. Gas cans tied on the racks of our Mitsubishi Pajero, our eight vehicle media convoy was ready to move. As we drove into the dark, Sam handed me a two-way radio and asked me to set up the right channel. The leader of the convoy, who at this point was Rod Nordland of Newsweek, confirmed everyone was on course using the radio. Sam broke the silence again with his Yankee humor:

"Mark, this is the Pharaoh. I am right behind you, copy."

"Roger, this is the Sheikh," Mark replied.

Now that the Times crew had their field names confirmed, the convoy continued through to the border. We all had doubts about getting into Iraq. With the sky brightening up, I could spot English signs on the sides of the road with names of U.S. military camps; like New York, Texas, and Camp Commando. Before the war started, Northern Kuwait was closed up for security purposes because most of the U.S. military training camps were based there. I remembered working on a story with Tony Perry exploring the anguish of the camel herders moving their camels down south into the Kuwaiti desert due to the military occupation of this part of the country. A month later, not only am I going to Iraq to report on the war, but I also have to pass by New York and Texas on the way!

After an hour of driving, at the closed up United Nation's camp, we stopped our convoy for a quick stretch and prepared ourselves for the border checkpoint a mile away. I had mixed feelings about seeing this huge well-built UN camp closed down by massive sealed metal gates. Watching the symbolic UN flag on top of the white camp, I remembered how the UN had failed to stop this war. Before pondering the issue longer, my chain of thoughts was disturbed by the loud continuous barking of a white dog trapped behind the gates. I was relieved to see my partner Sam stop and feed the poor canine, just as we were pulling out. In my mind, I felt safer that Sam was a humanitarian, sensitive enough to care about an abandoned dog. Especially, that as soldiers do, we were now expected to watch each other's backs. A family man and father to three kids, Sam had confessed earlier that he was hiding some of the truth about his duty here from his wife.

Ten minutes later, we reached the border. At this point the sun was shining, yet the American soldier's dull reaction was simply: "Turn back to where you came from."

Not shocked at his words, yet determined to enter, we all turned our SUVs around and parked in a straight line meters away from the border, refusing to leave. Watching some of the journalists haggling with the soldier, it was obvious that his orders were clear. So our convoy still waited as we joined other journalists who apparently had arrived before us and were still determined to go through. Among the unilateral teams we met on the border were the Chicago Tribune, Washington Post, and a few other European TV crews. I watched as everyone grouped together scanning one big map, looking for other off-roads across the border. I was so impressed with the dedication of these journalists. As a good hour passed by, a Kuwaiti police car drove around us, then stopped. I took the liberty of finding out what these cops were about. Surprisingly, they were not here to send us back or bother us. The two officers were simply shocked when they found out we were trying to enter Iraq. One of the officers yelled at me in his weak broken English, "You Iraq die!" When I spoke to him again in Arabic, he simply expressed his respect for our courage. Suddenly, a U.S. army convoy consisting of twelve vehicles appeared, heading our way towards the border. Since the cops were originally here to escort the U.S. convoy across Kuwait City, they drove out as their mission ended. Running back to our SUV, I was smiling at the sight of all the journalists turning their ignitions on, and tailing the last vehicle in the military convoy. Watching the plan fail from the passenger seat of our Pajero, I grinned at Sam asking, "Do journalists always think they can turn transparent or what? "Clearly, unilaterals don't take no for an answer.

We parked back in the same place after the soldiers ordered us back again. Cold from the desert wind, I sat alone in the SUV dozing off as I watched groups of journalists discussing how to get across. Listening to the local radio station unfolding the war news, I daydreamed about what could lie across the border. Being the optimist that I am, I was confident and fearless at this point. The fact that my crew was not covering Baghdad relieved me. The Los Angeles Times already had brave reporters like John

Daniszewski in Baghdad. I fantasized some more about my Iraqi girlfriend living safely away in the United Arab Emirates. I knew one of her dreams was to be on the ground reporting the story and covering such a war zone especially since this was her country. Suddenly, my thoughts were interrupted, as it appeared that a Chicago Tribune reporter had figured out a winning plan into Iraq. Laurie Goering, a blonde reporter from the Tribune remembered an off-road route she had taken days ago that led her to a section of the border controlled by the British army. A few moments later, our army of SUVs filed out slowly away from the border and back onto the highway towards Kuwait. Following Laurie now, Sam and I had our doubts that this would work.

However, a good twenty minutes later, Laurie's voice boomed across our two-way radio confirming that she had located the off-road and that she was turning back off the asphalt into the desert on the right. Moments later, like an angel, Laurie's voice sailed through the radio: "We are in. I am in Iraq!" A minute later, we crossed the rugged sandy border separating Iraq and Kuwait. Before I could even comprehend what was happening, I could see a huge British Challenger battle tank cruising beside my side of the Pajero.

Sam and I were delirious with happiness and I could feel the adrenaline rise in my body. As Sam and Mark cheered each other through the radio, I spotted a big card board sign positioned by the British reading: "The First Fusiliers Welcome you to Iraq." Not sure what Fusiliers meant, we waived at the British soldiers as we drove through the light sand. What caught my eye right away was that the Iraqi desert was much greener. With the sight of military in position, the trenches, and the soldiers in full gear, I was now rushing with energy and I could feel Sam reaching this level too, as he commented, "Mohamed, we are about to witness history."

Off the desert and onto a well-asphalted road, we were now driving towards Umm Qasr (Iraq's major trade-port city) which had been declared secure two day ago by the U.S. Defense Secretary. On the road we encountered the first group of Iraqi civilians hanging around a white bus as they yelled and waived at us. I rolled down my window and informed Sam that I heard them complaining in Arabic that the army would not let them pass through. They were ordered to go back to where they came from.

Just like us Unilateral, they were stubborn as they kept driving their bus back and forth hoping the army would change their mind. Meters after we passed them, our convoy stopped along the road since many journalists wanted to ask soldiers about the status of the roads up ahead. All the reporters were ecstatic to be finally in Iraq, some were snapping quick photos with their personal digital cameras. As I leaned on our SUV, I watched Sam and Mark take down notes as they interviewed an African-British soldier standing alert on top of his battle tank, right on the side of the road in the desert.

As soon as I got back into our truck and closed my door, complete chaos hit the scene as a huge blast accompanied with loud crackles of machine–gun fire disrupted my thoughts and scared the hell out of me and everyone around. I reacted instantly by rolling back my car seat and lying flat on my back. Seconds later, I raised my head and peeked out to find most of the reporters panicking, some of them were crouching behind their SUVs or hiding behind the closest battle tank. It was obvious that the area was dangerous. My crew jumped back into the vehicles. I watched Brian quickly put on his helmet and bullet proof vest, which were marked clearly with the word 'Press.' Still panicking, Sam and I turned our Pajero around and followed our convoy away from this scary road back towards the village of Safwan. Now on an adrenaline rush, both Sam and I got into our heavy bullet proof vests but not the helmets yet. Not so sure about what just happened I listened closely to Sam and Mark's conversation on the radio. I was glad to hear Mark relay what the soldier had informed him during their brief talk before the gunshots. Mark's words relieved me as he calmly explained, "It's just the U.S. and British forces working to take out a number of "guys with guns" who had shed their uniforms and put on civilian clothes."

Far from the danger, we reached Safwan, the closest Iraqi settlement north of the Kuwaiti border. I watched the long coalition convoys heading north. The security and tranquility of working in Kuwait out of five-star hotels had evaporated into this battle zone within a couple of hours. I was impressed to hear that my crew had completed a war survival course in London, England. Finally, our convoy spotted a British military point. As we approached the Brits, we realized that the scene had much more to offer. We parked our cars along the road in a highway clover-leaf where the British kept thirty-seven Iraqi prisoners of war who had surrendered and were being held in a barbed-wire enclosure on the edge of the road in the sand. With our excitement at its peak now, we tried to talk to the prisoners as our photographer rained them with photos, but quickly British troops ordered us away from the POWs. Under the hot sun, the Iraqi soldiers seemed very anxious. Farther to the right, six higher-ranked officers were imprisoned alone by another set of barbed-wire. I was surprised when Mark told me to yell at them and ask what had happened behind the Lieutenant's back. Not able to do that, I smiled at Mark, and at this point realized that he is the type of reporter who would do anything to get his story right and deploy the truth. Across on the other side of the road, there was a bunch of confiscated weapons that consisted mainly of old rifles and Klashnikovs, yet they were still capable of killing people. A British soldier was busy pounding and destroying the weapons with a big sledgehammer, as many photographers surrounded him, clicking away at their cameras. I could see many of the writers were trying to get information from the soldiers, so a military officer decided to brief the reporters.

Naturally, many Iraqi boys and men were also watching helplessly and this is where my job as a translator started. As Sam was busy listening to the Lieutenant's briefing, Mark decided to interview the civilians standing around. Of course, the local men were all complaining about their desperate situation and the dark days they have endured since the war started days ago. Most of them were stranded away from their farms and were also very scared of the infamous U.S. Apache helicopter. Mark was interested to hear many of their individual stories; if they had seen dead bodies around, where they were staying now, and if they had lost any family members in the attacks. One man explained how he buried two civilians killed by helicopter gunfire. Translating to Mark the details of their anguish, I realized that many other reporters were listening in to our conversation and taking down notes. We tried to avoid sharing our information, but it was hard to dodge these reporters and I had no problem translating to four or five people at the same time since I was not repeating myself too many times. What worried me were those TV cameras documenting these interviews as I feared for my mother spotting me on television, standing in the middle of a battle zone wearing a beige bullet proof vest. I was amazed at the credibility of journalism as Mark always insisted on documenting the full name, age, and occupation of anyone we interviewed. Later on, he explained that quotes were not to be published without this personal information.

The chaos continued as loud screams emerged from the distance; a woman approaching us in an old white pickup truck meters away. The vehicle finally stopped at the British checkpoint and I could see the lady was wailing and waving her hands. As everyone stood shocked, a military officer asked me to come quickly and translate to him what was actually happening. As I got closer to the pickup, I realized that on the floor of the truck lay two dead men. Everyone inside was covered in blood. Apparently, the screaming woman was hysterical mainly because she had left her sister behind. The mother was sitting in the back with blood splattered all over her dress. She remained silent with a look of total delusion drawn on her face.

I finally understood that it was an Apache Helicopter that had destroyed their farm. This frantic scene only lasted minutes as the military officer ordered them to head to the clinic in Safwan. He then looked at me sadly and added, "There was nothing we could do… They were already dead."

Back with Mark, we had the exclusive details of this sad family. We were now both cautious not to share information with other journalists. I relaxed by our car and drank some water. Locals approached me with complaints. They were glad to know that someone spoke Arabic. They asked questions like: *When will this war end? Are there any refugee camps at the Kuwaiti border? Why are they killing our civilians?* Many children came up to me asking for food and water. Older men approached me with requests to use our satellite phone to call their relatives outside of Iraq. Many locals claimed dozens of civilian deaths and injuries, but nothing could be confirmed.

Before I could relax, another speeding pickup truck stopped by the Brits. Running to the truck to help, I realized that this time it was less intense. A woman lay on her back screaming in pain as blood gushed out of her badly injured foot. She was accompanied by her tearing mother, her daughter, and still kept her baby boy close to her chest. I explained to the soldier treating her that she had been hit by shrapnel from an explosion near her farm. With the bandage tight around her foot, I instructed her to just rest as the truck rolled away towards Safwan.

The nature of my job was now clearer to me. All the journalists parked their cars by the bridge on the sandy highway cloverleaf. I felt secure only due to the presence of the British troops. From across the street, I could see the Iraqi prisoners of war were eyeing me constantly. Some of them even waived their hands implying that they wanted to talk. I watched the BBC crew broadcast live from our location at the cloverleaf. The afternoon sun was at its peak now as more media vehicles rolled in from Kuwait, and they all parked their SUVs around us too. The Reuters media crew caught my eye since they had an armored jeep with thick bullet proof windshields. Now, the inevitable diffusion of journalists was starting as different crews headed toward their headline stories, hunting down whatever they could get their eyes on. For that sole reason, the cloverleaf was nicknamed; "spaghetti junction"

Thankfully, our wise team did not head towards Basra. Our writers decided to check out Safwan's clinic just about 200 kilometers up the road. Walking towards the entrance of the medical center, we were welcomed by the men standing outside as they waived us in. Mazen Abdullah, a volunteer at the Safwan Center for Health, welcomed me and expressed his happiness that the press were there to reveal the crisis they were facing. Our writers immediately started asking him questions about the situation in the past days and how the center was dealing with the wounded. I translated Mazen's words and emotions, as Mark noted: "People need food and water. The ambulance can't even pick up people because of all the soldiers. We need doctors here. People are burned. There are shrapnel wounds. All we have here is the most basic first-aid."

Walking through the shabby littered hallways of the center, Mazen along with a crowd of employees led our team to show us a wounded patient. Abbas Fadel, a 20- year old student, lay flat on his stomach on an old bed with gunshot wounds to his lower back. I translated to Mark the details of his story, once again, this was another innocent man caught in cross fire.

Walking out of the clinic, the crowd surrounding us got bigger and angrier as they all complained to me in Arabic about the food and water situation. Mark and Sam dug deeper with questions like: *"Are you happy the U.S. is here to liberate you?" "Aren't you happy that Saddam Hussein's regime will end?"*

The crowd got bigger and more opinionated with their own questions too. One loud angry Iraqi yelled: "Their helicopters hit the parked ambulance and the doctors' offices!" We all then walked to assess the damage. Still digging deeper, our reporters were out to expose the truth but Mazen replied, "Mohamed, they will all lie to you, everyone is scared of Saddam. There are Ba'athi informers standing in the crowd around us right now."

Mazen then informed us that there was a dead corpse in the mosque. After quick negotiations, Mark and Sam agreed that they wanted to see the body. Walking towards the mosque to see the corpse, I was nervous. I asked Mazen if our presence might bother the family of the dead man. I could foresee their anger. Three white American journalists wearing flack jackets accompanied by an Arab translator could very possibly cause a riot in the mosque, which was located right behind the Safwan clinic.

Just as I expected, the mosque's Imam refused to let us in and the crowd outside the mosque who were witnessing the washing of the dead body were angry with obvious rage in their eyes. Mark directed his questions to a man in the crowds,

"Do you think this war will fix Iraq's economy and improve your life?"

I translated back the man's exact answer as he said:

"We should be a rich country," said Muhsen Salem, 24, a farmer. "We have oil, farming, we grow tomatoes, and export food. But we've become poor and the government comes and takes our crops from us, claiming there is uranium in them."

Still interviewing the crowd of Iraqi civilians, a man interrupted and yelled in Arabic, "We're very happy about the bombing of Saddam's palace in Baghdad, but we're very sure he's not in the palace." As I translated the last phrase of the comment, I spotted what seemed to be the Imam of the mosque approaching us with boiling anger in his eyes. Ahmed, the Imam, was yelling furiously,

"Is this peacekeeping? We welcome the attack and this is what they do. If we had power now, we would hit the Americans."

Now leading us into the mosque to see the body, Imam Ahmed left us standing by a broken down crying old man, the father of the dead man we were about to see. The old man's wrinkled face was now full of tears as he pounded his chest in grief over his son's death. Mark immediately asked me to take him aside so we can find out what happened.

"Ask him what happened exactly," said Mark, as he pointed towards the torn up man.

"He was such a good son, my only boy, Khamat, always taking care of me!" cried Fizah Abuaid Thekyal, as I translated his words back to Mark.

"Were you guys outside or inside the house when your son was hit?" I asked the old man in Arabic.

Still crying and now grabbing on to my shirt, the man answered, "We were sitting in the living room when suddenly the house got split in half with a missile from a helicopter... We had a white flag on the house... don't understand... I want to see him... I want to see my son."

Entering the room with Mark and Brian to see the corpse, I spotted the man's cousin sitting on the ground crying, covering his face with his hand. I then walked into the small room to see Khamat's body lying naked on a metal stand. I stood frozen as my eyes measured the damage. A portion of the man's intestines had lashed out of his right side, his right hand hung on the side of the bed separated from his arm, and shrapnel had carved two huge cylindrical gashes right through his foot. Leaving the depressing room, I watched Brian as he clicked his camera documenting the precious dead body of Khamat.

Still weeping loudly, Khamat's old father approached me with shrapnel in his hand and explained to me that he also had been slightly injured when shrapnel from the same explosion slightly scratched his lower back. We rushed into our Pajero as we expressed our condolences for the death of Khamat. I promised everyone that we would print out the truth to the whole world in the next day's newspaper

Back at the cloverleaf, most of the journalists had returned as we parked our jeeps adjacent to the Newsweek team, close to some of the other journalists who were in our original convoy from Kuwait. I watched the scene closely. Most of the journalists were writing their articles. News from the wires and the radio kept us updated about the war. My job for the day was over. I watched the writers and photographers work at beating their deadlines. A reporter's job is never easy. Not only do journalists have to risk their life and take notes during their interviews in a war zone, but they also have to write up the story at the end of the day and file it back to Los Angeles. The British troops were still in the same position and so were the Iraqi prisoners of war. I could see the POWs were causing trouble when the British called me over to translate and explain their orders to the prisoners.

"I'm hungry," said one of the men, who identified himself as Abdul Karim. All the prisoners stood up when I approached them. They bombarded me with questions about their future, wondering about their date of release. One of them yelled, "We have been here for three days, sitting in the desert under the hot sun!"

Some complained about the cold night and the long wait. The British soldier then asked me to inform them that they will be moved to a POW camp today or tomorrow.

I was happy to see one of the soldiers taking down each prisoner's request as I translated their simple demands for cigarettes and blankets. A British officer then escorted me to talk to the six higher-ranked officers who were imprisoned separately. They were glad to vent their complaints, but got more restless when I reminded them that they will be moved to POW camps, where they will be questioned then detained indoors under more comfortable surroundings with three meals a day.

Exhausted after assisting our British hosts, I attempted to cross the street back to my Times crew with a sincere desire to call it a day and eat some food. Before I reached our vehicle, a British soldier came running towards me and asked me to translate for them again, since they had a badly injured Iraqi civilian who was dropped at their checkpoint. "We have a penis injury here!" yelled the concerned humanitarian soldier.

In the back of the British medical aid vehicle, an Iraqi man lay on his back with blood covering his pants down around the groin area. The trained soldier slowly unzipped the man's pants then started cleaning the gash using the first-aid kit available. Watching the soldier raise the injured man's penis, I explained to the crying Iraqi that he was getting first-aid treatment and then he was going to be transported to a British field hospital soon.

9:00 pm. The ghost of the night surrounded our jeeps as most of the journalists worked hard to file their stories. The continuous echoing sounds of the generators actually brought peace to my mind and reminded me that all the reporting we did was actually being transformed into data and print; into a reality people will analyze properly. I could barely see what was going on around the vicinity, but I was sure the POWs and the soldiers were not going anywhere for the night. Not interested in the various political interviews on the radio, I just checked in with Mark and Sam for summarized news off the wires.

Exhausted, I rolled the car seat back and covered my head with a blanket ignoring the glow from Brian's laptop. Falling asleep was tough. I had decided to keep my boots on. I did not know what to imagine in a hostile war zone. However, I had expected this entire situation before I left Kuwait. What I could not have imagined was the sight of dead bodies and journalists caught in the crossfire. I shut my eyes, but could not delete visions of the corpse in the mosque and specifically the man's pink intestines lashing out of his side. I interrupted Brian and helplessly complained, "Man, I can't get over the body in the mosque. I see it every time I close my eyes."

"It usually takes a day or two," answered Brian, as he stared at his laptop's screen.

Brian then threw the blanket back on my head and said, "Moody, this is our first day here..."

Monday March 24, 2003

Awake in my new so-called bed, I rolled down the window of the car to welcome a bright sunny morning in Safwan. I watched quietly as my crew boiled water for coffee. The Iraqi prisoners, the British soldiers, and the International journalists were still in place paying their dues to Operation Enduring Freedom. I brushed my teeth and drank as little bottled water as possible. I was glad to wake up to a cosmopolitan group of top-notch journalists. About forty other vehicles occupied the sandy lot. Obviously, more journalists had filed in from Kuwait during the early morning, while I was still sleeping. A strong coffee, a 600-mg pill of Ginseng, and I was ready to hit the road with my LA Times team to wherever they wanted to go.

Driving along with a couple of other vehicles, we headed to Rafidiyah, a small town between Umm Qasr and Safwan. On the way, in the village of Muwailhas, at a deserted Iraqi military base, a very symbolic situation was taking place. We all decided to stop because the scene was a great photo opportunity for our photographer. Four younger Iraqi men were crouched down on their knees, hands behind their backs facing a stone mural of Saddam Hussein. Coalition soldiers with the Scottish Black Watch Regiment had arrested them as one soldier stood behind them with his bayonet pointed to their heads. Brian did not waste any time and went on photographing the scene.

"Why are they detaining you?" I yelled at the four men.

Walid Khalid, the third guy from the left, turned his head towards me and answered, "We were just coming here to take furniture and batteries for the radio…"

While translating to Mark, the man then interrupted adding, "We are not soldiers."

Before we could ask more questions, the British soldier informed us that these men lived across the road and they had not taken arms against the troops, but had to be humiliated as a message to the many villagers watching. Just as we were departing the scene, Mark asked me to translate the Arabic writing on a red cloth banner hanging outside the base. The banner read: "May God Protect Iraq and Saddam Hussein"

Further North towards Rafdyiah, we stopped again. This time a crowd of people and journalists surrounded a burnt supply truck that had crashed right into a number of street signs. Our photographer ran to see the body of the burnt dead soldier in the driver seat. Mark and I preferred to stay back as we checked another military truck that had been bombed in a U.S. air strike. This truck was definitely a perfect target since it carried a load of Klashnikov machine guns that were now charred and partly melted as they lay scattered on the pavement. I was sad to see barefoot kids touching the useless weapons and playing around the truck. Many of the villagers who witnessed the action stood around us and described the exact scenes. Mark took down notes carefully as I translated the villagers' words: "A U.S. - led attack on Friday left the two military vehicles in flames. One was a supply truck, they said, and the other carried about a dozen Iraqi soldiers who fled for cover when they heard aircrafts coming."

"Did you see anyone killed or injured?" Mark asked.

Mahdi Ali Sharif, 73, who lives in a brick house down the street, popped out from the crowd and added, "Only two Iraqi soldiers were injured. I took them to my house, gave them some civilian clothes and some first aid, and they left."

Mark questioned him again as I translated, "Were they scared?"

"Yes they were scared, but their morale seemed good," Mahdi answered.

While interviewing the villagers, a suspicious angry man approached me with accusation in his tone, "Are you Kuwaiti?"

"No, I am not Kuwaiti," I answered quickly.

"I hate Kuwaitis for letting the U.S. into my country. Look at them they are right behind you acting like they own the place."

Standing behind me were a couple of Kuwaiti journalists who had just crossed the border and were careless enough to leave their car plates on. Until this moment, I had not felt any threat from the locals. I was now paranoid, wondering if one of the civilians would pull out a handgun and shoot me. I could be called Mexican or Indian due to my dark complexion, but I did not want to be labeled Kuwaiti. Still nervous, I caught myself adjusting my bullet-proof vest as I yelled back, "The Americans are here to liberate you from this Saddam and you will be happier people!" Some faces in the crowd welcomed my words, while others argued against my outburst.

"All of a sudden, we have no water, no electricity," said an old farmer, as he puffed on his cigarette. Just before I could reply, I felt Mark pat me on the shoulder as he whispered in my ear, "Moody, don't take a stand, remember we are here to do our job and we must remain neutral."

Mark was suddenly interested in the suspicious man in the crowd, who later identified himself as Muqadam. The man pulled out patches of military gold stars from a pocket in his robe the waved them in the air shouting, "I am an airman with the Iraqi platoon that was scattered!" Still unconvinced of this man's credibility, I watched villagers gathering around him yelling all sorts of insults. One elder man pointed at him and hollered, "You should surrender!"

I translated to Mark as another man shouted at Muqadam and said, "There is no point in staying. The foreigners will fight... fight... and fight. You should go to the next checkpoint and maybe the British will take you in as a prisoner and give you food and water."

Muqadam raised his fist high and answered, "No, I won't go... I will not surrender... I am with the Iraqi air force!"

The scene was interrupted when even a weirder man drove his white pick-up truck towards us. This angry Iraqi waived his middle finger towards the villagers and stared at me as he shouted, "They are all liars. They all hate Saddam and they are all scared!" Before I could register what he had said, the man stepped on the gas and disappeared into the asphalted horizon towards Safwan road.

With news that the road to Basra was dangerous, we headed back towards Safwan, to our "spaghetti junction." On the way back, I watched Sam complaining to Mark over the two-way radio about the Kuwaiti journalists following our convoy. After failing to lose them on the road, we simply pulled their jeep over and asked them to either remove the Kuwaiti plates or stay away from us. There were already rumors about journalists being attacked across the country. When we reached the clover-leaf, we heard even more unconfirmed rumors about the death of a famous ITN journalist. The mood at the clover-leaf was tense. Unconfirmed reports of dead journalists raised the level of paranoia among many of us. A French journalist approached us and described a story about his colleague who was ambushed by Iraqi civilians. Apparently, the civilians tempted the journalist when they asked him to accompany them to see the dead body of a coalition soldier at the entrance of their building. The French journalist got beaten badly and robbed of all his possessions before they let him go free. Trying to ease my worries, I opened a can of tuna, and ate my stress away.

With the tension rising, I watched Keith Richburg from the Washington Post explain to Mark how he almost got ambushed on the way to Basra between two Iraqi pickup trucks. With more of these stories announced on the radio, I had to call my girlfriend and my family. "Don't worry; my crew is cautious and well trained. We don't rush into any area until it had been cleared and secured by the army," I lied, trying to calm my woman, who had heard of journalists being attacked on the daily news.

1:00 pm The midday sun was at its peak now. Mark and Sam were busy talking to our British hosts, gathering some intelligence about the war.

I avoided the Iraqi POWs who were now more restless than ever. Two Iraqi farmers approached me on the road with a handful of tomatoes. The modest and kind men were very happy when I asked them to get me a whole box of tomatoes and some bread. They were literally jumping with glee that they could actually help. When I asked about the price of the products, both men smiled and said, "We are Arabs like you." Shocked at their kindness, I turned my attention to the British medical team who were busy treating three Iraqis who were badly injured and burnt in a motorbike accident. The British soldier then asked me to inform two of the men that they will be moved to a hospital in Kuwait. One of the injured men lay on his side with a second-degree burn to his butt. The other man suffered a serious burn to his foot, which was now more contaminated with exposure to the sand and dozens of flies. I could see the men were calmer when they heard the word Kuwait but still both of them demanded a painkiller or Morphine. The third man, who had been treated for a slight cut to his hand, walked up to me and said, "Can I go to Kuwait too? I want to go please."

Watching the two men carried onto a stretcher into the medical van, I could see how luck plays a major factor in a human's life. Here, sat their third partner wishing his injury was more intense knowing it could have been his ticket out of Iraq away from this nasty war.

Back at my jeep, I watched my new Iraqi friends hurling at me with happiness as they carried a whole box of tomatoes and bags of home-baked bread. Reaching for my cash, I asked them how much the goods were priced at. "There is no way we are taking money, you are our guest in Iraq and we can not accept cash," said one of the men.

"You have to take the cash, you are at war and I already know of the Iraqi kindness," I added, as I handed them the cash.

"We are Arab Bedouins. This is our Iraqi pride. We will not accept money. If you want any more food let us know."

Now feeling guilty, I thanked them but tried one more time to squeeze the money into the man's pocket, "Well, I can't take this food then. It would not be fair to take your family's food during this war."

"Saddam distributed six months of food rations before the war to each family. We have lots of flour, rice, sugar, and tea," added one of the men, as he hugged me, ending my hopeless attempts.

The Newsweek team informed us that on their drive around Safwan they had discovered a gas station. Although each vehicle had cans of gas strapped to their racks, many journalists were concerned about the long run situation. Sam and I volunteered to go fill up gas for our team and for other journalists who had given us their empty cans. Another Italian journalist accompanied us since he was specifically doing a story on the shortage of fuel during the war. Not sure what to expect, we drove only a mile into Safwan where we witnessed another sign of chaos and war.

Looters had broken a valve in a humungous gasoline tank set-up by the government. The gas station was closed, but people were jamming the tank as the gasoline cascaded like an endless waterfall. No one was paying for the gas. People were filling up metal buckets with free gasoline. Not ready to wait in line, I jumped on top of our Pajero, untied the empty gas containers, and handed them to an Iraqi man who seemed to have authority over the rest of the guys hanging around the tank. Standing a couple of feet away from the pump and worried about the quality of the gas, I held a funnel as the man carefully filled each can. Sam took notes of the hectic situation then laughed when I asked him for a cigarette.

"Moody, this is your chance for a quick shower, you've been complaining all day," Sam commented, with his humorous Yankee sense of humor.

Upon roping all the full gas cans on our truck's rack, I handed the man six Kuwaiti dinars, (equivalent to eighteen U.S. dollars) which were literally a fortune at this time of war. When I reached the cloverleaf, I found Mark surrounded by a small group of farmers who were complaining about their miserable life. Most of the men in the crowd were asking for water while others wanted to use our satellite phone to call their loved ones outside Iraq. I immediately reached into our truck and handed one of them a full bottle of water, urging him to share it with the others. Mark saw an opportunity to interview them so he opened his notebook saying, "Ask them where they get their drinking water…"

"If we don't get water soon, it's going to be get very bad," said Sukni Falah, a worker for the state utility. "The electricity has been cut off. Many people can't draw water at all. We can pull up little water from a well by a hand bucket, but it's salty and there are dead insects in it."

With more pain drawn on his face, Falah added, "We can't even bury our dead." I got really depressed as I translated this last quote to Mark since I knew very well that it was an Islamic duty and ritual to wash corpses before burying them.

Mark expressed his anger with the situation then we both retreated back to our SUV since he wanted to write the day's story and file to LA right away. With the sun almost setting into the horizon, the British troops called me over again for a quick translation deed. This time there was no blood or injuries:

"Tell this man, there is nothing we can do help his daughter," the soldier yelled, as he pointed towards the most beautiful baby I had seen in years.

There stood a veiled Iraqi woman with her sick daughter nestled in her arms. The baby continued to cry and cough as the father attempted to appease her. I was shocked to find out that she had symptoms of asthma. I quickly placed my hand over the baby's forehead to check her temperature as her father explained how she had been sick for days and would not eat or sleep well. Her father then asked me if the troops had any cough medicine for her.

"Tell him we have no medicine here, and that we are only trained for first aid. Also tell him to come back tomorrow, and maybe we can transport her to the hospital, but tonight we can't do anything for them," the British soldier added, as he walked away.

Completely discouraged by this situation, I ran back to our Pajero and picked up a sachet of orange juice. Seconds later, I tried helplessly to force the child to suck on the straw for some vitamin C. To my surprise, the child coughed out every time she attempted to swallow the drink, and then I left the case to her mother who was in tears. Touching the baby's cute cheeks, I held in my own tears trying to explain to her father why he should forget about his idea of making a run for the Kuwaiti border since there was no refugee camp built there. When Ahmed, the father, asked what I wanted to eat for dinner, I fantasized yelling, "Any hot meal and bread!"

The early night had fallen over Safwan, as I watched our crew and most of the journalists typing their stories. Not sure what to do with myself, I walked over to the Canadian CBC crew and introduced myself. I felt really close to the four man crew as I had seen them struggling earlier without a translator. It was awkward to practice my French with a Jean from Radio Quebec, right in the midst of a war zone in Southern-Iraq. I felt homesick when he revealed the location of his office back in Montreal, which happened to be blocks away from my neighborhood. Still avoiding the POWs, I walked along side the British vehicles and watched with amazement at the amount of water and organization they had going for them. I was shocked to see them receive their mail right from London via Kuwait. After a little bit of eavesdropping, I got appalled to hear one of the soldiers complain that it took ten days for him to receive a letter from London.

9:00 pm. I was just standing at the side of the road reflecting on this mysterious war and wondering about all the injuries and casualties I had seen since I have been here. I knew the roads up ahead were filled with stories and pain, but I really did not want to see more dead Iraqi civilians. The long convoys of coalition vehicles I had seen until now did not contain any battle tanks or APCs, (Armed Personnel Carriers) but I was sure the serious action was in Basra. Before I could enjoy the glittering stars in the dark peaceful sky, a British soldier called me over for another quick translation session.

This time, another veiled Iraqi woman was screaming although she was not injured or hurt. However, her mind was devastated as she tried to explain how she had lost her young son during an Apache attack. The old woman was half naked, pounding on her bare breasts with sheer hysteria and frustration.

"Cover yourself please and tell me slowly what happened," I said to the woman, holding a flash light onto her tanned wrinkled face.

"They killed my husband and my cousins and they took my son away!" screamed the woman, as she grabbed on to my hand.

"Who are they? Who took your son away?" The British Major asked, as I translated to the poor woman.

"The same helicopter that killed my husband… the Americans snatched him into the helicopter and took him far away," cried the woman, then once again uncovered her breasts and wailed loudly.

Not sure if she was making any sense, I asked the family members escorting her about the details of the story. Still confused, I translated back the facts of the attack about how her husband was killed in a crossfire between Iraqi troops and Apache helicopters while she was out in the fields. Since their house was destroyed and she could not find the body of her son, she immediately believed a rumor spread by the kids in the village about U.S. soldiers kidnapping her son. I watched the Major radio a description of the boy to his headquarters. I was glad to see a translator arrive in a British military vehicle. Finally, this unit got their official translator from Kuwait. The man was wearing his bullet- proof vest, his helmet, and seemed extremely terrified at the setting. He came in right at the moment when the old lady exploded into a series of hysterical screams and tears.

With my translation deed done, I started walking on to the sandy clover-leaf, towards my crew for a reality check. Before I could reach my jeep, I heard someone on the street calling my name, so I walked back on to the asphalt and peeked through the dark night. It was Ahmed, the man with the sick daughter, but he had a tightly packed bag of food for me. Barely recognizing his face in the grim night, I thanked him for the food as he apologized for the small portions he had cooked due to the short notice. Again, like many generous Iraqi Bedouins, he refused to take any money and promised to cook me a bigger meal for my whole crew tomorrow. Not sure of our reporting plans, I asked him to come early so we can figure out what to do with his sick daughter.

Sharing the sautéed eggplants with my crew was great since they needed a break and of course I also needed an update on the war. Mark joked around as he called Brian over, "Come see what Moody has on the menu tonight!"

I knew my LA Times crew had a few hours of work to go, so I spared them the details of my incident with the Brits. However, trying to sleep was not an easy task. Rolling my car seat back into the sleeping position, I smiled hoping tomorrow would be a brighter day for Ahmed and his sick daughter.

Tuesday March 25, 2003

Insomnia had always been a serious concern in my normal life back in the city. In this war zone the saga was obviously intensified as I sat wide awake in the front seat of our Pajero. Brian had chosen to work on the sandy ground as he sat by the front wheel with his precious lap-top. It was midnight and I could not sleep as I replayed the long daily events in my mind. Most of the journalists were up writing their pieces. The darkness hovered over the trucks as the writers used headband flash lights or interior car illumination for vision. The sky was also unusually clear without any life and extremely dark. However, the skies also kept the secret of the darker events this spring night had in store for us unilateral.

I had thought the British army would leave me alone since they got a Kuwaiti interpreter. However, my short hours of peace evaporated into the quiet sky as I watched the white face of a British major pop right at my window, politely asking, "I am sorry to bother you, but we need your services again, if you don't mind."

Walking with the Major through the sandy cloverleaf, towards the road where the military vehicles were parked, I understood that the Kuwaiti translator had gone out on a military operation for the night. Following the major's flashlight, we came to a stop right under the Safwan Bridge harboring our cloverleaf.

"Could you explain to me what these three men are saying please?" The Major asked.

Relieved to see the scene did not involve any blood or injured people, I listened carefully to one of the three men as the Major pointed the flash light right onto the man's dazzled face.

"We came to warn you, we are simple farmers and we live in Safwan village and we don't want to be killed by helicopters or air-raids," one of the disturbed men complained.

"There are armed guys that are preparing to raid this unit and the journalists," I translated, measuring the farmer's words carefully.

Now extremely concerned, the British Major grabbed a notebook from his vehicle and handed the flashlight to a soldier who was standing on guard.

"Ask them where these men are exactly. Who are they?" the Major commanded, as he took notes.

"They are fifteen men and they are right behind Safwan gates. We heard them planning their attack today behind the supermarket and we tried to stop them," answered one of the men, as he pointed towards Safwan gates, which stood only a mile away from our position.

"What kind of weapons do they have?" the Major asked, sketching a small map on his paper.

"Machine guns and rocket propelled grenades."

I excused myself right after I translated these last words and left the scene as I watched the Brits prepare to investigate this shocking threat.

Crossing the road back onto the sandy cloverleaf, I caught my mind playing tricks on me. *Could they be just lying? Are we really safe by the British army for the night or are we a live target?* Hurtling between the rows of cars without a flashlight, I lost my way for moments, then stood still in front of an Italian news team. "Put your lights down, what is wrong with you?" I screamed at an Italian woman sitting in the middle of the desert cooking pasta right under the brightest lamp in the camp. Not interested to hear the Italian curse words this naïve woman had thrown at me, I ran to our Pajero and started packing the car quickly. I interrupted Sam and Mark who were working together on a story and informed them briefly about what I had just heard. Not sure what we were going to do, I realized that the British Major had sent a soldier inviting one representative from each media agency for a quick briefing on the current situation. The message did not translate through to all the reporters since some of them were either; sleeping, working, or cooking.

"We have to leave," Mark said, as he came rushing back from the short briefing.

Curious to hear what the British were doing, I ran up again to the Major, only to find him seriously busy ordering his troops to their new strategic positions.

"I want two guys on each side of the bridge, and two guys up ahead on the road with our Rovers," The Major ordered, as he put his helmet on.

"Now, I will robustly tell these journalists to leave immediately," the angry Major hollered, charging towards our parked jeeps.

Running back to our jeeps, I realized that some of the crews were preparing to leave but at a very slow pace. Mark was dismantling his tent, while Sam was already in the front seat of our Pajero, ready to go. Just as he planned, the angry Major followed me seconds later bursting into nonstop orders shouting his instructions repeatedly, "Get the hell out of here....Go Go... leave right now.... Clear the area!"

The chaos that hit the scene could well be the same as that of Baghdad being bombed: Shock and awe struck the camp as jeeps pulled out one after the other towards the road without a clue about their destination. The dusty air from the commotion made it harder to see and many vehicles had fled and left some of their belongings behind. We also got caught in a quick panic as we had misplaced our car keys. Leaving Brian to search for the keys, I ran and tried to help Mark dismantle his tent. Amidst the confusion, I just carried the tent and shoved it in the back seat of the jeep knowing that time could be a matter of life or death.

Moments later, Brian had found the keys and both our LA Times vehicles were now out in the exposed dark streets following the rest of the convoy. Many of the journalists who fled had no idea why they were leaving. I was not sure I felt better since I knew the exact story. My fear evoked spine-chilling visions of rocket-propelled grenades striking our trucks with loud orange explosions tearing the black sky amidst screams of bloody innocent people. Since we were now on a road in the bare desert, in the middle of a war zone, not only were we worried about Iraqi militias but we also remembered that the coalition air force could easily mistake us for the enemy and strike us down from the sky.

With no clear destination, the 4X4s were following the unknown leader of the pack. Confusion was at its peak as many jeeps overtook each other blocking the road. Glad to be in the front of the convoy, we all decided to park our vehicles on the left side of the road for a quick strategy meeting. The emotional status was high, at red alert, as we all put our flack jackets on. Faces of familiar journalists appeared from the dark when we all stood around one jeep and discussed our helpless situation. The drama increased as one Yarmikolav from the Wall Street Journal warned, "Stay on the road! Don't step on the sand! We don't know if there are land mines in this area!"

Still unsure of where we stood, I asked a Newsweek reporter for a cigarette as I listened to the many useless ideas. Once again, Laurie Goering of the Chicago Tribune came to the rescue with a superb idea: This was a situation that called for a Central Command decision. Not only did Laurie get some vital advice from the Brits on her way out of the camp during the peak of the confusion, but she also had the CFLCC landline phone number at hand. Laurie calmly explained to us how the British Major had advised her to drive ten kilometers towards a U.S. army point on this same highway. Her words were a big relief. There was a new sense of security with news that there was another army point up the road. One main problem remained: This U.S. convoy had no clue we were coming their way, which could lead to friendly fire and us dead. Puffing on another cigarette, I hung on to Laurie's every word as she pinpointed our GPS location to the Central Command. Indeed, there was another British point down the road and they were now expecting a herd of 4X4s to invade their privacy.

The quiet drive towards the British haven was extremely slow since we could not use our car's headlights for security reasons. I kept myself busy using Brian's one-eyed night vision goggles and watched the magical desert, trying to spot any signs of Iraqi military. To me the situation was unreal. I felt like a reconnaissance soldier trying to spot the enemy before they got me. In my mind's eye I could see images of trees turning into soldiers waiting to attack us. I even handed the goggles to Brian while he was driving to verify what seemed to be an Iraqi battle tank. The fact remained clear; there were only farms all along the road, and there was nothing there but stray dogs and some big power generators.

I gave into listening to the on-going dialogue between the journalists up ahead through the two-way radio. It seemed like the reporters were gaining more confidence as the jokes and sarcastic tone of the conversations brought a sense of hope.

"Is that you guys right behind us?" Mark asked, through the radio.

Still stressed, I handed the radio to Brian.

"Yeah, we're right there."

"Who's leading?" an unidentified journalist asked.

"It's Laurie..." Rod Nordland responded.

"Do you guys see any Fedayeen out there?" Rod asked.

"No, these are all abandoned farms on the sides of the road," I added.

Trying to relieve the tension, Mark interrupted the conversation and commented, "Mohamed, do you think there are any farm girls around?"

A good fifteen minutes later, a British vehicle welcomed us but only to disappoint us with orders that we had to stop our convoy and park on the right lane of the highway. Moments later, a long U.S. convoy consisting of supply trucks, tank carriers, refueling trucks, and humvees appeared from the far dark horizon down the road as they came to a full stop right on the left side of our road. Apparently, the convoy was scheduled to pass through Safwan until they heard through the British that the road up ahead by the cloverleaf was unsafe, with a possible attack by Iraqi militia. I watched through the dark as a couple of U.S soldiers took defensive positions by the bridge in efforts to protect their convoy and us journalists. A soldier then approached each jeep and relayed his orders firmly:

"Do not leave the vehicle, and do not use any car lights or laptops whatsoever."

With the ground rules set and clear, the mysterious scene remained silent and gloomy. Jailed in the car, I felt nicotine fits coming on as I radioed in for help, "This is Moody. Hadi, where is your jeep? I need a cigarette."

Hadi, an interpreter with Newsweek, replied quickly, "I am in the front of the convoy, should I send it to you by DHL or UPS?"

I had quit smoking months before the war. My weakness for smoke started again today and I was craving the evil nicotine once more. The sight of the Italian jeep right in front of mine did not help since the aroma from their continuous smoking stirred my appetite more. I gathered my courage then opened my door and snuck out of our jeep without waking Brian, who was fast asleep. Quietly, I approached the Italian driver. Surprisingly enough, it was the lady journalist that had cursed me earlier for warning her about the bright light at the cloverleaf. Five Italian journalists were cramped smoking cigarettes and complaining about the situation. Accepting her apology, I rushed back to my jeep and sat on the road by the front tire puffing my troubles away, waiting for this nightmare to end. Suddenly, my satellite phone rang and echoed across the desert: It was my brother Adel calling from Kuwait at the worst time possible.

"How are you doing? We all miss you… Are you safe?"

Picturing the comfort of our living room and our big screen TV, I whispered, "I am *perfectly* fine… I'm very *safe* here in Safwan! I'm in the middle of something. I will call you guys tomorrow."

The unexpected entertainment does not stop here. Out of the dark, pops out a British female journalist and kneels down beside me then whispers, "I have to take a leak, I am in the Ford behind you. Do you mind looking the other side please?"

My options were now limited, so I crawled back into the passenger seat and slept hoping this two hour wait in the cold desert would come to an end soon. Minutes into a deep sleep, I nudged to the sudden jolt of the engine, and watched Brian driving slowly behind our infamous convoy towards our next station. With a full update from Brian, I was happy to learn that we were to camp with a British convoy just a mile off-road into the desert. Again, using the night vision goggle, I gazed at the bulldozers, tank carriers, and military vehicles occupying our new camp. The vibe was totally different than that at the cloverleaf. This base was supposedly a top-secret location setup in the middle of the desert.

Sure enough, the SUVs filed in positions one after the other like an army of unwanted bandits. Fortunately, the full moon hovered over our location lighting the desert with a new hope. By now, many journalists were considering returning back to Kuwait. This war like many others represented a chance for many reporters to prove their talents and push their careers further. Many of the journalists had covered wars like Afghanistan or Kosovo yet they all agreed that they have never seen such hostility towards the media. The British major in charge of this unit showed up from behind a bulldozer and urged the many divided angry journalists to gather for a quick briefing on this terrible situation. Waiting for the anticipated speech, I counted the nearly two hundred reporters surrounding the one man with the "juice." In a heavy Scottish accent, the Major relayed his orders about our desperate situation.

"I understand your problem back in Safwan. You will be safe here as this area is secured as far as we know. We have been informed that you were coming here and you are welcome to stay tonight, but I must inform you that we will be heading off up north."

"This route on the left will lead you to the highway." The Major said, pointing towards the asphalt road.

Still trying to decode his Scottish accent, I listened carefully to his militant instructions.

"This area where your vehicles are parked and about a hundred-meters ahead has been cleared of any land mines. Do not walk further ahead of this range. If you want to use the bathroom, try that spot on the left," the Major added, as he halted for any questions before retreating to his quarters.

Most of the journalists at this point were facing the toughest professional decision on whether to stay or go back to Kuwait in the morning. Caught between pride and a life decision, many journalists surrendered to sleep while others shared their thoughts on the unknown future of this war. Our LA Times team was split in decision too as we discussed our strategy. I watched Sam light a cigar as he strolled alone into deep thought. He later told me he was thinking about was his wife and children. I had watched the dare devil come alive in Sam during the chaos as he handled the confusion pretty well and balanced his driving amazingly. Mark was around mingling with the other journalists, gathering intelligence on a possible plan for the morning. I also did a little damage assessment myself and listened to the angry Canadian crew explain how they had lost their tent and some major equipment back at the cloverleaf during the rush out.

Finally we agreed on a new strategy: We decided to leave early at 5:00 am, but in a smaller convoy of eight jeeps. There was no way we were going to get caught driving around with forty other jeeps under the broad daylight of a war. The plan was already in process as we parked our vehicles right ahead of all the others avoiding any logistical obstacles in the morning. I observed my team sleep after an intense depletion of emotions. Now running on low energy, my insomniac habit remained intact as I wandered around. Some journalists remained alert drinking alcohol and smoking in their cars, while others were snoring hopelessly. I engaged in seriously depressing conversations as I listened to a Lebanese reporter complaining:

"This is nonsense, I was doing a live feed today and a mortar landed meters away from me. We should go back to Kuwait until the situation calms down."

Another angry Italian journalist responded, "I covered Afghanistan, but this is different. I don't want to die reporting a story."

To make things worse, the rumor spread earlier in the day about the death of Terry Loyd (the famous ITN journalist) had been confirmed by the wire services. The exact story was now devastating everyone in this camp, especially since the ITN crew had also camped with us earlier at the "spaghetti junction", except they had decided to push further towards Basra. The ITN jeep was caught in a crossfire between an Iraqi pickup truck loaded with soldiers and a coalition tank. The driver of the SUV kicked down the accelerator as he ducked, got lucky, and survived. However, the vehicle flipped over and Terry, who was sitting in the passenger seat died instantly from gunshot wounds. The French camera man and the Lebanese translator sitting in the back seat remain missing.

With all this negative energy in the air, I closed my eyes and shut my mind to a forty-five minute sleep in the passenger seat of our Pajero. Before I could enjoy what seemed to be the beginning of a dream, reality took over with bright sunrays conquering my dreaded sphere. Our convoy was in motion right at 5:00 am. Since Rod Nordland from Newsweek had orchestrated this plan, he was again the leader of the pack as we rolled out quietly away from the rows of parked 4X4s. It was a good idea to move in a small convoy to avoid attracting attention. Another reason was simply that more journalists in one place led to more paranoia and extra opinionated strategies that led to confusion. Only ten minutes down the asphalt road towards Safwan, we stopped our convoy in order to discuss our exact destination. Breathing the fresh morning air, we all stood encircled around a map trying to guess where the safest route would be. Our assumptions and decisions were based on the intelligence relayed to us through CENTCOM. Suddenly without a warning, two white buses approached us speeding through the horizon. My reflex reaction was to duck, as I waived screaming, "Watch out, there is a bus coming this way!" Without a doubt, every single person in our convoy took precautions and hid away behind their trucks. The buses were only transporting civilians and drove right beside us in peace. Abandoning the map, we all agreed to return to our old "spaghetti junction," to meet our British host and gather information on safe routes. By now, I had no confidence in anyone's decision or the army for that matter. However, I was really curious to see if the British were attacked by Safwan's fifteen men militia and if the tip really checked out.

Driving into our cloverleaf, my mouth literally dropped with awe at the bare scene. The POWs were gone, the British unit had disappeared, and there was not a single Iraqi civilian in sight. The bright blue sky hovered over a horizon of beige desert silently like an abandoned painting. The only life in this endless sphere of no man's land was a shaggy white dog freely going through the garbage we had left behind.

As expected, other journalists started showing up and once again we were driving around the battle zone in long convoys, separated looking for Coalition Forces. More journalists were now defiantly going back to Kuwait. The bad news continued to pour in, as the radio announced the intense resistance up ahead in Basra. There was no reporting to be done today; it was all about survival and making the right decisions. Journalists who attempting to return back to Kuwait, reported scattered Iraqi military across the desert. With this news we almost cancelled the option of making a run for the Kuwaiti border.

After a good hour of driving under the afternoon sun, we finally spotted a British military base. Dictating our desperate situation to the commander of the base, we waited impatiently under the hot sun for his orders. The only civilians on the scene were two Iraqi teenagers. As we waited, Mark decided to make up for the loss of time when he interviewed the two kids and jotted down the details of their sad war story. The two boys displayed a fresh attitude. They confirmed the many reports about Iraqi soldiers deserting the army and taking on civilian clothes. They explained how they fed and treated two soldiers who had showed up at their farm days ago. It was great to get an inside view on the nature of the Ba'ath Party ruling Iraq and how these kids were approached in school by the Ba'ath and forced to join training camps. These boys were rounded up at schools and forced to join Fedayeen camps where they were brainwashed and trained to fight American Zionists. I enjoyed translating their stories, as many journalists jotted down notes. The spotlight shifted suddenly to the commander as he walked towards us with updates on the status. The man stood tall on top of a bunch of rocks by the road announcing the sad news:

"I am sorry to tell you that you guys can not stay here at the base and we must ask you to leave. I recommend going back to Kuwait for the time being. I understand that you have had a rough night but there is nothing we can do here."

"Did the British unit at Safwan confront any Fedayeen last night?" one of the European TV journalists asked.

"I can't confirm that, I really don't have information," the commander replied, with his disciplined military demeanor.

With nowhere to go I listened to many theories. Some journalists were now planning a daring escape back through to the Kuwaiti border. Without a military escort, I was not ready to dash through Safwan at high-speed through bullets and RPGs. I watched an Italian cameraman documenting the confusion on tape. He sat on top of his Ford Explorer filming the British base and the reporters complaining about the army's negligence. I personally did not expect the army to escort us back into Kuwait since they had argued against our presence in Iraq at this early stage of the war. Sitting alone in the Pajero, I called my girlfriend and informed her that we were now figuring out the safest route back.

In a flash, my eyes caught a U.S. convoy, which seemed to be heading for the Kuwaiti border. The rampage of unilateral SUVs fired their engines and in seconds we were all trailing behind the long convoy. I spotted the British commander laughing out of control as he waived farewell. The commander was extremely happy to be caught on camera with Euro news since he knows his family will see him alive and well when this TV footage airs tonight on the daily featuring Iraq. The U.S. convoy was a gift from God and we were all smiling now with extreme confidence knowing the Kuwaiti border was minutes away. Passing through the gates of Safwan towards the border, I lost my thoughts and gazed with pity at the hundreds of kids giving us the thumbs up, as some yelled, "Water….Mr, Water!" The burning sun left them desperate with no water, security, or stability. About a hundred-meters away from the border, I jumped up from my passenger seat, opened the back door of the Pajero, and started throwing out all sorts of goods to the desperate kids. No doubt, they were shining with happiness when I showered them with bottled water, cans of juice, boxes of cereal, candy bars, fruits, and cans of tuna. It was the least I could give to the masses of helpless kids caught in the middle of political egos, under the mercy of blind Apache helicopters.

On the highway to Kuwait city, the sight of civilization, cars, traffic lights, and well-fed people brought tranquility to my reshaped soul. I stared at a mega size advertising billboard portraying a juicy Burger King Whopper. Sharing my gut feelings with Brian, we both smiled when we heard the sirens announcing that another Scud missile had broken the Kuwaiti airspace. The country was still a mess, just like we left it. Kids who went to school were carrying their gas masks and major companies were closed down. By now Saddam had launched six missiles towards Kuwait city, which have all been intercepted by U.S. anti-missile Patriots. After our short reporting interlude in Southern Iraq, no alarming siren was going to move us. All I wanted to see now was my clean bed, hot plates of food, cold water, and above all; a long shower accompanied with bubbles of perfumed soap.

II

ROAD TO THE NAKED TRUTH

Chapter 2: British troops forced to fire over the heads of civilians outside Basra after Fedayeen Saddam chose to use their own people as human shields. Photo by Brian Walski.

TUESDAY MARCH 25, 2003

Relaxed in the cool atmosphere of my air-conditioned living room in Kuwait, staring at the big screen TV, I watched the war on television and remained shaken. I just spent almost three days in a war zone, and here I was disoriented, alert, and subconsciously already planning my return back to Iraq. Our LA Times crew thought the same way, except that we needed to regroup and take on a new plan. My mind drifted to Vietnam veterans, as I tried to imagine how disoriented they must have felt going back home after *years* of fighting. My curious thoughts disappeared instantly with sounds of another warning siren announcing an Iraqi missile penetrating Kuwaiti airspace. Kuwait was a round the clock target for Saddam Hussein's short-range missiles. With reassuring news of Patriots intercepting every Iraqi missile, the general public felt safer. However, as I glanced through the local Arabic paper, the headlines read: "Forty- thousand Arab nationals return back home evacuating Kuwait due to the war."

As I took a long hot shower, I remembered the look in the eyes of those thirsty Iraqi kids. I retreated to my room after listening to my family's theories on the war. The situation has become unbearable in Kuwait. Stores were out of duct tape and gas masks. People were actually carrying their gas masks along with them to work, and some were putting them on in the streets every time they heard the loud warning sirens declaring an attack. The sight of my family trying to perfect the use of their chemical kit made me anxious. I lay in bed feeling depressed knowing that my father was having a hard time putting the gas mask on within the eight seconds required in the expected case of a chemical or biological attack.

By now, Kuwait's government had designated and advertised the location of special bunkers for residents of every neighborhood in the country. Shutting down to sleep was not hard this time. However, I was now hooked on the war and willing to do anything to help Iraqi civilians and to discover some truths that no television screen could show me, or anyone else watching for that matter.

Wednesday March 26, 2003

The musical ring of my cellular phone, early morning could not have brought a more optimistic voice than that belonging to reporter Mark Magnier.

"Is your bag packed? We could leave any moment, I am trying to work out a way back in."

"What about the Kuwaiti border? I heard it was closed for journalists too, after the chaos we caused last time?" I asked, with my eyes half shut.

"Moody, have faith in me. I am trying to make a deal with the Red Cross. Just keep it hush-hush." Mark added, as he reminded me to read his new daily article in the paper.

With my eyes poised on the television and the news, I saw images of the war with blood baths in the city of Nasiriyah and less fighting at the port city of Umm Qasr. Now, reading Mark's article on the LA Times website, I was happy that the humanitarian relief efforts were not neglected. The article quoted State Department spokesman Richard Boucher saying, "There is a massive humanitarian and reconstruction operation, including U.S. government multilateral assistance for the Iraqi people, that is ready to begin as soon as the port of Umm Qasr can be reopened."

Since we had witnessed serious chaos and artillery the first day we broke through into Iraq at the highway leading to Umm Qasr port, I was not too sure this would happen soon. Digging deeper into the article, I was happy to read that the Red Cross has acknowledged that its biggest priorities are securing water supplies and getting medicine to hospitals treating those injured in the war. At this moment, a flashback hit me, with the vision of the baby girl stuck with Asthma in Safwan, with no medicine, and the memory of her crying desperate mother. Magnier's article also stated a separate briefing on the administration's relief and reconstruction efforts for Iraq. Andrew S. Natsios, administrator of the U.S. Agency for International Development, said more than half of a 62- member "disaster assistance response team" had arrived to Kuwait.

Never was I so politically aware, and with death and chemical warfare round the corner in Kuwait, you could not help not being alert. I now felt the need to contribute with passion. I made a long-distance phone call to a friend in Egypt. I wanted to reach the director of the *Sot El- Arab* (Voice of Arabs) radio station. Luckily, through my friend, I spoke directly to the director of the station who was very happy to know I was volunteering to give her a daily update from Iraq. After speaking to the studio manager, I was instructed to call them from Iraq just minutes before broadcasting whatever I was reporting.

Chapter2—Road To The Naked Truth

The Kuwaiti Ministry of Information now banned the media from entering Iraq until further notice. However, a one-day media trip was organized to Safwan, Iraq to cover the aid relief distributed by the Kuwaiti Red Crescent Society.

Later that night, after supper, at the Sheraton hotel in haunted downtown Kuwait, our Times crew discussed the strategy for tomorrow's bus tour to Safwan. During my brief acquaintance with Terry, our multi-media producer, the loud warning sirens announcing another Iraqi missile sent us right down to the bunker in the hotel. With the lights out and everyone ushered to the basement of the hotel with their gas masks on, I felt the stress in Kuwait too. Japanese journalists were actually documenting the whole process on video through their gas masks and the lens of their Cannons. Italian journalists were the only ones jumping into the full chemical suit. This mental stress continued. We had to go through this routine three times in a matter of two hours, to accommodate Saddam's missiles. The third time around, a Syrian lady receptionist in the hotel explained to me that it was mandatory to enter the bunker, so I dragged myself there with no mask on this time. Before I knew it, an older German journalist sitting beside me on the floor of the bunker explained to me how vital it is to learn to place the mask on perfectly within eight seconds.

We were set for tomorrow, Brian, Mark, Terry, and I were ready to cover the historical humanitarian aid planned for tomorrow morning. Sam was staying back to cover the action in Kuwait especially since there had been unconfirmed rumors that some of Saddam's intercepted missile heads were loaded with chemical weapons. The mood in Kuwait was boiling with tension.

THURSDAY MARCH 27, 2003

Media credentials hung on my chest; I literally pushed my way onto one of the seven media buses designated for the coverage of donated aid distribution in Safwan. Parked in front of the Sheraton as a meeting point, journalists of various nationalities were shoving their way to ensure seats on the buses. Those holding cameras for television broadcasting were burdened as I pushed to make space for the rest of my team. Kuwait Ministry employees already over-worked on their weekend today lost their patience and ordered the buses away leaving behind many reporters. Competition in the media never ends and now it had grown inside me as I smiled to see the buses leave behind some reporters representing major competition to the Los Angeles Times.

Almost sure that most of the journalists on the bus had never crossed the border to Iraq; I watched them prepare themselves psychologically for the unexpected. For me, I felt safe that the buses were escorted by Kuwaiti police up to the border, then a U.S. military escort took over and followed the entourage into an open field on the edge of Safwan. The town looked just as hungry, broken down, and old as we left it days ago. Incidentally, the day witnessed a vicious sand storm that left everyone on their toes. Of course, the hungry Iraqi civilians awaiting the boxes of aid were dancing at the sight of the trucks rolling in. Three 40-foot trucks with the slogan Kuwait Red Crescent Society imprinted on the side brought an uncontrollable crowd of people running towards us. Brian, our photographer, placed his back-up bag on my shoulder as he jumped out of the bus towards the action, with his favorite camera. Terry disappeared into the crowd with his video camera, which left Mark and I running around interviewing the locals. Survival of the fittest was the name of this scene. Younger stronger men jumped right into the aid caravans throwing the boxes outside to their partners. Older women stood helplessly seeking any help. Little girls cried as they watched the rampage. Sad to ignore the elderly asking for my help, I followed Mark as he interviewed a calm man watching the whole run riot. I introduced our selves as reporters representing an American newspaper while Mark prepared his notebook.

"What do you think of this?" Mark asked, pointing towards the crowds toppling the truck.

Abdullah Yassin, an engineer, looked at me implying that he understood the English question and answered in Arabic, "Is this the freedom George Bush is talking about? These hoodlums taking the food are not Iraqis. Iraq has pride and history."

Translating his words, I realized where Mark was going with this story.

"Do you think there could have been a better way to distribute the rations?" Mark asked.

"Listen, this is Kuwait....The Kuwaiti government is doing this on purpose to embarrass Iraq and bring us out as animals fighting over food... Look around you at the poor farmers and kids. What about the media show organized by Kuwait? They want the whole world to see this embarrassment," Yassin replied, as he looked at me for backup.

Translating his wise words, I was sure Kuwait did not operate in this evil fashion, yet I was surprised at the lack of organization.

"My last question to you Sir; do you think these people still fear Saddam's regime with the presence of the coalition?" Mark asked, shouting over the ruckus of the horrific crowds.

"They are all supporters of Saddam. They are just here to take the food."

Looking with awe at the rumble over the boxes of aid, Mark and I interviewed a lady who stood amidst the crowd holding a can of tuna that had slipped out of one of the aid cartons. The boxes contained juice, bread, slippers, milk, tuna, and crackers, and were labeled with a sticker stating: "This is a gift from the Kuwaiti people to our brothers in Iraq."

Sad to see that Saddam had planted an eternal seed of hatred into the minds of his people, I decided to relay the big picture back to the media in Egypt. I called the desk of the *Sot El Arab* radio station and informed them that I would be calling back in three minutes to broadcast a live update from Safwan. As I watched Mark interview U.S. officers supervising this operation, I bumped into a Japanese female reporter who was obviously being harassed by a younger Iraqi rebel. The man was infatuated by her beauty as he tried to grab her hands. Before I knew it, the lady held on to me, and then with a quick smile the aggressive man released her and shouted; "I will leave this white *duck* only because you are an Arab!"

When I found myself free I called the desk at the radio station, and waited for them to give me the ok to start my three-minute broadcast report about the chaos. Coincidentally, a fistfight started at the center of the food distribution. Before I knew it, I was just rambling on about all what I saw with spontaneous passion trying to picture the average Egyptian man on the street listening to my words. I got so excited that I forgot to use classical Arabic, which was a major mistake. The station did not like the fact that I used the word 'barbaric' to describe the fighting over the aid boxes either. Before I could even finish the piece, a huge crowd of men added to the chaos as they danced and chanted for Saddam.

I was dissatisfied with my radio broadcast, the sand storm, and the organization of this whole aid distribution operation. So I just translated the words of the chants to Terry as he captured the whole performance on video: "*We sacrifice our souls and blood for you, Saddam!*"

Mark and I were probably the last journalists to head back onto the buses. On the bus Mark realized that his satellite phone was stolen from his backpack. With our team intact, we welcomed our peaceful trip back to Kuwait. The buses glided through the dark highways, lit in the horizon by the networks of oil refineries Kuwait is best known for.

In my living room with the family, I watched the short clips of this humanitarian relief broadcasted on Euro news and other major stations. Excerpts of the aid distribution were broadcasted under a silent program called "No Comment"; a montage of news footage basically portraying hotspot areas in the world without the voice-over reports. I had no comment myself, and all I was thinking about was Basra and Baghdad.

FRIDAY MARCH 28, 2003

To wake up on a Friday, the day of peace and prayer for Muslims, to a national warning siren announcing another Scud missile is nearby, remains a very depressing beginning. I lay in bed for minutes, staring at the ceiling, waiting for the siren announcing the end of the danger. Most Kuwaitis I had interviewed with Mark and Sam were positive and agreed that Saddam could not do more damage than what he did back in 1990 when he invaded Kuwait. All I know is that in the first Gulf War there were no scud missiles penetrating Kuwait and chemical weapons were not such a devastating threat. Packing my bag again, I heard the Friday call for prayers emerging from a neighboring mosque. Wishful thinking and lots of prayers were evident in times of distress. I could just imagine the Imam's across mosques in Iraq motivating their people to stand and fight the American Zionists. I had no doubt in my mind that most Iraqis wanted Saddam out, especially those oppressed Shia'a Muslims who like the Jews during Hitler's time were massacred by Saddam on a regular basis and dumped into mass graves. My short interlude in Iraq last week proved that rich active Ba'athi Party members and Saddam loyalists were counting on such a stir of religious emotions to support resistance and win the war against the so-called infidels, the Coalition.

Charged with ideas and hungry for Iraq, I switched to the big screen TV just in time to catch a segment on the price tag the U.S administration had placed on the relief and reconstruction of Iraq.

The news stated that a $ 74.7-billion supplemental spending bill President Bush is sending to Congress this week includes $ 3.5 billion for relief and reconstruction in Iraq. Of that, $ 2.4 billion will go towards food, housing, security, electricity, water, health care, and road and bridge building in Iraq.

Once again, my cell phone rang with news from Sam that we were moving in half an hour towards the border. Our team met a man working for the Kuwaiti Red Crescent who claimed he had good contacts with the Kuwaiti border police and we would be able to cross through. In a rush like a soldier, I checked my chemical kit, tied the laces of my combat boots, packed my vitamins, hugged my mom, and jumped into a cab towards the Sheraton. On the phone in the cab, I learned from Sam that they had met the Red Crescent employee in the lobby of the hotel.

Since the early deployment of coalition soldiers and intelligence into Kuwait during the pre-war phase, hotel lobbies were a theatre for transactions. Some off-duty military personnel were making deals selling used humvees to media teams. Kuwaiti officers were monitoring the scene from behind their coffee mugs as they hunted for media interviews, for a chance to shine and make it in the local paper. Drivers and translators hunted down jobs with high paying media organizations. As a matter of fact, the ITN Lebanese translator who is still missing in action was a taxi driver working outside the Sheraton when a tempting salary as an interpreter pulled him into Iraq. The CIA was my favorite; conducting their recruitment and interviews in the private halls of the hotels. A little bit of eavesdropping and disguised newspaper scanning proved very helpful in many cases.

When I arrived to the Sheraton, our SUVs were parked outside and just as my instincts forecasted, the man had over heard Sam and Brian conversing in the hotel lobby about their struggle crossing the border so he offered his service. An hour later, at the border, I realized that the two lane road leading to the border had switched to a one lane, in efforts to tighten security. Waiting inside the vehicle for the man to conduct his *magic* with the border officer, I realized from their hand movements and facial gestures that this was another failure. The man was not getting paid, and it was my turn to use whatever Arabic charm I possessed to lighten the situation.

"Sir, we have all our credentials and we are just going to do our job just like you are doing your job…. please let us through," I pleaded.

"I am the top official here, but I have a boss too, I can not let you through. I have orders," answered the officer, as I saw the reflection of my face in his sunglasses.

Now addressing him with his name, a lie, and a touch of humor, I added, "We will not tell anyone, besides we really need to meet up with the rest of our team to supply them with food and water."

"My friend, it is extremely dangerous on the other side. The other day a helicopter dropped a lost journalist right there," he answered, pointing towards an empty sandy lot.

"Sir, I understand your responsibility for the whole district, but this is our job. What would it take to convince you now?" I asked, with total anticipation for his reply.

"Look, do not try to bribe me. A Newsweek journalist tried that yesterday and I told him never to show me his face here again."

Lost for words, I stared at the Red Crescent representative and listened to his words as he told me to forget about it.

"What is your boss's name?" I asked the strict officer.

Pretending that I knew his boss, I played around with my cell phone dialing an imaginary number claiming that I knew him well. Watching the officer's face for any signs of mercy, I gave him more time to think claiming there was no response on the other side.

With no luck and the sun dimming into the late after noon, we retreated. On the drive back to the city, I listened to the radio announce that Umm Qasr port was relatively peaceful and that the British forces were in the process of clearing the harbor of mines. Sam then informed me in the jeep that more than 130,000 tons of food was sitting in warehouses in the region, and the British ship Sir Galahad is positioned offshore to deliver more food and water to Umm Qasr. To me that meant feeding the mouths of all these beautiful kids I encountered last week in Safwan. I was still positive about the war and I knew the only way the coalition would win this war is through the hearts and minds of the Iraqi people.

Still persistent and sure that we would cross the border the next day, Brian and I went shopping for more supplies. Stove canisters, batteries, a wider variety of canned food, pots, and more bottled water were among the top items on the list. We all knew that once we entered Iraq again, there was no coming back to Kuwaiti bureaucracy and that our trip would be indefinitely long.

Back at the hotel, or what we called headquarters, we learned that there was another media excursion organized by the Kuwaiti government covering more food distribution in Safwan. The trip was scheduled for the next morning at 7:00 am and only two representatives from each media team were allowed onto the bus. The plan was simple; Brian and I were to stay back among the villagers in Safwan after the buses leave. Mark Magnier, who never ceases to amaze me, was to wear the typical camouflaged U.S. army uniform and drive our SUV right behind the buses entering Safwan. Laughing at Mark practicing his army salute which he would not have to use the next day, I could not imagine him in a soldier's uniform. Our crew then laughed again at the publicized scandal of the Newsday reporter who entered Iraq before the war as a human shield. The wild man applied for a visa to Iraq from Jordan as a loyal human shield to Saddam. I wondered what Saddam's regime did to him when they discovered his lie and detained him. Entertained with this story, I headed back home leaving my bag in our SUV, awaiting tomorrow's perfect plan.

SATURDAY MARCH 29, 2003

7:00 am. We are on the buses headed towards Safwan to witness the second aid distribution in three days. Luckily, Sam was able to join Brian and me on the bus as Mark followed in our Pajero. So far his military outfit had tricked Kuwaiti border officers as he remained in the car and followed us when we entered Safwan. Like the last aid distribution, the chaos continued with people concerned about the thirst and hunger more than anything else.

Once again engulfed by starved Iraqis fighting over the packages from the aid caravans, Sam and I interviewed more people about this dilemma. I spotted a helpless skinny farmer standing on the side watching the madness, which included men punching each other and women complaining that they and their children had no chance at scoring any packages. The farmer identified himself as Nasser Shami and then said, "I would like to drink some water." With no water to offer the man, I tried to avoid him then heard him yell, "If this is freedom… then we don't want it!"

With electricity cut off, many residents said they have no news about the war in the north. Rumors were spreading as one man approached me stating that 17 Americans had recently surrendered at nearby Az Zubayr. Sam listened to this statement then asked another bystander what he thought about that.

"Yes that is good." Ahmed Jabber replied, "We want the Iraqis to beat the Americans. We are Iraqis, after all."

Translating the words of another civilian watching the humiliation of his people, I realized that educated and illiterate Iraqis all had the same views.

When asked by Sam if he believed the forces where here to liberate Iraq, Mohamed Attul, a petrochemical worker answered, "I don't trust that at all. They are coming to overpower us and take our oil. They are conquering us like Palestine."

With the Red Crescent trucks picked clean of every aid package, the trucks started to roll out. Kuwaiti officials used microphones calling all journalists to board the buses. I could see Brian was acting invisible as he walked farther into the desert. Sam left and jumped onto the bus then screamed at me, "You sure you want to stay?" I was too busy acting invisible too and I ignored the last call for journalists to board the buses. As the buses moved away, for seconds, I felt uncomfortable standing alone surrounded by hundreds of hungry people. U.S. helicopters were flying over and raining the area with black bits of paper known as 'Char,' which was made of material that distorted radar devices that might be used by the Iraqi army. Smoking a cigarette, I watched other reporters waving to me through the buses then Mark came to the rescue with our SUV. Moments later, Brian jumped into the back seat completing our bulletproof plan.

Driving through the city of Safwan, Mark removed his military outfit and hid it in the Pajero. Fired up with full concentration, we tightened our flack jackets and headed towards Umm Qasr. The road was safe yet filled with young kids giving us the thumbs- up along with cries for water. Obviously, they had interacted with hundreds of coalition soldiers and convoys and picked up the thumbs-up sign implying that everything was under control. Deserted or destroyed Iraqi battle tanks and anit-aircraft vehicles were spread around the highways and the desert. Empty trenches and sporadic weapons lay across the desert too. Indeed, everything at the port was calm. Almost deserted, the port was closed and guarded by U.S. soldiers who were anxious to move up north and engage in actual fighting.

The British were now facing intense resistance in Basra, Iraq's second largest city. As we approached the outskirts of Basra, we stopped at the road leading to Az Zubayr Bridge. British Challenger tanks and units were positioned on the two-way road, with soldiers spread across the road trying to control crowds of civilians. There were a few reporters on the scene taking notes and talking to civilians fleeing Basra. I watched Mark gather information from the army while Brian went on with his photography. Securing the location of our jeep, I watched the slums and the dry desert surrounding us. Signs of the air strikes were obvious as many buildings were demolished while some destroyed Iraqi tanks lay out of service. Not sure what to think, I locked the car and joined Mark and listened to the British officer's update. The major news was that Iraqi militia, firing machine guns and grenades, mounted on jeeps had forced civilians to turn back to Basra. Not too happy to hear that, I understood that this would hinder the efforts of British troops to bring humanitarian aid to Basra. It was no way near secured as the officer acknowledged that the city's water supply remained under the control of Saddam Hussein's forces.

Walking towards the people rushing away from Basra, Mark asked me to choose someone to interview. My eyes fell on a middle-aged man who seemed ready to explode.

"How bad is the situation in Basra?" I asked with genuine curiosity.

Fizal Abid Naser, 38, said, "We're very afraid"

"They were killing children and women at the crossroads," Naser added, referring to Fedayeen Saddam. Led by Saddam's eldest son Uday, *Fedayeen* (martyr troops) are the most loyal and viscous followers. Several witnesses confirmed that Fedayeen were breaking into homes and neighborhoods, forcing people to fight. British forces had hoped for a public uprising in Basra by the Shia'a Muslims who were suppressed and executed for years by Saddam. Unfortunately, British troops did not get this break and now were avoiding street fights against Saddam's loyalists. The complexity of the situation remained that residents were not allowed to leave, which could lead to a higher toll of civilian deaths. Squadron Leader Simon Scott, a British military spokesman revealed how ruthless the Fedayeen were when he pointed to the bridge and explained how just yesterday he witnessed Fedayeen firing at masses of civilians attempting to flee the city of 1.3 million residents. In a position to attack, the leader of Britain's 7th Armored Brigade had to watch them go to avoid killing innocent people.

Mark and I then approached a Mohamed who refused to give his full name since he feared for his wife and four children still trapped in Basra.

"The foreigners are afraid of losing their army. There are a lot of Fedayeen, maybe as many as 10,000 troops and militia fighters too, inside the city," Mohamed complained.

Mohamed then confirmed the many reports that Iraqi soldiers were taking over people's houses and using them to launch and plan attacks on the British.

"Where are they based? Have you seen them execute civilians?" I asked, in Arabic.

Translating his words to Mark, I kept looked behind me at the maneuvers of five British tanks moving robustly in the direction of Basra. Armed soldiers dressed in civilian clothes organized checkpoints at major intersections in the city. For a second, I stopped to think and realized how confusing that could be for the British soldiers. No wonder the only attack by U.S. or British forces had been through air raids or artillery fire.

"Yes, some civilians have been killed by Fedayeen," said Mohamed. "Just saying the wrong thing can get you killed."

Before leaving Kuwait earlier in the day, I listened to the radio announcing a major revolution in Basra. Evidently, everyone thought that would be a repeat to the revolution in 1991, which was oppressed by Saddam's regime. Such a revolution would have weakened the Iraqi army and the moral of the regime too. Unfortunately, it was a modest revolution in the Al Kaad neighborhood in Basra after Iraqi soldiers had confiscated people's houses for strategic reasons.

The highway leading south from Basra hosted a row of trucks, ambulances, cars, and carts fleeing the danger.

"Most residents are too loyal or afraid of reprisals to rebel. There was no revolution," said Mohamed Abas, 29, a farmer.

Still shocked at the responses, we continued our interviews as I approached a pick up truck. Introducing ourselves as journalists working for a paper published in California, I smiled to the driver's wife and three children jammed in the cab of the truck. Mohamed Saleh, a merchant fled with his family after the horror he witnessed in Basra.

"I just came from Basra, It's very dangerous," he said. Before I could elaborate on my question, an artillery shell exploded far in the direction he had come from.

"I could see that," I added, staring at Mark who was too busy taking notes and thinking ahead.

"We saw a lot of crossfire. I'm worried for my children," Mohamed complained, as he drove away.

On the other hand, across the road, ten miles outside the city, more than a hundred men were restless to enter back into Basra. Many were farmers who were working at the fields when the war started and never made it back home. The British Major manning the checkpoint explained to us that they were worried that younger men would join the resistance in Basra so they were very selective on whom to let through.

An old weary man approached me when he realized I spoke Arabic. "We've been stuck here for weeks," said Hamdani, "We're reduced to sleeping in the road or at the mosque."

I felt sad for the man but could not do anything. I knew the British were having a hard time identifying loyal Ba'ath Party members.

"The soldiers at the checkpoints search us, but don't let us through," Hamdani wailed, as he waived his hand to me for help.

Standing under the hot sun, I finally felt the roaring pain of the war. My mind blocked food and water. I did not even know where we were sleeping tonight. The story was right there in front of my eyes. Hours into Iraq and here I was observing the true facts, living the sad nightmare of those peaceful Iraqi people.

I stopped a happier man who was just given permission by the Brits to cross back into Basra. Salem Hasson, a 47-year old tea merchant, carried two bags of vegetables and a small bag of eggs that he was bringing back to his children. The prices were ten times higher in Basra after the air raids. The British army was aware of that as they let through herds of trucks loaded with onions and tomatoes grown in Safwan.

Walking away towards our jeep, a dark well-built Iraqi man approached me waving his hand, implying that he wanted a word with me.

"*Hallaw Hallaw*, You speak Arabic?" the stranger asked.

"Yes I do, Go ahead....what is your problem?" I asked, expecting him to complain or tell me another sad story from the archives of the war.

"I am an Iraqi intelligence officer, and here is my card to prove it."

Staring at the man's red identity card, his name read *Saddam Hussein*.

"I want to turn myself in. Could you just explain that to the Brits?"

Walking with the shady man towards the British officer in charge, I informed Mark that this he was turning himself in. I was also checking his demeanor and trying to read his mind.

Before we could interview him the British Major stopped us and just asked me to explain to Saddam that he will be transferred to regional headquarters for questioning.

As the soldiers took him away to the side of the tank, he looked at me and answered a question I asked him quickly during our short conversation.

"I decided to surrender because I had little to fight for," Saddam said, as he pointed towards the sky adding a quick prayer; *Allah Kareem* (God is kind)," "I don't own any land or houses in this country. Why should I fight anymore? My family and friends are dying over this."

With the sun an hour away from setting, I headed back to our jeep and took off my bulletproof vest. Most of the other journalists on the scene were so competitive to the point that they would not even reveal where they were sleeping for the night. Mark and Brian were advised by the British to sleep at Basra International Airport, which was a major base for the British forces. Sad and quiet at the events of the day, I stared outside the window for any signs of hope

"When do you think Basra will receive humanitarian aid? Whatever happened to that British supply ship Sir Galahad?" I asked Mark, with mixed emotions of anger and despair at the sight of people struggling for eggs and water.

"The ship docked after Umm Qasr port was cleared of mines. According to Col. Chris Vernon, Basra is clearly nowhere near their hands, and they have no way at the moment of getting humanitarian aid into the city," Mark answered, as he drove towards Basra Airport.

Driving into the airport, through the airplane run ways, I was happy to see an arsenal of British tanks and vehicles parked in an extremely orderly fashion. The soldiers were at ease, sitting around smoking, eating, or washing their clothes. After negotiations with Mark, the British commander permitted us to stay for one night only. I finally relaxed and called my family. Like every man in the desert, I was thinking about my woman too. Her mother was born in Basra. Her voice was medicine and I confessed to her that I saw her and her dear family in every civilian. Relaying the events of the day to her, I caught myself surprised at my own words. Verifying to her that there was no uprising in Basra, I realized again the responsibility of the media.

Leaving Mark and Brian to their laptops and deadlines, I strolled into the arrival hall of the airport. The place was dark as a cave. I followed the beam from my flashlight looking for a comfortable place to sleep. British military technicians had set-up their computers and maps inside. There was a unique peaceful silence that I had not felt all day. Broken windows let in a steady spring breeze and the airport's marble floors provided a cool atmosphere, very fit for sleeping. Without a doubt, I found my way to the transit hall and surrendered to a long row of brown cushioned seats.

Sunday March 30, 2003

My eyes let loose, ending a deep sleep. I lay down staring at a huge crystal chandelier hanging from the airport's ceiling, listening to British soldiers commemorating and shouting orders through the airport's halls. I did have vague dreams, but I was sure the roaring blasts of continuous artillery at dawn were real. Looking down the row of cushions I saw Mark's body crumbled in a quite sleep. We were so exhausted, that not even the night shelling of Basra grabbed our attention.

Up and ready, Brian and I boiled water for coffee and noodles. With his light humor Mark reminded us how lucky we were to be in Iraq. The stories were coming to us just for being here, and Mark's articles were already on the front pages of LAs' favorite newspaper. Our plan for the day was to pass by the old Ba'ath party headquarters, which is now a major British base, just a couple of miles from the airport.

Driving towards the base, we learned that it was located in a little town called Shuaybah. A center for oil, the town hosted the Shuaybah refinery, which was nothing more than a network of old rusted pipes and neglected offices. Still a source of income for many villagers, the refinery provided jobs for many of the men in the town. Now, closed and robbed, the rest of the refinery's trucks, furniture, and equipment were still threatened by looters. Approaching the base, I was not surprised about the slogans painted on the walls of what you used to be the Ba'ath Party headquarters; *"Iraqis will unite to fight the evil oppression of the American Zionists."*

Walking past the barbed wire through the gate, we were welcomed by a British soldier of Jamaican origin, on post under the hot sun. Inside the building it was clear that the British First Fusiliers army was in control of the area. Forming their base in what used to harbor the ruthless Ba'ath Party headquarters was an elegant symbolic approach to win over the support of the local villagers. Listening to a Fusilier brief Mark on the situation, I was sorry to hear that Iraqi mortar shells landed in Shuaybah before dawn, destroying two houses. Not surprised that the British artillery guns roared through out the day, firing rounds into Basra, I walked outside the base to converse with some of the Iraqis who were now friends with the soldiers.

With hesitation in their eyes, many villagers whispered as they talked to me. There was total distrust and men in the crowds were cautious about what they said. Mark flipped his notebook as I translated the complaints of the poor people.

A villager named Hamdani, who like many others, refused to use his last name then complained quietly, "Civilians are caught between two armies.

Where can we go? What will the Americans and British do, and for how long? They said it would take forty eight hours to reach Baghdad, but it's already been ten days. People are scared. Bush stays in America, Saddam in Baghdad, we're in between."

Now that the language barrier was resolved, the villagers surrounded me, offering me cigarettes and asking my name. I felt safe and realized that this group of men was not like the rebels of Safwan. They were more educated and extremely loyal to the Shuaybah refinery. However, whenever I asked questions about Saddam Hussein, their faces dimmed, others lowered their voices, and many spoke then pleaded for anonymity. During my conversation with them, I could hear heavy artillery, far around Basra city. A younger guy approached me and warned that there are spies around every corner, maybe even in the crowd among us. These villagers were glad the British were in their poor neighborhood and kept asking if they were here to stay and for how long. The wiser men, held on to memories of the 1991 Persian Gulf War, when the U.S. relieved Saddam after the Iraqis had started a revolution only to find Saddam just as strong, appointing his cousin, Ali Hassan Majid- better known as " Chemical Ali"- to crush them with mass executions. People were talking about the famous news footage of the unidentified man gripped with catharsis and beating a painting of Saddam with his shoe. A rumor was spreading across the south that he had been executed by Saddam's troops.

As I walked around, guys bombarded me with questions that I could not answer. I had no idea when the war would be over or the destiny of Saddam. I was now dedicated to understanding the principles of the Ba'ath Party and how they got so strong and influential. I learned that some villagers were hesitant to accept aid packages and water in fear of execution by Saddam's spies for collaborating with the enemy. Capt. Joe Butterfill of the First Fusiliers clarified the situation more when he said, "The biggest thing exercising people is whether we're here to stay or not. If they're seen to collaborate with us and the regime comes back, they fear being executed."

On the move to report on a shipment of aid arriving in a poor Shuaybah town consisting of nothing but a collection of dirt houses, I wondered if this distribution method would be different since the army decided to apply a new system allowing the Iraqis to control the distribution. Following U.S. humvees and British Land Rovers into the town, I was excited to see several hundred people waiting behind a barrier of white tape as soldiers urged them to be patient. Once again, I was the only bilingual person on the scene, and I found my self sucked into helping the army with pleasure. I kept relaying the soldiers' orders in Arabic telling the people to stand in line, reminding them that there is enough for everyone. A local leader held a bunch of ration cards belonging to the head of each family. The cards were issued under the U.N. oil-for-food program. Each card stated the father's name and number of children in his family.

With the sun at its peak, I walked with Brian towards a blue U.S. army water tanker that was surrounded by women and kids pumping fresh water through one thick hose right into their pots and barrels. Instructing them to stand in line, I realized the poor people were not listening to me. Just as I leaned to help a woman carry her full barrel of water, a loud echoing explosion broke my wisdom and left me scared for seconds as I instantly ducked feeling weak at the knees. Surprised that I was the only one who reacted, I smiled with embarrassment when a veiled Iraqi woman said, "You are scared? We are all used to this, it's far from here." Unscheduled ammo detonations confiscated by the British army really bothered me. It came with no warning and left a huge brown sandy cloud of smoke in a distance. By now, I was picking up slowly on the difference between *incoming* and *outgoing* firing.

Looking for Mark, a man grabbed my shoulder and offered me a cigarette and then asked me to publish his words in the paper. Jotting down his quotes for Mark, the man whispered, "Hussein has robbed the national wealth for his personal use, but Bush would not have attacked Iraq if not for the oil."

The man refused to reveal his name then asked, "There are dictators every where. Why us? "

"I will give your comments to our reporter. Thank you," I replied, weighing the phrases in my mind.

With the distribution under way, I was asked by Major Doug Stellmack of the 402nd Civil Affairs Unit to assist his soldiers and the local Iraqi leader controlling the crowds. "We want to see equitable ownership and have them take over. We tried to put a lot of thought into this. We want it to be a template," Major Stellmack added. Not having a microphone was a major obstacle, so calling names over the natural noise of the big crowd was a joke. The system was working slowly, but many villagers were growing impatient as they stood for hours under the sun waiting for their name. I stood on top of a truck shouting at the locals, urging them to stand in line. Mark approached me and whispered, "You don't work for them. You don't have to do that."

For almost an hour, two guys standing behind the aid caravan continued to wave at me, asking for help. They carried no ration cards and came walking all the way from Az Zubayr. They looked smart and were smiling as they kept whispering in my ear that they wanted food for their wives and families. Feeling guilty for raising their hopes and stalling them, I walked over and introduced myself. The two men introduced themselves as former soldiers and Ba'ath members. For a second, I saw a window of opportunity, a chance to get a full understanding of this seedy Ba'ath Party. Following the good old bartering system, I promised them three aid boxes if they told us everything they knew about the Ba'ath.

"With pleasure, I only fear God," Ayat Jaber Farag yelled, with a laugh of desperation.

Back with the boxes I had promised them, Mark joined us as we sat in the sand close to our jeep away from the escalating chaos.

"Why did you join the Ba'ath Party?" I asked, relaying Mark's question in Arabic.

"Many people join the Ba'ath Party to enter university or obtain a good job. Only Ba'ath loyalists are allowed to work in strategic industries, including broadcasting."

"How does the recruitment work?"

"They bother us at school. They used to pick us up from elementary school and force us to train with Fedayeen Saddam. Like animals, these guys literally eat dogs!" Farag laughed.

His friend then added, "They come days after the training and try to push us into signing up with the party. I used to skip school sometimes after the training to avoid haggling with them." After high school, as a member, you progress until you reach the high ranks. Finally, at the top after many years, hard-core members intimidate opposition, form internal spy teams, and file reports to the regional headquarters in Baghdad pointing out traitors, which leads to their execution in many cases. These brainwashed groups of loyalists are the main threat to the coalition, fearing that they will be punished severely under any new regime.

"Why are the people still afraid of Saddam today?" Mark asked.

With his open sarcasm, Farag laughed and said, "Hussein doesn't have to be here, just his ghost makes them afraid."

"People will only stop feeling trapped in the middle when Saddam is taken out. He has been in power for thirty years, that's all people know."

"So you are not afraid?" I asked, with admiration.

"My whole life, I've seen Saddam on the wall, on television. You see those people chanting for him and clapping on television? They are all rounded up...shoved into buses and transferred to these parades," Farag responded then asked for another box.

When I refused to give him the fourth package, he stood up, laughed, hugged me and said:

"There is a joke in Iraq, that even television static is the sound of Saddam snoring!"

4:30 pm. Back to the crowds of angry villagers, we were exhausted. The situation was out of control. British soldiers were shouting at the crowds, the people were pushing forward, and the hysteria began. People rushed into the aid caravan and just like the first two attempts in Safwan the scene turned bloody with kids punching each other and older women crying for help. I stood helpless as I watched the British bring in the tanks to serve as barriers while the troops urged the people backwards again. Minutes later, the army retreated in frustration and left the savage scene. Once again the aid caravan was picked clean. I watched Mark quote Capt. Mark Ellwood of the 1st Cheshire Battalion as he commented; "We did our best, but at the end of the day we're not getting support from the locals. They don't like to stand in line."

Our home for the night was Umm Qasr Port. We parked our jeep next to the four U.S. soldiers guarding the entrance. I got acquainted with the soldiers from San Jose, while Mark and Brian set-up the generator. The soldiers were wearing their Oakley sunglasses and bored with their post. The port was deserted, with only a few stray hungry dogs roaming around our car waiting for any leftovers.

Monday March 31, 2003

Waking up to young boys banging on our Pajero's window, asking for food and water was a good new reality check, reminding me that in Iraq every bottle of water was valuable. The night was calm except for interval roars of coalition convoys driving through. The skies had been lit with flare bombs used by the British to light up the night sky for ground operations. That night I spotted three sets of orange pumpkin shaped flare bombs that just popped up high in the sky and descended slowly for minutes, lighting up the perimeter for vision.

Mark had picked up the news from wires that resistance in Basra was just as bad, except now there was news that huge explosions had been reported around the outskirts of Basra. Driving towards Az Zubayr Bridge, outside Basra, we could see two separate rays of black smoke from a distance, ripping through the sky. Ten minutes later, we were facing Az Zubayr Bridge, the black smoke was now right above us hovering over the clear blue sky, and the massive amount of civilians detained by the British was much more than those we had witnessed days ago. With our vests on, Brian and I followed Mark as he approached the British officer for a briefing on the situation. There were hundreds of women clutching babies and men carrying their possessions in duffel bags. Groups of younger kids waived at me and shouted their hellos in Arabic. I was actually recognizing faces in the crowds from the few days I had been here. Glad the crowds were under control, I walked to our Pajero to pick up my own camera.

Without a single warning, the now familiar loud rattling sounds of machine guns rained the place with terror. A signal had been given by Iraqi undercover scouts in the mud huts surrounding the bridge. Iraqi militia in white pickup trucks, far within the swamps, fired at the British checkpoint. I knew very well they were incoming shots. I leaped onto the asphalt and hid behind another media jeep. I could see Mark and Brian were taking defensive positions. Immediately, a scarier incoming shell rammed in from another mud hut, then a mortar shell landed meters away from the British checkpoint. Now lunging with my head ducked moving back farther from the scene, I spotted my crew panicking. Both Mark and Brian were flat on their faces on the street behind a man made sand dune, with their hands on their helmets.

Mothers and children screamed with desperation and filled the air with more panic. The once calm crowd, were now racing towards the British soldiers for help. Watching the nose of a British Challenger tank rotate towards the mud huts, I ducked again to the continuous thunderous banging blasts of artillery as the Brits returned fire. Soldiers were panicking too as they struggled to protect themselves and control the crowds. The refugees lived the horror as they raced away from the scene caught between the cross fire. I had never experienced such fear and never witnessed such contradictions. If war permits fair game military killing, then what belief justifies the Iraqi military using their women and children for human shields?

Considerably calmer, I ran towards Mark and Brian. They were still crouched behind a sand dune. Only outgoing fire ruled the sky now, as the tanks continued to fire their shells towards the maze of huts outside Basra. Hiding along with Mark, were four Iraqi high school teenagers, who were waiting for a chance to run too. A true professional, Mark flipped through his notebook to gather more information on Basra. I asked the boys if Iraqi military was using their school for bases. A teenager by the name of Jalal Abdel Karim, confessed that there were tanks parked in the playing area of Al Marbad Elementary School. I freaked out when he said that there were rooms filled with gas masks and mortar shells.

With a pause in the battle, scores of people including us ran fast towards the south away from the bridge. The black clouds of smoke were now darker and the whole perimeter was just unbearable. Mark jotted down the reaction of Major Peter Macmullen with the 1st Battalion of the Irish Guards, as he sat on the curb commenting, "In a way we can't do an awful lot. The Iraqis work in groups of two or three, driving white trucks dressed in civilian clothes. They have no position. They're moving and use the slums to our left and right, making it difficult to fire back." I knew the administration on the British political arena and in Washington was pressuring the coalition military leaders to push forward faster. Evidently, Major Duncan McSporran of the 1st Fusiliers knew his orders as he commented, "We've got to go in." Mark later informed me that McSporran's unit had secured one of the main bridges leading into Basra several days ago in a 36-hour operation that included crushing an Iraqi attempt to blow up the bridge with explosives. After a week of shelling Basra from the perimeter, the city was expected to fall soon. So far they had established forward observation posts, which they planned to use for launching artillery attacks on Fedayeen and Iraqi military. Recent British loses included one British Royal Marine in a British commando raid on Southern Basra.

Peace did not last long enough, as once again sounds of 60- and 120 millimeter mortar rounds blasted towards the edge of the bridge. This time at least three hundred poor Iraqi refugees lost it as they ignored the British soldiers shouting at them in English, ordering them to stay put and lie down on the sand. They just rushed forward. Men pulling their old mothers, veiled women struggling with their babies on their shoulders, and families of numerous children struggled to keep up. Crouched behind our jeep, I breathed heavily watching the British troops resort to their last option as they defended themselves firing their machine guns over the heads of the refugees. Everyone bolted in their space and knelt down on the ground. The situation got even worse when an Iraqi shell landed close to our position toppling an electric tower leaving a cloud of smoke and dust. That was *it* for me, I jumped in the driver's seat of our jeep and steered away crossing the muddy sidewalk separating the two-way road and slipped right in between two tanks, and headed south.

Farther from the danger, most of the refugees confirmed that Fedayeen were bribing people or keeping them hostages so they could stay and fight. As we briefly interviewed several people, Jabber, 34, a fleeing oil worker commented, "They find people give them a weapon and force them to fight." I was disgusted to know that lately the Fedayeen were offering people promissory notes worth $10,000 to stay and fight.

"There are no banks. Where are you supposed to cash an IOU?" I asked the small crowd around me, not expecting any logical answer.

Most of the refugees confirmed the sad truth that Fedayeen, Baath loyalists, and Iraqi military, and militia had taken over schools, civil buildings, and some hospitals for use as shelters, ammo dumps, and tank storage. The picture in my mind was so drastic. I was not asking anymore questions. Angry men were just raining Mark and me with their queries. A man who quietly informed me that he was a soldier until two days ago, shared his opinion with me saying, "Fedayeen are very good at street wars. I don't think the British and Americans are brave enough."

"If they go into Basra there will be a slaughter house," added the man, who later identified himself as Aris Darraj. Later, Mark explained that even though street fights are dangerous, the British were well experienced after their missions in Somalia, Kosovo, and Cyprus.

A couple of miles away from the nasty scene at the Az Zubayr Bridge, we regrouped as we parked our SUVs at another British checkpoint which was totally secured. Ironically, the soldiers at this checkpoint were frisking people hoping to enter back into Basra. Abdullah Aziz, 25, explained how he went to get food and got stuck for days outside the city.

"I'm scared to go to Basra, but I've got to get my family and get out," Aziz complained, with tears in his eyes.

A strange scene was taking place at this checkpoint as four Iraqi men sat in the sand with both hands placed on their heads. Soldiers pointing guns to their heads ordered all media away and refused to give statements.

Curious, I walked closer to the Major in charge and offered to translate. Surly, the officer called me over. I focused really hard to memorize the names and details for use in our articles.

The Brits were suspicious about Ba'ath loyalists trying to sneak back into Basra to support the resistance. I asked them about their occupations and reasons for entering Basra as I jotted down their names on military forms designed by the Brits. Of the four men, the most suspicious was a 38-year old man called Ali Zein Abdin. The soldiers found a thick brick of cash hidden in the side panels of his late model pickup truck. The Major was very upset when the man insisted that he was a farmer.

"Ask him why his hands are so soft and where he got his expensive watch," the British major shouted, as he ordered his troops to take him in for further questioning at headquarters.

After several hours at the checkpoint, both the army and the locals were frustrated, so the Brits let everyone pass through towards Basra. Hundreds of young men rampaged past the soldiers and the barriers shouting pro-Saddam Hussein slogans.

"There is a fear they'll rejoin," said Capt. Sam Devitt of the Irish Guards 1st Battalion. "But it's a checkpoint not a blockade."

Mark was hunting for more information as he pushed me to concentrate just a little longer before we called it a day. As a youngster living in Kuwait, I always heard about Saddam's brutality, and how he cut the ears of men deserting the army. Well, Mark caught one of these tortured souls, as the man walked alone away from Basra. Walid Nabil Ibrahim, 31, complained that he had no family and that he was fed up with the regime. I felt him seeking help as he turned his head revealing to us his right ear or what was left of it, a third of it was missing. Walid then removed his shirt and showed us the acid burns on his back. Then he confessed that he was tortured in jail for three years by knives, electricity, and chemicals. He finally paid his way out after working for a low wage inside. Watching Brian photograph his ear, I walked away speechless, looking for solitude.

"Moody, we're leaving right away just tell me what this man is saying."

Murtada Qadi walking with his wife and children, including their sweet 1-year-old son had caught Mark's attention since he had left Basra without any of his possessions. He decided to leave after air strikes started hitting Basra around 6:30 am.

Caressing his son's cheeks, full of despair, I translated his words like a robot, as he complained, "They use us as human shields. They put us in front…themselves in the back….They control every corner of Basra."

Our home for the night was outside the gates of the British 7th Brigade base, located off-road in the desert, five miles south of the Az Zubayr Bridge. Mark decided that we should stay close to Basra in case the city fell to the British the next day. Our new home was safe yet the non-stop mobilization of tanks and convoys bombarded us with dust and lots of noise.

Trying to relax, I called home and checked in with the family. I avoided talking about any details of my day because I wanted to hear their side of the war news. After all, out here in the desert we had no television and very brief radio news did not give us a complete view of Baghdad. Mark and Brian were busy sending their information through the net. We used satellite phones to maintain an internet connection. We were safe with the 7th Brigade. However, after what I saw today, I was now fully aware of the dangers surrounding me.

Using bottled water to scrub the dirt off my body, I stood under a tree wondering about tomorrow, looking forward to a positive end to this war. Every single face and quote I encountered today was engraved in my mind. I had been blocking the idea of Saddam actually using chemical weapons in efforts to deter the coalition. Today, that kid confirmed that his school was filled with gas masks. I did not know what to expect. I did get good chemical weapon training before coming here, but my imagination could not grasp it. Should I expect a speeding plane tomorrow morning dropping a chemical or biological bomb? I headed back to our truck, and lay flat in the back seat, knowing that my chemical kit and mask were somewhere in the car in case that animal Saddam lost his mind. Why not? He did it in 1988, when he ordered his cousin "Chemical Ali" to use chemical weapons and wipe out five- thousand Kurds in Halabja.

III

HEARTS AND MINDS

Chapter 3: Flyer distributed to Iraqis at British checkpoints outside Basra. "This time we are here to stay. Let's cooperate together for victory!" Photo by Mohamed Fahmy.

TUESDAY APRIL 1, 2003

Awake and alone in our jeep, I covered my face with a light blanket, hiding from the bright sun. I could hear Mark and Brian preparing coffee and cracking jokes at my heavy sleeping habits. Because of the noise made by the continuous military vehicles and tanks passing in and out of the gates of the British 7th Brigade base, there was no chance for anymore sleep. Keeping my boots on while asleep proved to be a hassle, yet my feet felt better as I walked towards our stove for some boiling water and fresh coffee. Mark saluted me as he continued to dismantle his tent. Brian informed me that the U.S. army was encountering serious resistance on their advance towards Baghdad. The Sunday Telegraph crew had parked in close to us at night but did not identify themselves until the morning.

With no warning, I panicked at the sight of a British guard hustling towards us, yelling repeatedly, "Gas alert…! Put your gas masks on… put your gas masks on!"

Confused at the sight of the guard placing his own gas mask back on right after he relayed his orders to us, I ran to the jeep. Brian was fast as he placed his gas mask on immediately. Mark was not sure where his gas mask was, yet he dug through the bags in the back seat until he found it and put it on quickly. I, on the other hand had no clue where my mask was, so I simply wrapped my head tight with the blanket like a mummy and jumped back into the front seat of our jeep. Moments later, Mark unlatched the door and handed me an extra gas mask he had brought along. Now, looking through the glass of my mask, I could see no signs of an attack, yet I was not sure what to look for. The Sunday Telegraph crew were all wearing their masks too and standing around waiting for further instructions from the British. The Iraqi children and sheepherders hanging around us must have thought we were aliens from Mars. Ten minutes later, the same guard ran back again with news that this was a false alert and we could now remove the masks.

Barbara Jones from the Sunday Telegraph walked up to me and expressed her anger at such a scare. She then complained that she was having a hard time reporting without a translator. Her crew then teamed up with Abu-Dhabi TV and left towards their story of the day.

With no real destination in mind, we headed towards the Az Zubayr Bridge to see if the British had advanced towards Basra. Coming off the dirt road and onto the asphalt, I could see the smashed up SUV of the late Terry Loyd from the ITN station. Unfortunately, their truck was nothing more than a landmark for other journalists to pinpoint their locations. At the bridge, the situation was still the same with black smoke from the burning oil wells conquering the sky. Waiting for Mark to come back with new information from the British Major, I observed the ground and collected some of the leaflets that had been dropped by the coalition before the actual air strikes days ago. One Arabic leaflet covered with faces of children and parents stated in point form:

- Don't interfere with the coalition forces
- Stay in your homes
- For your security, the coalition will enforce a curfew
- Set your radio frequency to the information broadcasting station for the latest war news.

Not too sure how the Iraqi community reacted to thousands of leaflets dropped from airplanes before the initial air strike, I translated another flyer decorated with battle tanks and the face of Saddam Hussein:

- The Iraqi people are not the target of the coalitions' military operation.
- The strict violent regime is the target of the coalitions' military operation.

Mark returned with news that the British were now using nighttime raids to explore Iraqi defenses as they waited for the anticipated fall of Basra. With the situation at status quo, we headed back down south to Shuybah towards the old Ba'athi headquarters for more British intelligence on the war.

Inside the Shuybah base, I had a chance to interact with British soldiers relaxing indoors away from the heat. Some soldiers were cooking while others were writing to their girlfriends and families back home. My favorite was a soldier too busy to talk as he played a war game on his lap-top trying to defeat an enemy of battle tanks. They all agreed that capturing Basra would definitely be an important strategic and political goal. One of the British Fusiliers escorted us into a back room full of surface-to- air missiles and artillery shells that the Iraqis had left behind before fleeing the headquarters.

On our way out of the base, the Iraqi civilians who were now sharing their village with the soldiers expressed their happiness as they bombarded me with more questions about their future. Not too sure about the outcome of the war, I just guaranteed them that Saddam Hussein would never return back again to haunt them.

Mark and I had been relying on eating Iraqi dates for replenishing our energy. Stopping to restock at the Umm Qasr market, we were glad to see people resuming their life normally. The open market was full of vegetables, some fruits, and small amounts of eggs. Very little canned food sat on the shelves, but most of it was expired. We interviewed some of the merchants and villagers who were all peaceful and hoping for a better future. Umm Qasr was generally faster to recover than Safwan because it was a port area with more working Iraqis. However, it still remained drenched in poverty, and like the rest of the south, their major problem since the war began was lack of security, water, and electricity.

Parked for the night outside the quiet port of Umm Qasr, we followed the news of the war in the north through the BBC station. Listening to different analyses of the war on Arabic radio channels got me thinking about the Middle East in general. Since the historical attacks of September 11, I had faced minor problems myself while working in Canada, for having a name like *Mohamed.* Working as a customer service representative for a company based in Canada, yet serving clients in America, I was instructed by my boss to use another working name on the phone to avoid doubt and gain the customer's trust. Now, I was in Iraq witnessing history and trying to put the pieces of the puzzle together.

Wednesday April 2, 2003

Our sleep at Umm Qasr Port was fairly quiet, but the mosquito attacks never stopped. I caught myself chasing one with a magazine inside the Pajero. That night Mark and Brian were sleeping as I watched the skies light from a distance. I was happy to spot sets of flare bombs light the sky throughout intervals of the night, knowing that the British were conducting night raids.

In the morning, we woke up in a rush. We drove through Umm Qasr right towards the old Ba'athi headquarters for updates on the night raids. Outside the British base, an American Hummer belonging to U.S. Special Forces was parked and surrounded by villagers, who were just as curious as I was. A big American officer with sunglasses to suit his robo-cop style, stood alert with a high-tech remote control as he tilted his head towards the sky trying to control a small plane. Trying to figure out their job, I approached his three other team members and introduced myself. The team was conducting a reconnaissance operation over the outskirts of Basra using a state of the art spy camera connected to the agile plane. The villagers had never seen one, and I have only seen it in movies. Minutes later, the officer brought his eagle back in. I watched them dismantle the long fiberglass wings and the body of the plane. To everyone's surprise a spy plane with the size of a baseball bat was now safely packed into a box as small as a first aid kit. As the Americans drove away, a villager friend of mine stepped out of the audience and laughed as he approached me sarcastically saying, "With all the oil in Iraq, does Saddam even have a spy plane like that?"

Excited to hear about the British night raids, I walked inside the base to find Mark, Brian, and the British Major sitting on the only couch in the room.

Apparently, the night raid took place at Al Garma Bridge, the first bridge outside Basra. As the night descended, 25 soldiers slipped discreetly into no man's land. Most of the Geordies (term used to describe residents of Newcastle, England) felt nervous about such a risky operation to snatch a man out of Iraqi territory. It was not an easy task, as it did take longer to complete the operation. The men struggled through mud up to their ankles, to reach their target, a house at the edge of Basra. Moving through the muddy fields, they stayed 30 to 40 feet apart, to avoid exposure. After a good hour, the soldiers hid outside the intended house that had been used as a reconnaissance base by the Iraqis and to launch mortars on British points and civilians. Some soldiers were using night-vision goggles while others relied on mere nightlight. The soldiers then radioed artillery strikes behind and to the right of the house, so the Iraqis thought they were being attacked from those directions. Surveillance aircrafts using heat imagery quickly warned the soldiers about the presence of two guards, whom they avoided. Within seconds, half a dozen Fusiliers kicked down the door and rushed in, grabbing their man with his weapon at hand. Two other armed Iraqi militiamen attempted to escape but they were killed outside the building. Two of the bigger Geordies dragged the prisoner out the door as the other soldiers opened fire to cover their retreat. Three Cobra helicopters circled the skies overhead for additional protection. As the soldiers evacuated the dangerous area, an artillery air strike was called in to secure the premises. Armored vehicles met the soldiers with their prisoner at Al Garma Bridge for a speedy retreat back into British controlled territory.

Major Paul Nanson, who led the raid explained to Mark the importance of such attacks as he added, "By extracting someone in their midst, it unsettles them. I expect the next night they didn't sleep... The last thing you want is to wake up and find 25 Geordies in your bedroom."

I took notes for Mark as he interviewed a couple of soldiers who were actually involved in this night incursion. They all agreed that such operations help build their moral as they waited for the big attack on Basra. They all felt that it boosted their confidence when it sent the message to Iraqis that the Brits can reach them anywhere. Now encircled by a proud Captain Craig Taylor and Major Nanson, they both agreed that these operations destroyed the eyes and ears of the Iraqi military. "Taking them effectively makes the enemy blind. They might know you're there but not where you are."

"Do you think high-tech weaponry gives the soldiers a little more edge?" I asked, with hesitation.

"These operations are ultimately about guts. At the end of the day, you're going head-to-head with the enemy," Major Nanson answered.

Driving towards the south, Mark and I were quiet and sad that Brian was leaving back to LA. Brian had admitted to falsely combining two photos into one, therefore breaching the basic rules of photojournalism. After twenty-five years of successfully fulfilling his ethical job, Brian just broke down in the blunder of stress this war had laid down on him. We had to drop him close to the border or find someone driving back into Kuwait to give him a ride across the border. I would have loved to escort him into Kuwait and back in aim for a shower, cold drinks, and a good night sleep in a bed away from mosquitoes and the night blasts of artillery. However, the Kuwaiti border was just as strict, only a minimum amount of journalists had passed through within the last days. On the way to Safwan, we spotted a Kuwaiti media bus that transported reporters into the Umm Qasr port for a day trip.

Loading Brian's luggage on the bus, I wondered if I would ever see him again.

Now waiting for the bus to leave, I watched a beautiful black female approach me from the desert with her little baby girl. Like a dream, I stared at the woman's blue eyes and her straight silk hair with total shock at her voluptuous well fed body and the top of the line designer clothes she was wearing. The lady was subtle about her problem when she explained how she lived in the United Arab Emirates, but was left behind during a vacation in Iraq with her husband. Her man had left for a two day trip, but never returned due to the air strikes, leaving her alone with her young daughter in a war zone. The desert heat was peaking now, so I grabbed the child and took her in our truck. The girl's eyes shinned when I gave her juice and candy. My eyes were bolted to the mother as she screamed with tears through my satellite phone, telling her family how bad her situation was. Without money or a place to stay they were in trouble. There was no Western Union, banks, or any way of transferring money to her, and all the Iraqi borders were shut. We personally could not take them along with us due to the dangers of the job and the liability. I stared at the woman's sad blue eyes and informed her that her best bet would be to flag down a Red Cross truck and ask them for help. After all, the Red Cross is specifically responsible for displaced people stuck in the war. I was still speechless as I handed the mother twenty dollars, then retreated to my air-conditioned Pajero. I quietly watched her pull her 4-year old daughter into the hot desert towards the road.

Thursday April 3, 2003

After a long hot night of restless sleep in the backseat of our jeep, I welcomed the morning without a shirt. Walking grouchy around the vehicle, I yelled grouchily at the kids surrounding the truck. I was worried someone would steal our equipment or phones. With Brian gone, Mark and I were inseparable as we continued to support each other gracefully. I was fed up with the mosquitoes and did not know what war strategy to use to get away from them. With hopes that the British might have advanced towards Basra, we headed to the Az Zubayr Bridge again. The all too familiar scene at the British checkpoints remained the same, but this time the checkpoints had advanced ahead declaring a closer victory towards Basra. Most of the troops dispersed across the south were more relaxed as they took off their helmets to swap for their floppy hats, berets, and bare heads. I thought that strategic change was due to the hot temperature. However, I listened to a British Captain explain to Mark that the troops were now patrolling the recently secured towns of Safwan, Umm Qasr, and Shuaybah, trying to adopt a softer touch and pretend to be at ease as quickly as possible. "This is just one of the tactics the British military has developed after decades of operating in riotous quasi-urban environments in Northern Ireland, the Balkans, and Cyprus. " I think we are probably the best anti-guerrilla warfare army in the world," said Captain Mac McGuire's of the 1st Fusiliers, a veteran of confrontations in Northern Ireland and Bosnia.

Weighing his words in my mind, I did not vocalize my thoughts, as I knew that Iraq could never be compared to those countries. An Islamic country like Iraq fumed by the treacherous beliefs of the Ba'ath Party could be a major obstacle in this war. If the majority of Muslims view this war as an occupation rather than liberation, then the situation could lead to Islamic Jihad. What we witness today in Israel and what Osama bin Laden preaches through Al Qaeeda is the Jihad against crusaders fighting the freedom of Islam. Already signs of such holy war surfaced when four Marines were killed last Saturday when a suicide bomber drove his taxi into a checkpoint and detonated a bomb near Najaf, in central Iraq. The British understand the sensitivity of their mission. Troops were attempting to separate two objectives of urban warfare: alleviating the fears of the civilians to gain support as they strike the "baddies" as some called them.

Major Nanson of the Irish guards elaborated more on the lessons learned from Northern Ireland as he specified the importance of checkpoints. Outside Basra, these checkpoints are used to reduce the smuggling of weapons and fighters into Iraq's second-largest city. They also help in capturing Fedayeen

Saddam and senior Ba'ath Party officials trying to escape. In addition, the checkpoints allow the troops direct contact with the local residents without attracting much attention. After years of trial and error in Northern Ireland, the British have designed their checkpoints carefully in Iraq. At the Az Zubayr Bridge checkpoint, the last one before the no man's land outside Basra, the British have assigned two Challenger tanks well ahead to warn the troops by radio when unidentified vehicles approach. A search area follows the checkpoint, which is protected by four observation towers to spot snipers. In the middle, tanks and soldiers surround a 'dead zone' just in case someone does slip by. However, these checkpoints were established mainly to maintain a flow. Lt. William Hawley with the Irish Guards' 1st Battalion commented clearly: "We're trying to let normal life continue as much as possible."

Watching the soldiers handing out a new set of leaflets printed by the army, I walked over and picked one for myself too. The flyer designed to win the hearts and minds of the Iraqis portrayed a green caricature drawing of a soldier and an Iraqi, shaking hands under a message that read:

"Residents of Basra, we're here to liberate Iraq. Our enemy is the Ba'ath Party, not the people. This time, we'll stay together with you until the end."

Standing at the checkpoint, I stopped a bus driver who had just picked up the leaflet. I wanted to see his reaction and asked him if such flyer would win the villagers over. "Quite honestly, this paper isn't going to do anything," Ali Abdel responded.

"I'm going to take it home and show it to my wife and kids for a laugh."

Troops also added that patrolling the area constantly built trust. I felt safe myself when I saw a British patrol, but I did not know how valuable it was for the army. I sat on the curb sharing my water bottle with a soldier as he explained how patrolling taught him to foresee danger. He explained how in Northern Ireland a neighborhood with most of its windows open usually meant a bomb was about to blow. Simple banging of garbage cans also meant locals were trying to signal the troops' arrival.

"What about Iraqis, have you figured out their techniques?" I asked my new soldier friend.

"We are a long way from understanding Iraqi customs and culture, but there are common-sense indicators of danger. For example, a usually busy market that is suddenly empty is a sign of danger," added the soldier, as he handed me a paper with his girlfriend's email address back in England. Like most soldiers, he was isolated from the world with no phone or internet access. I was glad to email his woman that night to inform her that he was fine and trying to win the hearts and minds of Iraqis here.

"We don't want to be aggressive if people are with us, or nearly with us," said Captain Andy Bell of the 17-Port and Maritime Regiment. The British were now doing anything they could in advance to weaken the resistance up ahead in Basra. I was glad to hear that, as I knew very well that Mark and I were going to advance in right behind them when Basra does fall eventually. I listened to Major Hawley again for clues as he added, "I'm sure Basra is an absolute rabbit warren of sewers, alleys, and the like. I don't think we'd ever win like that. It would become like Vietnam."

An hour later, Mark and I arrived at the southern village of Safwan to check on a water distribution point, where British guided Iraqis one at a time to a water truck to fill their needs in the blazing heat. The scene was chaotic with crowds of women, men, and elderly trying to load up as much water as possible. I sat in our jeep trying to hide as I sipped hot water out of our own stock. We were low on water supply too. I gathered all our empty bottles to go fill them up from the same truck serving the poor residents.

Before I could leave the car, a lady covered with the Arab traditional black veil knocked on my window and then started pleading for some help as I opened my car door. She needed medicine that was not available in the local pharmacy. Heartbroken, I listened to the woman complain about everything in one breath. My mind drifted to my own portable pharmacy trying to remember if I had the medicine she needed. Before I could react, a tall dark Iraqi man with the typical Saddam mustache wearing the traditional Bedouin head wrap approached us, and yelled at her:

"Hey woman, you think this Arab *traitor* will help you? He is an agent working for the Americans! Don't ask him for anything… Come with me, I will get you everything you need!"

Watching the woman yield to his assumptions and loud aggressive accusations, the lady walked away with him leaving me angry and helpless at the situation. I did actually have the exact antibiotic pills she needed, but was left threatened before I could offer my assistance.

Back with Mark, we observed the scene as the soldiers urged everyone to back off and stand in line. One female soldier pushed a younger boy back, as the kid tried to bypass a number of women ahead of him in line. As I filled our own water bottles from the tanker, a man approached us complaining,

"We're Arab they are British, and they must go home," he said, "By giving us water, they're just giving us what we already had before."

The British were sharing information with the Americans on Iraqi weaknesses and strategies. However, resistance in the south was also relaying ideas on British weak points north to Baghdad.

Camping outside the British 7th Brigade for the night, I found Barbara Jones from the Sunday Telegraph. It had been almost two weeks since we showered or had a real meal. Excited to hear feedback from such a brave female reporter, I wondered how Iraqis perceived her. As we exchanged stories of the day around a hot meal she was cooking, I gave her a piece of my mind too. Coalition soldiers came to Iraq with a fixed ideology leaving their kids behind, just the same way Iraqi militia vow resistance every morning following their own beliefs too. The emotions of fear do not always result in a rational reaction. What worries me is the reaction of a whole population afraid of the new white man. War is not just a brief parenthesis. Yes, a lot of the Iraqis want Saddam gone. What *comes* after that? The British hope to win the hearts and minds of the residents, but can the Iraqis accept the white man, even as he arrives in the image of a liberator?

Saturday April 5, 2003

The pressure of the war was now lingering in the air. Associating myself with the civilians, their suffering under the Ba'ath Party, and their aspirations for the future, left me intrigued at Saddam's power of manipulation. I was still looking forward to see the North; Basra, Baghdad, and Hillah (Babylon). Until now, I have seen no signs of the architecture, history, and the Iraq that is always associated with the title; "The Cradle of Civilization."

In the past day, I had encountered some U.S. soldiers and had realized that they were more aggressive with a more 'trigger happy' attitude than the British troops. Come to think about it such attitude could be justified by the 'Anti-America Hysteria' rising up in the Gulf and the Middle East. I was now worried about my family at home with news that two of Saddam's missiles actually landed on *Al Sharq* (the east) mall in Kuwait, fortunately at dawn, causing no casualties and leaving only the front sea side section of the mall slightly damaged. Word on the street in Kuwait was that the Americans let the missiles go through deliberately to remind Kuwait and the Arabs that opening their land for the U.S. troops was a wise move. Such pathetic accusation was no surprise to me, as I had learned to read between the lines and ignore rumors and street talk during this controversial war.

On our way to the British base at the old Ba'ath Party headquarters, Mark and I stopped by a recently decapitated Iraqi tank to check the interior and assess the damage. Looking inside the tank, I was shocked at the lack of technology and the primitive equipment. The soldiers using this tank had obviously deserted the area leaving behind their military uniforms and pots of tomatoes. We collected a lot of documents and even found their ID cards hidden among the uniforms. Grabbing their cheap Iraqi helmets, I wondered about the whereabouts of the oil profits Saddam had incurred. Did he actually think he was going to win a war against the coalition with outdated Russian made tanks?

At the British base, back in Shuybah, we realized that the Fusiliers had added another set of barricades due to the continuous threats. The villagers gathered around me, offering me cigarettes as they relayed a story of how they caught an Iraqi man last night who was trying to place a bomb on the roof of the base. A British spokesman later confirmed the story adding that the man seemed drugged as he failed to accomplish his mission.

The long arm of the Ba'ath Party was still evident as the man confessed about his masters. In an attempt to show who is boss, the 1st Fusiliers used tanks to smash a mural of Saddam Hussein that stood in front of the Ba'ath headquarters. The village was basically controlled from this headquarter as the electric switch trip for the whole village was marked clearly in the halls of the base. In an attempt to restore order and sustain life, the British had planned to turn the nearby Basra Refinery Police Station into a clinic. Moments after I learned this news from a Red Cross official also at the base, Major Doug Stillmack of the 402nd Civil Affairs showed up, parked his Hummer, then announced that the building was on fire. Major Stillmack was an older optimistic American service man. He was full of high-spirits like a character from the old MASH TV action series. In a rush to report the fire, he waived at Mark and I as he shouted, "You've got to believe someone overheard us! It's very disappointing.... It's fully engulfed in fire.... I didn't see any fire a few hours ago when we passed!"

Mark and I immediately ran over to the burning police station, before anyone got there. Half the one floor building was on fire, yet the entrance remained untouched. We walked around the building and peaked inside one of the rooms. Undamaged files and folders with documents were left behind. Mark and I stormed into the building as we went through the files picking and choosing what could be useful for our new quest to reveal more secrets about the Ba'ath Party. We were both focused on choosing files marked with hot titles such as **[executions, recruitment, top-secret].** Amidst the light smoke blowing from the other side of the building, I spotted some gas masks, a 9mm gun without its magazine of bullets, and remains of food. Minutes later, we were joined by familiar faces from the village. Boys joined us looking for anything valuable as they ripped the place apart. They walked us through the building showing off the still intact jail cell with nothing but flea-ridden blankets. The kids looked for anything to scavenge among the ashes as they expressed their happiness to see this place fall apart.

A thirteen year old kid called Jalid Ibrahim handed me a forgotten copy of a book written by Saddam Hussein: "Principles, a Way to Life, and its Crown."

Hyper and filled with excitement the kids led us through a smoky torture room as Jalid explained, "I'm very happy it's burning... My friends were locked up in there, accused of stealing....They were beaten and tortured...I am very afraid of this place." Smoke still billowed from several windows caused by smoldering mattresses where policemen once slept. We dashed out of the blazing building carrying the huge piles of documents. On my way out I snatched a Ba'ath manifesto hanging on the wall.

Breathing fresh air again, I stood across the street from the burning police station and guarded the piles of documents. I waited for Mark to drive by with our jeep, which was still parked at the British base minutes away. A white pickup truck slowly stopped in front of me, and then the driver leaned out and yelled, "The Ba'ath set this fire. They are very jealous and angry right now and want to create chaos!" As soon as Mark arrived with our jeep, I loaded the back seat with the documents, trying to operate as quickly as possible before the arrival of the army. Like a treasure, we covered the documents with a blanket away from the eyes of other journalists.

Today was probably the hottest day since we had been in Iraq. I wore a tank top and protected my face with sunglasses outside the Umm Qasr Port. We came back to Umm Qasr specifically to pick up our new LA Times photographer, Don Bartletti. I was looking forward to meet him due to his reputation for being a 'cowboy' photographer ready to jump into any scene to get the best photos. Mark and I were nibbling on the tastiest Iraqi dates when two guys approached us hoping we had time to listen to their sad past. Indeed, stories about the cruelty of the Ba'ath Party never ended. One of the men identified himself as Yousef, and explained why he was hiding in the port away from the invisible eyes of Ba'ath Party officials.

"They used a heated knife and cut me here with a machete," said Yousef, lifting the sleeves of his shirt to show us several long swollen scars.

"Why were you tortured?" I asked, relaying Mark's question.

"I deserted the army in 1998. It was so painful. They also used electric shocks on me."

"Was that the only reason for this torture?" I asked, handing the man a bottle of water.

"They tried to make me admit that I was an Iranian, an Iranian agent, or an enemy of the Ba'ath Party," Yousef replied.

He was passionate to expose the real tyranny of this regime. He said he was caught and detained in the Laith Abid jail in Basra serving a seven-year sentence during which he was tortured for three months. After each torture session they would throw him into a dark tiny cell the size of a dog cage. After three months, he was forced to sign a confession even though he was illiterate and had no clue what it stated. Yousef was then transferred to a jail near Baghdad where he served out four years of his sentence before a general amnesty set him free last year.

"Where did you go after that?" I asked, with concern.

"With no other choice, I returned back to the army and I was forced to plant land mines against the Kurds in the north, even though I am of Kurdish origin."

Mark shook his head in shock and I was trying to weigh the psychological pain this man endured.

"I'm very happy now," Yousef said. "I won't really be able to relax, however, until Baghdad falls."

Human rights experts have documented many stories breaching the boundaries of humanity under the Ba'ath Party rule. Most of Saddam's victims that I had met had agreed unanimously that those who crossed the Ba'ath Party had witnessed quick and lethal retribution. Just as we finished interviewing Yousef, a white Cherokee rolled in hauling Don Bartletti, our new photojournalist. Don was upset as he explained how kids in Safwan had stoned the jeep and smashed the front windshield. Terry, our multi-media producer, was devastated at the situation as he clearly expressed his intentions to return right back across the border to Kuwait. Don loaded our jeep with his equipment and bags while I singled out their food supplies for reinforcements. I was excited to see a variety in their diet so I picked up their energy drinks, cans of V8 tomato juice, Gatorade, spiced canned sardines, and lots of Chinese noodles. Moreover, I also stacked all their gas cans on the rack of our jeep since we were struggling for fuel or as the Arabs call it: *Benzene*.

On our way to the British 7th Brigade to camp for the night, I asked Don and Mark to refresh my memory about the origin of the Ba'ath Party. Sitting in the back seat surrounded by piles of top secret Ba'ath Party documents, helmets, gas masks, and boxes of supplies, I listened to Mark explain how the party was originally a secular Arab nationalist party. Arab unity and freedom of colonialism were the bases behind it. The Arabs needed to reinforce their presence after years of foreign influence. It was introduced in Syria by Zaki al-Arsuzi, Salah al-Din al-Bitar, and Michel Aflaq in the 1930's. By the 1940's these same men extended their movement to Iraq to revolt the British presence there. By the end of World War II the movement took on the name *Ba'ath* (Arabic for resurrection) and became a party. The party was then founded officially in Damascus, Syria on April 7th, 1947, carrying a constitution and an executive committee. Expansion of the party took place outside the Syrian border after lack of unity by the Arabs was blamed for the loss of Palestine to the new state of Israel. Finally, In February 1963 the Ba'ath Party came to power in Iraq.

Parked outside the gates of the British 7th Brigade, I noticed an unusual amount of military activity. More tanks were being mobilized out of the base and of course each time that happened, a tremendous cloud of dust raged towards our vehicle. Across the fields from us, only a couple of miles away, the same barn that stood there for days was now on fire. The dark orange color of the flames emerging from the roof of the structure blended in quietly with the fading sunset. I was excited to see the Sunday Telegraph crew again after days of separation, but no one had a clue what had hit this burning barn. I boiled water for pasta and listened to Don describe how he followed Central American youth as they traveled a perilous route north into the United States. 'Enrique's Journey' remains the name of his photo series nominated for a Pulitzer Prize. Proud to be working with top-notch professionals I watched Mark pacing around the desert, talking to his wife and son Tyler, back in Japan.

Personally, it has been exactly two weeks for me without a shower, my skin was dry along with a ferocious tan, and my body ached literally from the humidity of the desert. I sat in the back seat of our Pajero waiting for Mark so we can attack the mountain of documents we had obtained from the Basra Refinery Police Station. Mosquitoes were getting on my nerves. They were very attracted to the glow emerging from the screen of my laptop. A pattern of dead ones covered the screen of Mark's laptop too. The same dogs that we fed days ago were still around but they would not stop barking.

After bombarding the stray dogs with rocks, I returned back and started the process of filing the documents. They had a stale ancient smell to them, symbolic to the Ba'ath Party and the atrocities that came with it. Translating the title of Saddam's book; "Principles, a Way to Life, and its Crown," I laughed at the fool's photo portrayed on the front cover of the book. I chuckled even louder as I translated some of the lessons in the booklet said to be drawn from past wars:

- Don't provoke a snake unless you have the intention of cutting his neck
- If you don't intend to fight to the death observe your enemy realistically, expose his true intention as an attacker and let the final punch be yours.

A major document that caught my eye was labeled Punishment Law 111, section 200, also known as the "execution section" The main decree states that party disloyalty leads to the mandatory death penalty. Such disloyalty includes hiding one's previous membership in another political party. Joining another political party during your Ba'ath Party membership also results in capital punishment. Translating the old hand written documents was tough, yet Mark and I forgot our exhaustion to try and figure out how Saddam Hussein maintained control and synchronized the daily life of Iraqis for a quarter century. We dug deeper into the personal files of different recruits.

Entesar Abdul Jabar's file begins with a hand written submission stating:

"Please accept me in the Ba'ath ranks so I can employ my beliefs and weapons in the fight for truth and whatever the Ba'ath Party asks me to do."

In her detailed application she declares that she has never worked with anyone who spoke ill of or worked against the party's interests, never been punished by the party, nor have any of her close male relatives. Entesar is employed as an administrative secretary and mother of seven children. She is listed as a member of *Jeish Al Quds* (Al Quds Army) organized by Saddam to liberate Jerusalem from Israeli occupation. I knew this army existed in Iraq but I had no clue women were involved too. I had also encountered stacks of personalized certificates honoring *Jeish Al Quds* memberships, back in the police station but left them behind. Moreover, the application indicated that she received training in the use of machine guns and that her "favorite weapon" is the Klashnikov rifle, which she had learned to use during a course offered by the 2nd Basra Army. Another handwritten submission in her thick file stated:

"I totally believe in all the standards of the Ba'ath Party and consider it the one true glory that serves the interests of the Arab world."

Clearer than ever, the terror in Iraq was emerging from each page I translated. In a section of her file stamped, "**TOP SECRET**" in red, senior Ba'ath Party members pass judgments on her request, asses her character, and assigned her duties. They confirm that she's never worked for an embassy, never traveled abroad, never been captured, and the regime has never tried or executed any of her friends or relatives. Her best quality, they deduce is her "calm nature." She is assigned as a spy with the duty of passing on whatever she learns to higher-ranking party officials.

More exhausted than ever, Mark and I stepped out of the car for a quick stretch. Now that I had been there for weeks, I tried to put myself in the shoes of the Iraqis. After translating these documents, I felt grim, hopeless, and depressed. The future seemed like murder. Don was preparing his sleeping bag and I just watched the sky, smoking another cigarette.

10:00 pm. Thunder blasts of artillery destroyed any peace we cherished in the past hours. Dozens of shells set off towards Basra, and the source was *right* inside the gates of our home, the British 7th Brigade. Every time the artillery blasted a set of shells, we could see a silver flash on the ground similar to that of a camera's flashlight. The shells left a long golden trail in the black sky. In a matter of minutes, we were accustomed to the loud ground artillery growls. Don was quick with his camera as he jumped on to the rooftop of our Pajero trying to capture images of the golden traces following the shells in the sky. I tried to count the hundreds of ammo launched that night, but failed. The artillery launcher on the ground would halt for a break then another long session would resume the attack. The sky reminded me of Christmas night. The uncountable amount of golden tracers left no doubt in my mind that tonight was the night we have all been waiting for. Mixed with emotions, I was hoping this artillery was landing on the homes of those senior Ba'ath officials and their loyalists. My mind shutdown, lost in the roars of the attacks, thinking the worst. I remembered that my girlfriend's grandparents lived in Basra. Months ago, when we both lived in Montreal-Canada, I had no idea I would be sitting at the source bombing their city. Tonight, I was confused, living the fears of many Iraqi exiles, yet also the hopes of many British Royal Regiment Fusiliers. Unlike the old days, the Fusiliers of today were not using light flint lock muskets. Mark continued his work while Don surrounded his sleeping bag with our own luggage to avoid the stray dogs.

Back in the jeep, I started to translate part of the Ba'athi manifesto I had picked up on the way out of the burning police station. The opening read:

"We fight for our land and people regardless of our opinion in the regime and the ruler, regardless of our relationship and opinion of this foreigner or that.....Our struggle with our Zionist enemy requires a rise by our nation.... preparing our military...economical and cultural weapons through a scientific advanced base of a high-civilized degree...."

Exhausted, Mark was fast asleep inside his tent, while Don slept in his sleeping bag with a stick in his hand. I maintained a cat like style of sleeping as my eyes wove in and out of focus. The shelling continued and sounded even louder now that everyone was asleep. I thought I was dreaming a couple of times as the Pajero wobbled through the more intense blasts of ammunition. I caught myself moaning and aching with extreme pain deep in my knee from the humidity in the air. Without a second thought, I reverted to a tranquilizer my folks had slipped in my bag. One pill of Ativan killed my anxiety and left me fast asleep away from the horrors of the war and the nightmares of the Ba'ath Party.

IV

BASRA: BEGINNING OF THE END

Chapter 4: Iraqi women fleeing Basra towards Az Zubayr. Photo by Brian Walski.

SUNDAY APRIL 6, 2003

The term used today by most reporters and military officers, is the "fall of Basra." I like to call it the "opening of Basra." For two weeks, our team like many other media crew reported around the British checkpoints near the bridges outside Basra. The city was situated only a couple of miles ahead. The British could have reverted to the quick air raids and dropped bombs, but they would have lost the hearts and minds of the Iraqi civilians and increased the number of casualties.

Today we woke up in a rush and drove quickly to the British checkpoint at the Az Zubayr Bridge outside Basra. The checkpoint was cleared and hundreds of soldiers were folding up and advancing forward. Before we entered the heart of Basra, we stopped outside the city to check the damage evident at the Basra Technical College. The covered body of a dead Iraqi soldier lay outside the gates of the college. We were not allowed to enter since the army was still checking for hidden explosives. I gawked at the burning roof and the artillery holes in the buildings. Bullet holes dotted the concrete walls. Iraqi snipers had been using this position and it was also used to store ammunition. I listened to a British spokesman confirm that at dawn several thousand British troops with 40 Challenger tanks and Warrior armed vehicles pushed into the city under the cover of helicopter gun ships.

Now anxious, I wore my flack jacket as we drove behind more British tanks at high speed right into the heart of Basra city. The mess was horrific. There were random holes in the streets where mortar shells had landed. People of all ages filled the streets cheering us with "thumbs-up" and loud ovation. Black smoke emerged from many partly damaged buildings. We stopped outside the University of Basra, close to a large black statue of two fish that was also partially damaged, but still standing. Locals were out to vent, looking for answers and solutions to their predicaments. Their attire was not restricted to the usual *dishdasha* worn by the farmers and villagers in the south. Educated men wearing jeans and worn out branded shirts stood looking for answers. U.S. humvees patrolled the secured neighborhoods with large microphones and announced taped Arabic messages that stated:

"We know you are worried about the war....We will not stop until we rid you of Saddam Hussein's regime....And that will not take long."

Don had been already running around the intersection documenting the damage with his camera. Mark and I hustled across the street to speak to an American Sergeant who was standing alert with his M-16 beside his Hummer, announcing the Arabic messages.

"Is this working?" Mark asked, trying to yell over the loud noise emerging from the helicopters flying overhead.

"It's going good. We are seeing lots of hand waving and thumbs-up signs. People come to me and think I speak Arabic because of the recording, though I have to explain that I don't," answered Sgt. Allen Mow, with the Army's 307th Psychological Operations Company.

Worried about our jeep, I ran back and greeted the masses of residents checking out our fancy SUV. One well-dressed man hugged me and said, "This car is from Kuwait. I lived and worked there for years."

Today was the worst fighting since the war began. Indeed, the city seemed scarred. Very few cars, mostly with smashed windows, passed us and tanks continued to roar forward. A charred bus drove by loaded with industrial machinery. Several carts loaded with stolen junk occupied the sidewalks.

Mark drove behind a British tank as I kept my eyes open for any surprises. Don handed me his hat then leaped out the window of our moving truck and clicked his camera at the disastrous scenes. We weaved into the urban city, surrounded with partially damaged or generally ill-kept buildings, haunted streets, rows of locked down shops, schools, one church, and very elegant mosques. I felt comfortable at the sight of a huge roller coaster standing clear over a closed entertainment park. A neglected fenced canal ripped right through Basra and various untamed trees surrounded the empty streets providing random pockets of shade. However, the atmosphere was still dubious. I watched signs of looting as boys carried stolen auto parts, furniture, and other small items. Carts loaded with stolen lumber, tubes, and aluminum windowsills occupied the dirty sidewalks. Meters ahead, we realized that we had just driven into the Ashar neighborhood, where there was still minor fighting going on.

Helicopters were patrolling the skies above us and sporadic fires emerged from strategic government buildings and previous strong hold Ba'ath Party positions.

We stopped briefly near a multitude of friendly citizens standing smiling, gossiping, and giving us the thumbs-up. As usual, Don jumped out of the vehicle and disappeared. Mark and I recorded their reactions on this historical day. There was no need to ask questions. Surrounded by at least seventy people throwing all sort of comments at me, I felt suffocated. To them we represented the outside world, like good will ambassadors. They loved the media and were glad to share their thoughts in Arabic. Mark urged me to concentrate as I relayed their valuable observations. A 35-year old teacher placed his hand on my shoulder and shouted, "I feel very happy because we have freedom for the first time."

Another 45-year old labor worker said that he considered himself lucky for surviving the past two weeks of fighting. He then added, "My family and I have been very scared. Many of our neighbors were not that lucky."

I did witness the intensity of the artillery and I knew the number of inevitable civilian casualties was not reported yet. On the other hand, earlier on the radio, I heard the British Defense Ministry confirm the death of three British soldiers. With the clear sounds of explosions close by and the sight of U.S. Cobra helicopters dashing up ahead, we felt unsafe. British military officials had informed us that many of Saddam's conventional forces had fled but they cautioned that they were not in full control of the city of 1.3 million. I also understood why Don Bartletti was reputed for being a "cowboy" photographer. Every time we stopped, he disappeared, and now we wanted to leave quickly due to the danger in the area. Only after I honked the horn of the Pajero, Don appeared from the entrance of a burning government building then we fled the Ashar neighborhood back towards the south.

Outside Basra, back at the Basra Technical College, which was now a new British base, we stopped to relax and pick up some more information. I got rid of my heavy flack jacket, and changed my dirty jeans. Behind our jeep, I slipped into a clean T-shirt and cleaned my face with a wet towel.

"*As-Salaam Alaikum* (Peace be upon you)!" yelled a man hiding behind another media vehicle.

"You want *khamra* (alcohol)?" The suspicious Iraqi man asked in Arabic.

"*Wa-Alaikum- Salaam,*" I returned the Islamic greeting back. I had the advantage of blending into both cultures easily. The man offered a bottle of whiskey and cans of hot beer in a bag he was carrying.

"How much for the bottle?" I asked in Arabic.

"I sold two to the Reuters crew for $20 each."

Coming from Kuwait where booze is illegal and a smuggled whiskey bottle costs an outrageous $150, I bought the bottle without bargaining and without the intention of drinking it today. This ironic man amused me. He started the conversation with the traditional Islamic salutation then proposed booze.

Fresh-back with Mark, I listened to an officer from the British Scots Dragoon Guards express his happiness that Basra did not turn into guerilla warfare. The new base was bustling with tanks and military maneuvers. Just when I thought the action for the day was over, a red pickup truck stopped in front of the base then two young men exited the vehicle with their hands up in the air. Walid Jawal, an 18-year old student had been shot in the groin as he tried to escape the Ashar neighborhood. Accompanied by his 25-year old cousin, Sachet Kasim, they both looked terrified.

"The Fedayeen didn't want us to leave. They fired their Klashnikov rifles as they yelled, 'Come back fight with us!'" Kasim said.

Discipline among the Fedayeen Saddam militia forces was weakening and their ammunition was running low. This was one of the main reasons the British decided to storm into Basra this day. Standing injured beside the pickup truck with a bullet hole in the windshield Jawal complained, "We stepped on the gas and got away."

Mark and I were done for the day and we invited the crew of the Knight Ridder daily newspaper to camp with us tonight at our secret location by the British 7th Brigade. Photographer Pauline Lubin and writer Sudarsan Raghavan were among the few reporters that stormed with us into the "opening of Basra."

Monday April 7, 2003

Waking up today was different than any other day. The fact that Iraq's second-largest city had crumbled down gave me hope that Baghdad and Saddam were next. I joked around with Mark, Don, and Pauline about my mission here in Iraq. Saddam had invaded Kuwait when I was studying there as a sophomore in high school. Alas, I was on my way to capture him.

I drove slowly into the intersection leading to the heart of Basra, and without a doubt the scene outside Basra University was breathtaking. The university was being looted as dozens of younger men raided the campus stealing everything from chairs to books to window rails. I parked close to a couple of other media jeeps. Don immediately headed towards the university and I wanted to join him, but Mark had spotted a more significant situation. Red Crescent volunteers and ambulances along with white pickup trucks sped right past us towards the east gates outside the university. Pauline, the photographer from Knight Ridder newspaper was way ahead of us as she waived us on to move faster. Mark stopped a kid who had precariously balanced 13 chairs on a handcart. He confessed that he was going to sell them. When I asked him where he got these cushioned seats, the kid proudly answered, "I got them from the university's economics and administration department."

We stopped at our jeep since Mark wanted a new notebook for his reporting. Within minutes the whole scene took a totally different vibe. Military trucks filed in one after the other and at least a hundred British paratroopers jumped out onto the streets. Militant looks drawn on their faces, the soldiers took defensive positions as they dispersed across the streets and outside the gates of the university. My calmness disappeared; I was extremely worried with no clue about this situation. Just like the soldiers, I knelt down on the asphalt close to our jeep and waited. I even yelled at one of the soldiers with a query about his duty and got nothing but a silent rigid look. Not too happy, I followed Mark and ran towards the Red Crescent volunteers. The soldiers then started moving towards Algeria Square, in a steady sweep, filing very cautiously towards their invisible enemy. Four U.S Cobra helicopters swept overhead.

Outside the gates of the university along a vast marshland that surrounded the campus; reporters, by standers, and Red Crescent volunteers stared at the dead bodies scattered along the dirt. Like a magnet, I was drawn to the bodies and tried to count them. The two bodies closest to the road were adjacent to each other, covered with cheap brown bare-threaded blankets. Right beside them in the dirt was a busted rocket-propelled grenade launcher. I walked further and then froze at the sight of another corpse lying face down in the water. Goose bumps hit my body as I observed every single detail in this fighter's dead figure; his shoes, his wet hair, the headband on his head. I lost my thoughts with pity for this human being. I wondered if he was fighting for a cause or just forced to do it. I heard but ignored an Iraqi bystander's comment that this man was a foreign fighter; a Syrian or Palestinian who had migrated to Iraq for a chance to die as a martyr for Islam. The sight was touching for every one watching soul less corpses floating in the water. Still in control, I then poised my eye intensely onto what seemed like a human leg floating in the water with its distorted upper-body following it separately. Confused emotions haunted the morbid scene. I asked an Iraqi man for a cigarette. As he gave it to me he complained,

"What is Saddam doing for them now?"

I translated quickly to Mark the remarks of another resident,

"Saddam paid $25,000 to the families of these brain washed Palestinian fighters."

Crowds continued to stare and gossip. Beside another body on the dirt were green canisters of ammunition, army-issue canteens, and a green vest. Locals pointed out a couple of hand grenades scattered along the side of the water. Registering the status of the seven dead bodies, I lost myself in a semi-trance and blocked all the noise around me. I visualized what these men might have seen moments before their death. I tried imagining their defeat. Were they fighting to die, against the world's most powerful armies, and with these primitive weapons? I do not raise this question with any philosophical intent. The nature of the war, the beast, I could *not* do it. Engulfed by clarity, I felt death squeeze my breath, heart, fate, and identity. For the first time since the war started I tasted tears sliding down my face, very well hidden behind my shades. Facing fear in this war, I remembered that death was inevitable. I also remembered a brief line from one of Saddam's manipulative speeches during the first days of the war:

"You brave Arab fighters. This is your chance to meet God and taste the fortunes of heaven."

Walking away to let the Red Crescent volunteers move the bodies; I realized many people were ignited with repressed anger, defeat, and despair. Six workers barged in and pulled one of the bodies from its blood stained shirt onto a canvas. The curtains dropped over this demonstration. The Red Crescent wanted the TV, radio, and print media to document these bodies. A female volunteer farther down the swamp continued to shout her comments to a radio reporter with anger; exaggerating,

"We have moved thousands of bodies....They are all stacked up like animals in fridges....Where are the Arabs? Don't they have jealousy over Iraq?" I watched her break down with tears of anger, humiliation, as well as fear.

Driving further into Basra towards Ashar neighborhood, I followed the canal lacing the city. Residents seemed much more confident that Saddam Hussein's despotic rule was over as they looted buildings and defaced all his familiar posters and billboards hung in public places. Since we entered Iraq I was disgusted at Saddam's egotistical humor, flooding the country with posters of himself in personas of an Arab nationalist with the head wrap , a business man in a suit, a soldier with military medals, and my all time *favorite*; a tough guy with sunglasses.

As soon as we parked at the Ashar roundabout, I saw masses of crowds cheering on a guy trying to rip off a 10ft billboard painting of Saddam's face. I had learned to read the degree of levity on the faces of Iraqis. It's always an instant signal of what is going on and this crowd was free with their own celebrations. I beat Mark and Don to the scene, and just asked them to stop as I helped a stranger hold up the painting for Don to photograph. Instantly, I rolled up the tarnished painting and saved it in our Pajero. Out of energy, I rested by the sidewalk and watched two British tanks stop by the roundabout. Iraq's second largest city was honestly enjoying freedom. One street cried with pain, while another street witnessed looting and greed, and the crowds of this neighborhood were jumping with glee. A captain Sarah Shepard of the 2nd Royal Tank Regiment jumped out and sat on top of her tank, removed her helmet gracefully, and revealed her blond hair with a joyful smile. Jaws dropped as men cheered and threw flowers at her. It was like a parade, a quick vacation from the war. I watched as guys handed her paper for autographs. A man came running to check her out and waived his hands yelling, "This is freedom! I have only seen women like her on TV!" Admirers continued to celebrate this symbolic moment. Her green eyes lifted my spirits too. Mark came back with her funniest quotes as he read them out loud to me:

"I've gotten a couple of offers of marriage. For them it's a real novelty."

Indeed, the macho soldiers of Iraq were always portrayed as strongly built men with Saddam like mustaches to complete their brave manhood. What a smack in the face it must have been for some of the soldiers that have melted in the crowds to see a gorgeous female with blond locks drive the enemy's battle tank.

Behind her tank, soldiers from her unit guarded a building marked with a huge sign, "Artist's Theater; Basra Branch." I was getting worried with no signs of Mark, Don, or Pauline. The crowds surrounded me with curious eyes. A strange man ran towards me, kissed my cheek then handed me a bronze-plated bust of Saddam's face that he claimed had stolen from his palace.

Inside the theater, I followed Mark as he noted the rooms filled with boxes of plastic explosives, grenades, dozens of mortars, and ammunition. Strolling backstage, I stepped into a recess room where partially melted ice cubes and a half-eaten meal were signs of how quickly soldiers had fled. In the room where the fighters slept, were old clothes, a bed, and a fusty mattress. I felt bad for the kindred spirits of four live rabbits and a loud chicken crunched in the corner of the room.

"We deduce they would kill a rabbit and eat one a day. They have probably gone into another area, or perhaps dissolved back into society," commented a Captain Edward Cones, with the Royal Artillery, as he walked us out of the secured building.

Outside, I waited for Mark and Don by our jeep. The crowd was getting bigger and louder. Boys peeked into our vehicle, pointing desperately at our phones, the food, and the luxury of the car. Just as we drove away, I caught a glimpse of a kid's hand as he succeeded in snatching something out of my bag tied to the rack on the roof of the car. Later, I realized it was only my cap.

Sitting outside a British base in what used to be the City Hall Building, Mark and I laughed and connected with the free kids who were looting at the ruins. The massive structure built to represent power and confidence had collapsed into a rumble of concrete and the steel supports had caved in after an allied air strike last week. A wild kid carrying two wooden chairs passed by me and smiled.

"Everyone is happy they hit this thing," said Latif Mohamed, a 16-year old student. He also added: "Before the war, the mayor walked around like a tough guy. After, he went shaking off to Baghdad."

Looking for some peace of mind, we all relaxed around the car, outside the gates of this new British base. Sharing our treasure of Iraqi dates with the soldiers was fun since they were sick of eating the same military preserved MREs (Meals-Ready-To Eat.) I tried to engage in a conversation with the young soldier at the gate but that did not last long because he freaked me out.

"Do you have a cigarette?" I asked the soldier.

"No. I am not too fine with this RPG pointing at me."

I glanced behind me, then turned back and smiled at him, "RPG? Are you seeing things?"

"It could smash our faces any second," Face grim as a bat.

This time I turned around, and realized there was a British soldier cleaning his RPG just meters away from us and the rocket propelled grenade was pointing right towards us.

"I thought you were hallucinating man. See you later," I sighed, then left this poor paranoid solider alone.

Our Times crew was still relaxing with the reporters of the Knight Ridder, and the crew from the American television program; Night Line. A very confused Aljazeera correspondent suddenly stopped his Cherokee by our corner and hysterically asked if I had seen his cameraman whom he had lost hours ago. He then wrote down his name and satellite phone number on a paper and then asked me to call him if I found his colleague.

The man was panicking as he stepped on the gas, and quickly yelled, "The Sheraton is burning! It's being looted! We were just staying there last week!"

Like a race, we all fired our engines towards the burning Sheraton. Still following the canal, we bypassed the Ashar roundabout right through to the edge of town where the Basra Sheraton stood burning from the outside. Across the *Shat El Arab River*, the hotel was being stripped of its carpets, towels, mattresses, and furniture. Kids on bicycles, teenagers, and young adults carted off with ceiling fans, floodlights, roofing material, and even simple stationary. Two men were busy hauling a grand piano at the entrance of the hotel. The chaos was unprecedented as Mark, Don, and I ran into the building to document what was happening. The escalators and once elegant hotel were dripping wet from the fire sprinklers. In rooms and suites young men unscrewed light bulbs off vanity mirrors. Some had established faster techniques as they threw doors, chairs, and bed frames from three-story windows to their partners downstairs. I was not too calm about this free-for-all fiesta. I wondered if that was a warning to what could happen in the capital, Baghdad, when the heavy hand of Saddam's dictatorship ended. I hesitated to relay Mark's general questions to the looters who were too busy and rowdy to even speak. Most of them were planning on selling the goods while others just confirmed that their parents had asked them to bring back some new furniture for the house. Across the street at the *Shat El Arab River,* docked ships were also being looted and some of their cabins were on fire too. The beauty of the river and the shore, decorated by hundreds of palm trees dimmed over the commotion.

At the river's boardwalk, some older men stood blaming the British and the Americans for destroying the system without creating a replacement. I pleaded with them to be patient since I knew the British were too busy eliminating the last pockets of resistance. The scene was too frantic for any Iraqi worried about his country's image and treasures. I spotted a Syrian priest watching the looting with his disciples. This was a man of religious knowledge, and I immediately bombarded him with questions about the fate of Islam in Iraq. I was worried a civil war would emerge between the *Sunni* and *Shia'a* Muslims. His words were full of hope. He outlined how Saddam had tried for ages to establish a religious *fetna* (internal sedition) between the *Sunni* and *Shia'a Muslims*, but failed. The priest assured me that there was also no bloodletting of any kind between the Muslims and Christians of Iraq and that they were all living like brothers. I had spotted this same priest in three different locations across Basra's neighborhoods today. I wondered if he was on a personal spiritual mission. The man then leaned over closer to me and whispered, "I want to tell you something important away from the crowds."

In our Pajero, the Syrian priest opened up and shared his views with us:

"I want you to know that the three percent of Christians in Iraq also suffered under Saddam. These Ba'athis don't know God or religion. They hide behind auspices of Islam and the anti-Zionist slogans, but at the end of the day it is all about black gold and money."

Inside the gates of the Basra Teaching Hospital, I never felt safer. Exhausted surgeons who had been working twenty days without a day off took a break outside and welcomed us in. As they led us into their haven, Dr. Ahmed Galibi explained that injured civilians hit by gunfire and shrapnel usually showed up two hours after an air assault or artillery battles. Doctors have been taking up the role of security guards, cooperating together to guard the hospitals against thieves. That same morning seven hoodlums had tried to rob ambulances and a Land Cruiser. The doctors informed the neighboring British troops. The thieves fled, except for one who failed to surrender and was shot on the spot. The doctors tried to save his life but could not.

The hospital was in good shape with electricity. We walked through the hallways until we reached the director's room, which was cool and air-conditioned with comfortable sofas and chairs. I watched Mark and Don chatting with the doctors in English, as I rested momentarily on the couch. We were not allowed to see the patients without the permission of the director, who was absent today. I stared at the troubled face of the physician in charge as he relayed the director's devastating story.

Apparently, the director was on night duty during one of the major air assaults throughout the first days of the war. He got a phone call from his daughter and she complained about the strikes explaining the family's fear, without electricity. At one point during the call, he heard a loud explosion and the line cut. When the director reached home he found his four daughters, wife, and mother buried under the rubble of his leveled home.

Alas, I asked for water as I felt my own heart beat fast accompanied with a body twitch. I swallowed an anti-anxiety pill right away as I watched the nurses tear and lead us to the wards to see the patients. I don't know if I was upset about the death of innocent civilians, the looting, the rape of this country, or maybe the patients I was about to see.

On the second floor, a father stood watching over his son who had been shot in the head by snipers. The man grabbed Mark's hands and complained to him in broken English, *"Please tell British... have someone, save son... to come here."*

I was speechless at the sight of sedated patients and the ones in comas from random gunshots. Watching Don photograph another wounded patient, I shuddered at the loud interruption of explosions that shook the ward. The nurses were obviously calmer with their war-long fear behind their backs. They reminded me that the worst was over and then I deduced that this was just another unscheduled ammunition detonation by the British.

I sat quiet and numb in the back seat on our drive back to our usual open-air home by the 7th Brigade, outside Basra. I watched the demolished buildings, oil fires, the random patches of smoke, and the happy *Ali Babas* heading back home with their loot. 'Ali Baba' was a name given to thieves by the soldiers. The story originated in the old ages in Persia. Ali Baba gained his wealth on the expenses of forty thieves when he figured their secret word that opened up the walls of the cave where they had hid their gold, money, and fortunes. Today, the Ali Babas of Basra did not need to yell the words "Open Sesame" to crack any walls open.

Tuesday April 8, 2003

Today was hot with southwestern winds blowing. I glanced at my watch; 10:00 am, later than usual. I welcomed the sun and stood shirtless looking for my phone. I had slept like a log in the backseat before any of my crew. Mark had spared me the daily privilege of editing his article before he sent it to LA at night. Mesmerized by my girl friend's soothing voice flowing through my mobile phone, I walked aimlessly in the desert listening to her updates on the war. Out here, we were isolated from TV and the bulk of the news relayed to the outside world. I listened to her complain with rage at the horrific scenes of looting broadcasted globally.

"Did you see what the coalition did? They let everyone loot to embarrass us and present Iraqis as barbarians!" she shouted.

"They were still eliminating scattered Iraqi militia and they are not trained for it. They will rebuild and fix it all," I answered calmly.

"Rebuild! That is what they said after Afghanistan. Is it rebuilt?" she asked, with a sarcastic chuckle in her voice.

In the background, I could hear a television broadcast, a loud dictation of an Arabic news presenter, with updates on the war. News has become a so familiar part of everyone's life in the Middle East that intimacy grew between the newscaster and the public. One newscaster's opening gestures was a signal of what type of news was to follow. I could hear the news presenter in the background saying the name Ahmed Chalabi.

"What do you think of Dr. Ahmed Chalabi? I think they might set him up as president," I asked, with no hidden intentions in mind.

"What? Listen, we will choose our own president and this man is a fraud," my girl added. "There is no way any Iraqi would accept such a *crook*!" she yelled, with fuming anger.

Her father had left Iraq in the 70s at the peak of the Ba'ath Party and Saddam's power. Her dear grandfather was also an active political figure, and at one point was also the mayor of Basra.

Outside our home, in the open space in front of the gates of the British 7th Brigade headquarters, various groups of civilians arrived with questions, requests for work, and inquiries about the lack of water and electricity. I covered my head with the traditional Bedouin head wrap and walked over with Mark to record their queries. At first, I approached a Saad Mohamed, a trader, who had been haggling with the soldier at the gate. I took him aside with a promise to help him converse with the guard later.

Mark immediately noted his name and occupation, and then asked,

"What do you think about the U.S. airlifting Iraqi National Congress head Ahmed Chalabi into Iraq from London. Do you think he will be president?"

"We don't want any leaders coming from London. They go out to bars, don't know anything about Iraq, were paid by the Americans and now think they can just take over the country."

A 50-year old employee working at a wheat trading company then interrupted the conversation with passion and added, "I never heard of him before. Why not opt for someone from inside who's witnessed the war and suffering?"

After mingling with the upset Iraqis, we drove towards Basra on the hottest day since we had arrived weeks ago. The wind was blowing fine sand at us when we parked our vehicle on the side of the road outside Basra. The British were pulling out of their temporary base at the Basra Technical College. The tanks roared one after the other towards Basra. Hundreds of looters waited with cars, trucks, and carts. They violently cheered their departure as they stormed the institute. Without a doubt, they rushed into the offices then the looting mayhem began. Mark, Don, and I ran in with them and watched them strip air-conditioners, television sets, desks, drafting tables, oscilloscopes, black boards, and computers. Some were arguing, dividing their new possessions, while others just stood there watching in sorrow. Mark called me over quickly to translate what a crying man was saying. "You must prevent this...This is horrible," said the computer scientist, tearing, as he watched his office being destroyed.

"The whole country will go down! This is very bad," cried the professor.

Following the canal into Basra, past Algeria Square, we stopped by the Sheraton again. The second day of looting in the city continued as thieves drove by with stolen trucks, cars, and huge government bulldozers. I asked Mark to stop at a street parallel to the Sheraton when I saw a crowd of men standing casually around what used to be a nightclub. The angry owner was sitting on the steps of his property preaching to his many local supporters. I interrupted him and introduced Mark; Don went on with his photography.

"What happened to your place?" I asked.

"You saw the looting. I assigned a security guard to protect my club from thieves. When they tried to rob my place, he fired warning shots in the air and it scared them away," Muhi Lefth explained, clearly.

"So how did your place topple down into rubles like that?" I asked, with astonishment at the collapsed concrete columns.

"You are a reporter, write this down. The British tanks patrolling the area heard my guard's warning shots and mistook him for militia firing at them," said the man. "They fired artillery shells and destroyed the whole place… my life savings."

"What are the major problem facing residents today?" Mark asked the man.

"People are very scared and distrustful," said Muhi, standing outside his nightclub surrounded by his many disciples. "Who brought Saddam Hussein back in 1991? The U.S. did. They should have gone all the way."

Muhi and the dozens of the neighborhood's residents agreed that the British would win their trust if they restored water, electricity, and security.

"British soldiers are letting people burn and loot. People don't trust anyone. They don't even trust themselves." Muhi complained, as he walked away.

2:00 pm. I spotted one of the very few restaurants open to the public. The street was haunted; many owners had blocked the entrance of their stores with brick walls. The heat was intense. A few men wandered the streets in their undershirts. The restaurant offered only *kebab.* The owner was happy to host us foreigners as he ordered his waiter to setup a table for us outside, away from the masses of flies hiding from the heat inside his restaurant. The crew from the Knight Ridder, who were now accompanying us on our daily reporting, joined us too as we cherished the first cold drinks we have had since we entered Iraq.

Mark sat sharing quotes with me that he had picked up from British officers on the security issue. The British lacked the manpower and the authorization to become a civilian police force.

"Here is what Major Tim Brown of the Royal Scots Dragoon Guards said, 'we can't provide law and order. Only a police force can do that,'" Mark explained, as he devoured his delicious salad.

"Listen to this; he also said, 'No one's actually started planning how it's going to go after the war. There's a real vacuum.' "

My attention span disappeared when our first hot meal in three weeks landed on our table. We jumped hands first into the hot minced meat. I gobbled down the meat with bread and a touch of hot sauce. Then I combined the salad, onions, meat, and bread together in one like I had never seen hot *kebab* before. We also ordered another round of cold Pepsi at a thousand *dinars* (fifty cents) a can. Indeed, I felt rejuvenated from the protein in the tasty *kebab* Iraq is famous for.

There were only three or four residents lurking around, watching us-the-outsiders eat in peace. I was not too keen on staying out in public in one place in such an unstable town. Yet, the smell of the grill was irresistible.

On our way to the car, a loud angry man dressed in the traditional Arabic *dishdasha* crossed the street and waived his arm yelling,

"You destroy our country and you come eat here?"

His loud voice drew some people over while others popped their heads out of their windows to watch.

"You are a Kuwaiti! How can you let the Americans in to destroy your Iraqi brothers?" The fuming man yelled, pointing his accusing finger at me.

"I'm not Kuwaiti Mr. I' m Egyptian," I responded, firmly.

"You are all the same. Husni Mubarak is the biggest CIA agent, letting *their* ships through the Suez Canal."

"No need for talk like that," I answered, peacefully trying to avoid a confrontation.

"All these Arab leaders are agents working for the America! Saudi Arabia and the King Abdullah of Jordan!" the man yelled, with a threatening look in his eye.

I got into our jeep, swallowed my pride, and locked my car door.

The man was still rambling on as I heard his last threats, "Go and don't bring those Americans here again! My gun is upstairs under my pillow. Saddam is the pride of all Arabs!!"

On our way to Basra Military Hospital, Mark continued to explain how the British have already began meeting with a local tribal leader in Basra who has authority and potential to help. The British have also consulted with retired U.S. Army Lt. General Jay Garner, who is to oversee the U.S. postwar occupation. Controversial opinions revolved around including former members of Saddam's Ba'ath Party, due to their knowledge of the locals, which is way broader than the Brits who have been in Iraq for two weeks only.

Inside the gates of the hospital, we were informed that the building was looted and its patients had been moved to another hospital. I was disappointed to hear well-educated doctors complain about their destiny, and I also wanted to speak with Iraqi soldiers with an urge to explore their hypnotized Ba'athi ideology. The manager of the hospital walked Don, Pauline, and I through the dirty hallways and damaged labs. The rooms were stripped of their mattresses, furniture, and piles of military uniforms were scattered across the floors. I left Mark chatting with the doctors and enjoyed the freedom of working with the photographers, as they documented the smallest details with their cameras. Our unconventional tour guide then led us downstairs towards the back entrance of the hospital where a bundle of destroyed guns and rifles lay in front of the door of a room marked with the words "spare-parts storage." The man paused as Don replaced his camera lens to accommodate the bright sun light. I entered the storage room first. What a surprise! The walls of the room were lined with rifle racks and wooden boxes filled with ammunition including bullets of various sizes. Don and Pauline stood clicking their cameras away as I read an Arabic memo hung on the wall which stated:

"Your weapon is your pride, perfect cleaning it and reassembling it."

Our guide, Mohamed, then informed us that he had stored three dead bodies of Iraqi soldiers in a big cooler trailer, meters away from the storage room. Without a doubt, we walked over to the room and followed him up the stairs of the cooler slowly. On the floor lay two dead bodies of Iraqi soldiers in uniform, covered with blood and numerous flies. Their faces were blue, and their open eyes starred with a motionless glitter. Walking deeper into the trailer, I gazed at the worst body of the three. Hit by a shell, this soldier's head was split in half, as his skull seemed outstretched. Agonized for a few seconds, I fled the cold trailer swaying the flies out of my way.

Outside, I listened to a doctor explain to Mark that the British troops had encouraged director Yaseen Taher to return. In addition to being a surgeon, Yaseen is a military general, a senior Ba'ath Party official and chief administrator for all military and civilian hospitals in the south. Confused, I listened to Flight Lt. Darren Finch of the Royal Air Force as he commented, "You have to divide the Baath Party into two parts—militia and administration." Not too happy about hearing this, I interrupted and asked how such a man could return back to civil work.

"If he committed heinous crimes; that will be investigated later as people talk," replied the lieutenant, as he adjusted his sunglasses back on his face and walked away.

Almost done for the day, Mark and I decided to extract more insights from the people about their future expectations. Hassan Sahar, a 45-year-old engineer stood at the intersection outside Basra and explained to us how most Iraqis feel it's too early to even think of the road ahead. "We can't say who the best leader is right now," he said.

"We've had 35 years of problems.... We need to listen to everyone and then after five or six months choose who is best."

A happier bus driver seemed more flexible with no preferences for an expatriate candidate like Chalabi or a local. "Any change will be a cause for happiness and celebration," said Hamid Fayed. "The way I see it, nothing can be worse than the old regime, no matter who it is." On our safe drive back, I relaxed to the sight of Saddam's tattered posters and billboards that were hung on every major school, hospital, and government building.

Wednesday April 9, 2003

9:00 am. No sooner did I want to hear today's news about the fall of Saddam. News poured in through the phones, announcing that Saddam's symbolic statue standing in the center of Baghdad had been pulled down by U.S. soldiers and dragged down the street surrounded by hundreds of jubilant citizens. Analogies to the demise of the Berlin wall and historical leaders left me in awe at the world we live in.

I noted the Metamorphosis: Friends and family who were against the war were now calling me with apparent tears in their happy voices about the "fall of Baghdad." Those for the war were totally suspicious about the sudden news of the paramilitary fleeing; the overnight disappearance of senior Ba'athi government officials, and Saddam himself. Such people could have been victims of Iraq's Information Minister, Al Sahhaf who became famous as the Ba'athi propagandist, an icon for his delusional speeches which included:

"Their infidels are committing suicide by the hundreds on the gates of Baghdad." My favorite was: *"Our initial assessment is that they will all die,"* and *"God will roast their stomachs in hell at the hands of Iraqis."*

Over the phone a friend from Egypt humored me with his serious speculations that the U.S. made a deal with Saddam in Baghdad airport. Others questioned the moments of darkness that hit the city of Baghdad when the electricity cut off although it was operating throughout the infamous bombing of Baghdad: "Shock and Awe"

Watching Mark and Don sip their coffee, I crawled into Mark's tent for a rare private moment with the slow Internet connection. Waiting for my hotmail inbox to open, I read some quotes and articles Times staff writer Paul Richter had sent to Mark from Washington. I supported the coalition's orders to the soldiers; to protect themselves first and concentrate on destroying the remaining pockets of resistance. A quote by a Pentagon official brought a smile to my face, it read:

"Obviously, soldiers who have just fought for two or three weeks are not going to be the best marriage counselors in Baghdad." The same official also added, "We want to hand this over to a credible police authority just as soon as we can."

A good five minutes passed before my hotmail inbox opened. I could hear the guys packing up outside, so I sent a quick email to my family and closest friends that read: "I am alive and well. Will head back to Kuwait very soon *Insh'allah*. (In God's will) We will not be going to Baghdad this time, but will pass by Nasiriyah tomorrow. I warn you, I might smell a little funny because I have gone without a shower for almost three weeks now!"

Before I disconnected I caught a glimpse about the sad news of the death of Vache Arslanian, a Red Cross logistics official who was killed Tuesday when a convoy of cars came under fire in an unexplained shooting incident on a Baghdad road.

Driving through the south towards Basra, I stepped on the brakes at the sight of more intense looting at the Bank of Baghdad, Basra branch. Don accompanied me into the bank. As soon as we walked in, the thieves stopped, looked at us and then continued stealing when they realized we were not soldiers. I was not too relaxed at the sight of armed robbers stacking old Deutsch marks and Iraqi *dinars* into plastic bags. Unlike other looters I had encountered in the two previous days since the fall of Basra, these guys were well groomed and operated in a very professional manner. Moments later, Don and I split the shady scene. Indeed, Basra seemed like the "Wild West." Convulsions of disorder haunted the city. The looting escalated; robbers were targeting homes, cars, and personal property. Mark caught an angry rich trader, who furiously criticized the coalition with his well-weighted remarks.

"Anyone with a car has to sleep inside or post a guard all night if they want to keep it," said Sattar Tamini. "They're even stealing our license plates."

As usual, we were surrounded with a crowd. Mark noticed another man in the circle who was mumbling in Arabic about the U.N.

"What is he saying about the U.N.?" Mark asked.

"He is saying that he wants the U.N. to come in quickly," I answered.

With the spotlight on him, Saef Ali Ahmed, then quickly added, "We need protection so we don't get killed, so our hospitals and schools aren't destroyed. It's turning into a jungle. I just finished university but I can't get my documents because the school has been destroyed."

An older sick man pushed his way through the crowd; pointed at Mark's notebook and shouted, "The coalition opened the bank for everyone to steal on purpose."

Such rumors inflamed the already sore citizens with more pain. Under the old regime they had never known the real meaning of the ancient words: *democracy, freedom, courage, honesty, civilization, creativity, liberty*. These words meant nothing to them just the same way they meant *nothing* to Saddam Hussein.

Sitting in the back seat, I flipped to the BBC on my shortwave radio. I was not surprised the International Committee of the Red Cross and the aid group Doctors Without Borders had suspended their operations after the death of Vatch Arslanian. I switched to Mark for some answers.

"So if the Red Cross is out, who takes care of people?" I asked.

"The U.S. and the British forces have the legal duties of an occupying power to maintain order and to ensure the populace has food, water, and medicine, according to the International law. Since the 1907 Hague Convention, the law has drawn a sharp distinction between military invasion and occupation," Mark replied, as he drove towards Basra.

"Meaning?"

"When fighting is underway, soldiers have the sole duty to destroy the enemy. They can not be expected to maintain order in the civilian populace. But the duties change as soon as the enemy is killed, captured, or driven away," Mark elaborated.

I was glad to hear the voice of General Vincent Brooks, deputy director of operations for U.S. Central Command on the BBC as he commented on the security issue;

" We're seeing a lot of jubilation from people who have been oppressed for years and years....We believe that this will settle down in due time."

The extreme lawlessness I witnessed put doubt in my mind about the success of the coalition's main goal; "to win the trust of the Iraqis." The U.N. and the Iraqis demand the 125,000 troops intervene the lawlessness and looting.

On a different front, Mark decided to approach an investigative trip about the evil legacy of Saddam Hussein. I already knew he was born in the poor town; *Alawjaa*, "the crooked" What I did not know was the famous rumor that he had a special gem implanted in his arm that supposedly repel bullets. We parked our jeep at the side of the road and strolled down into the desert to greet a shepherd standing amongst his animals under the hot sun. When he heard the name Saddam, the wise man smiled but hesitated to converse with us. After we established trust and handed his smiling kids some chocolate, the man opened up gracefully. Aboud Matter then sat on a pile of rocks, crossed his legs under his *dishdasha* and replied, "I would not believe he was dead even if I saw his body on television." I was admiring the old man's wise profile while he added; "I won't believe it unless I see it with my own eyes."

In spite of the detailed CIA tip about the location of Saddam on the first day of the war, Saddam had survived. The news that he survived the bombings and the extremely expensive 2000- pound American cluster bombs injected more pessimism in the minds of Iraqis. The Bedouin shepherd justified this power with the famous rumor that his special gem, which some said was red, others blue, protected him. To add more mystic about this rumor, the man explained how this gem had been tested on a chicken, which lost just a few feathers when it was shot at point-blank range.

Hunting down more people for a further investigation, I stopped a man down the road. As soon as I mentioned the name Saddam Hussein, the man ran away and disappeared behind a building. A retired man standing meters away displayed more bravery when he volunteered to answer my inquiry. "His mother is a magician and her love and her connection with the spirits has protected her son with a magical aura… I grew up learning that he was in touch with the occult," said Saaed Abdel Reda, a farmer. "And he has fortunetellers tap into the spirit world and tell him when people are trying to kill him."

I watched the man's pupils for signs of credibility. But, I translated his words with confidence, especially since a couple days ago I had conversed with an Iraqi soldier who shared a brutal situation he had witnessed during his mandatory service in Saddam's Republican Guard.

At one point, a soldier standing five rows behind Saddam had tried to kill him, but his 9mm Beretta jammed. Saddam quietly walked over to the soldier grabbed the gun and said, "This is how you do it," before shooting him dead. Others attribute his ability to survive to plain old paranoia. Hussein is known to sleep in a different palace every night, and trusts only a few in his inner circle. Occasionally, he bluntly fires his top guards and relies on relatives who he also subjects to capital punishment.

1:00 pm At the Umm Qasr market, we bought more supplies and exchanged some U.S. dollars for Iraqi dinars decorated again with the ugly face of Saddam Hussein. An old Iraqi Bedouin lady covered with the traditional black *abaya* (robe) welcomed us with joy, waved the flies from her face, and smiled into Don's camera. The naïve lady then wondered when her photo would be broadcasted on television. The woman's old tanned face wrinkled as she shrieked with laughter and prepared to tell us another fable. Discreetly, away from the customers at the *souk* (market), she relayed a story about a citizen she once knew, who used spit on his television screen whenever Saddam's face appeared. This hatred went on for years until the man and his daughter saw Saddam in person at a military exhibition. "That's the man you always spit on," the little girl cried innocently. Guards within ear shot distance snatched him immediately and shot him in public.

In the past days, the world had also been skeptical about the identity of the man portrayed in Saddam's last videotape broadcasted globally. With his son Qusay, Saddam stood on the top of his car saluting the masses of chanting crowds and supporters openly on the streets of Baghdad. This last video left the world puzzled. Was it a fresh-taped video or footage shot before the war? For years I grew up in Kuwait listening to rumors about Saddam's doubles, something like what we see in Hollywood movies, hopefully not clones!

3.00 pm. We headed down to Basra for a quick checkup on the status of water and electricity. The city was now on the verge of disaster without electricity or water supplies. Under the shadow of a tree beside the Basra canal, I spotted a man out to catch some fresh air with his kids. The sorrow in the children's eyes bothered me, so I modestly approached them with two bags of chips and a bottle of water. The boy's eyes lit with glee when Don also handed them some candy. Their father Ahmed Shab, a teacher, stood calmly by the canal and explained how this psycho leader was known to employ at least seven doubles, which led to world-wide speculation every time his face appeared in the media.

"There's a saying that Saddam Hussein does not even trust his own little finger," Ahmed added. With more crowds interested in the debate, an engineer calmly approached me with a logical question. "How can we really be sure he's gone for good?"

"I know he came back in '91 after the Gulf War and he executed thousands who had criticized him. Saddam today is finished, you must believe that," I replied, with confidence.

"We can't trust the U.S. and Britain. They left us once before!" yelled the engineer in English.

The rumors and tall tales of Saddam's super powers had been started with propaganda spread by the strong hold of Ba'athist surrounding him. His followers fueled many fables to keep the Iraqi people on their toes. One funny man I had encountered earlier in Safwan had it simplified in a comic connotation; "Lying is a sport in Iraq." Indeed, Saddam was falsely personified as a super man; an expert at archery, a world-class swimmer, a courageous fighter, a brilliant hunter, and *of course,* a champion equestrian representing the cream of the crop for all Arabs.

Karim Kasem, a *Shia'a* student who had also endured pain under the Ba'ath Party, shared his freedom with us when questioned about his views.

"His picture is every where—on our school books, our mosques, government buildings, and our money."

"Did you hear any stories or rumors about Saddam growing as a kid, maybe from your parents or grandparents," I asked.

"No, I just hated the fact that at school we stood up for Saddam Hussein and sat down for the Ba'ath Party," answered Karim, with clear despise in his tone.

With news that the U.S. had conducted thunder runs towards Baghdad and the disappearance of the regime over night, people guessed Hussein's next move. Some said he would fight till the end. Those who knew him better said he would rather commit suicide than be apprehended or tried in front of the world, possibly at the Hague, for his uncountable war crimes. I was actually worried that the extensive amount of burning and looting in Baghdad and Basra would reach documents needed for a future war trial. Many Iraqis were also certain that the U.S. will not be able to kill him and that he would get away like Osama Bin Laden.

Driving south of Basra, around Az Zubayr, we parked off the road on the sand to make way for a long convoy of U.S. military vehicles heading north towards Baghdad. A curious shepherd approached my side of the car and asked for water. Isolated from radio or television, the man knew nothing about the latest events of the war. I briefed him quickly about Saddam's defeat and waited to see his reply. Surprisingly, the shy shepherd confirmed that even if Saddam was out of power, many Iraqis would remain terrified knowing he was out there alive. Surrounded by his eight kids, Ali Abdul Wahed then expressed his opinion with confidence, "Every human being has a set lifetime. Even Mussolini and Hitler fell eventually."

"Do you think he will go to hell when he dies?" Mark asked, smiling with a glitter in his eye

"When he dies, he'll go to hell," said shepherd Ali. The man went silent for minutes then suddenly jumped like a stand-up comedian, gawked and shouted: "The very worst hell!"

V

HISTORY IN THE MAKING

Chapter 5: U.S. soldiers and journalists get a tour of the ziggurat and remains of Ur in Nasiriyah. Photo by Pulitzer Prize Winner 2003- Don Bartletti-Los Angeles Times.

Friday April 11, 2003

I woke up silently, pondering for the one-thousandth time since the war began, about the destiny of the Iraqi people, the severely oppressed Shia'a Muslims, and this day; my own fate. I had survived my own private moments with death in this war. Yet, strangely I did not fear death. I saw it as part of life. Mark and I had developed similar rashes on our hands for unknown reasons, probably lack of showering. The tension in the south had defiantly simmered. People were cautiously joyful. I sat still in the front seat of our car, my bed for the past three weeks. Don was standing by the gates of the 7th Brigade, surrounded by shepherds, kids, and Bedouins who were curious about their new life. I was in no mood to hear more tragic stories this early as I hid away from the eyes of the small crowd. I could hear someone's voice saying, "They have a guy who speaks Arabic. He is sleeping." Mark was still in his tent, probably on the net. Minutes later, I watched Don accompanied by a middle-aged Iraqi man approach our car.

"Get up you lazy son of a gun. They have *caught* Saddam!" Don hollered jokingly, as he handed me a paper.

That would have been the best news ever, had it been true. Instead, Don flashed an ancient paper in front of my face and asked, "What does this document say? I want to help this man."

I lit a cigarette and examined its dulled Arabic calligraphy, which indicated that it was death certificate No. 326624, belonging to a Naji Abbas. Accompanying Don was a Mazen Abbas, who had come to the 7th Brigade like many Iraqis looking for work or retribution for the uncountable executions Saddam had ordered, especially on to the masses of Shia'a Muslims. I asked Mazen to wait for Mark and then watched him politely drag himself to the curb where he sat quietly; a broken man.

Mark appeared from his tent and appeared with a fresh outlook showing off the cowboy hat he was wearing. He was the still the captain of our mission. I tied the checkered Arabic *kuffiyah* (head wrap) tightly around my head and embraced the sun's heat.

Mazen came hurled over and explained his family's pain. The death certificate in his hand belonged to his father, whom he claimed headed out of the house one day in 1985 to purchase medicine and never returned. Thirteen months later, the police informed his family of the whereabouts of his corpse at the Abu-Gharib prison near Baghdad. I knew nothing good could come out of this prison since Mark and I had worked on a story about the 605 Kuwaiti prisoners of war captured during the Iraqi invasion of Kuwait in 1990. Some of the Kuwaiti POWs who escaped during the 1991 uprising had described their devastating stories about the torture and breach of human rights conducted in Abu-Gharib prison.

Mark and the photographers were interested in spending a substantial amount of time with a Shia'a Muslim family. Don and Pauline wanted photographs of their homes, the daily lives of their overlooked women, and we all wanted to explore their grief under Saddam's Sunni-ruled Iraq. Mazen joined me in the back seat and led us over to see his family at their poverty stricken town of *Imanas*.

Cruising through the south of Iraq, past the Shuybah refinery, towards Imanas, our car radio was on constantly. Tuning through the stations, the latest reports revolved around the anticipated aftermath of the storm. Saddam was no where to be found, nor were his top officials and family members. Such rumors lingered; *"he fled to Syria,"* or *"he escaped with the Russian ambassador to Moscow."* I had hoped we would advance to Nasiriyah further north, but a day in the life of a brave Shia'a family was also equally exciting to me.

Indeed, there was a visual sense of new freedom on the road. The sixty-five percent Shia'a Muslims of Iraq were now ready to cross the all time "red lines" imposed by Saddam. For the first time in thirty-five years, posters of their Imam, Hussein Ibn Ali or leader of the *ummah* (nation) covered car windows and swayed on flags outside their homes. I admired Mazen's calm attitude, as he sat peacefully unmoved by the car's cool air-conditioning, the electronic gadgets, the comfort of the seats; luxury. His disciplined brain was programmed to disregard such comforts and concentrate on reviving his family's pride. Leading us through a maze of mud houses and rugged sand beaten pathways, Mazen finally opened up to me and complained peacefully, "My father was only guilty of being a Shia'a Muslim. He was tortured; an eye poked out, an arm broken, and his chest was burned with electric wires."

I nodded with respect as I translated the words to Mark. I suddenly remembered flashes of an interview we conducted weeks before the war with a Kuwaiti POW who had escaped the Abu-Gharib prison. I remembered the woman's tearing face as she described the dark torture chamber, and how she was hung from the ceiling on a metal hook like a piece of meat; raped and electrocuted on the genitals. Stopping outside his home, I could see Mazen's psychological wounds would probably take years to heal as he commented, "They destroyed our family."

The children of the family admired Pauline and stared at Mark and Don with curiosity. They had never imagined strange American white men with big boots standing among their dear family. I lay my shoes aside and so did my crew as we entered the family's sacred mud brick house consisting of only two rooms. The physical suffering was clear. Twenty family members occupied two rented rooms, what a pity. I crossed my feet and sat on the floor beside Mark surrounded by Mazen's brothers and an uncle. Their Bedouin hospitality bared their kindness, as they offered us cold water. We all waited for the mother of the family to join, so that we could get the exact story. I felt a euphoria of admiration at the way this family sustained with their impossible situation, as they offered us *estikanas* (small cups) of tea. I could see Mark noting down the devoid of furniture in the room, which only consisted of a wood vinyl cabinet and a large pile of well kept sleeping rugs in the corner. Pauline, who had been in the other room with the women of the family, reappeared followed by the mother and said,

"They have a baby crib made out of welded steel rods."

Rasmia Abdel Kazem, 40, sat beside a framed picture of her husband, adjusted her black scarf, and immediately opened her old wounds; "Family members were asked to pay 30 *dinars*, a month's salary for the bullets that killed my husband, before we could receive his body."

I translated, listened, and measured the pain. Today, this woman's eyes were fearless. With an outburst she described what passed as normal under the Ba'athi regime.

"I had to consider how I was going to survive with four children younger than eight."

The woman reminisced with precision about the hollowness of not knowing for thirteen months what had happened to her husband. Hamza Abbas, sitting in the far corner of the room, joined the conversation, and tried to portray what had happened to his brother eighteen years ago.

Naji Abbas was deputy head of a local Shia'a group and was open about his disgust with the cruel Ba'ath Party. His brother deduced that an informer from the neighborhood must have turned him in. Until this week, every district had a Ba'ath official who monitored the area and recruited new spies. It was easy to figure out who they were, since they lived in the best houses and drove late model cars in addition to having extra money to throw around. In the past years, the Ba'ath Party had tried to force Abbas's family to paint pro-Saddam slogans such as *"Yes, Yes, to the leader Saddam Hussein"* on the wall of their mud house. When the family refused, the party officials wrote the saying themselves. Since the advance of the U.S. and British troops, the family had gained confidence. They immediately erased the slogans on the walls of their house. Half-way through the conversation, Hamza leaned back with misery at his bleak past, and sighed,

"Every second person in Iraq has been a spy."

Without a warning, the mother interrupted with another surprise. After she received Naji Abbas's body she realized he hadn't been killed by gun shots despite the 30 *dinar* bullet charges, but rather by inhumane hanging. What hypocrisy, what insult to this family's intellect!

Instantly, the cousin sitting in the corner broke down in tears at this revelation. Their wounds were just as fresh as they were eighteen years ago. Hamza, the long time breadwinner of the family joined the conversation again adding, "After his death, our family was blacklisted. I was fired from my position as an engineering professor at the university and forced to work as a nighttime security guard by the Ba'ath Party." He made five percent of his old wage, $10 a month. Both Naji Abbas's parents died shortly after his death due to the intensity of the shock. "We had to sell our furniture, borrow, and live a very low life," Hamza added as he retreated away and lied flat on his back. Trying to avoid any more painful questions about the past, Mark shifted to the future as he directed his questions to Mazen, the eldest son.

The grateful family considered themselves lucky. At least they were able to retrieve Naji's corpse. "We know of entire families buried alive. There are cases where they put them in acid baths and disappeared without a trace," Mazen clarified.

"For eighteen years we hid symbols of our Shia'a faith, including pictures of our holy Imam, Hussein *Ibn* (son of) Ali," added Mazen's mother with a sheer of hope in her liberated voice.

Hussein Ibn Ali was prophet Mohamed's grandson. He had seized the caliphate after the death of his father Ali. The Umayyad Caliph Yazid killed him and his small group of supporters in 680 on the plains of Karbala, near Kufa in modern Iraq. Since then he had become a particular hero of the Shia'a, a reminder that it is sometimes necessary to fight tyranny to the death.

Listening to Mazen, I observed the frayed wires supporting the only fluorescent light in the room. Under the light, a well-hung picture of Imam Ali on horseback carrying a gold shield and a red spear represented their new honorable freedom. Days ago they pulled it out of the cabinet only on Shia'a holidays after covering the windows with blankets and ensuring that no spies were peeking in. The Shia'a view their Imams as the *bab* (gateway) to Allah, the *sabil* (path) and the guide of every generation. There was no glass in the windows of the room. I lost my thought staring outside at the kids playing freely. Saddam's strategy for a tight hand ruling revolved on a divide and rule basis, driving a wedge between the religious and tribal groups in Iraq. His hatred and suppression of the Shia'a was ruthless, also proven throughout his eight-year war with Iran, which is dominated by Shia'a Muslims. Some Muslims regard the incarnation obvious in the Shia'a views as blasphemy. I personally like to compare it to the Christian incarnation. In the West, people tend to stereotype Shia'aism as an inherited fundamentalist sect of Islam, especially since the Iranian revolution. The truth remains that most Shia'a are very intellectual and disciplined. The U.S. military and pilots were extra cautious during their maneuvers in the city of Najaf, where Imam Hussein is buried, a holy shrine for Shia'as across the world. I had interviewed Iraqi Shia'a exiles in Kuwait and their ever-long dream was to visit Najaf. Many claimed they were ready to walk from Kuwait to Najaf once the border opened up, no matter how tiring the long journey might be.

Mazen and his brothers led us outside to their small courtyard and escorted me right into their bomb shelter, dug by hand weeks ago when the coalition neared their attack. Inside the bunker, I had to crouch or sit down as I tried to imagine twenty people crammed in this claustrophobic cave. The ceiling was supported with metal bars. "It saved our lives during the 1991 bombing too," Mazen added, as he walked me out of the dark shelter. Outside the entrance of the bunker I posed with the men of the family for Don's camera. I smiled at the sight of kids playing war games, running in and out of the shelter screaming the "bang bang!" imaginary sounds of gunshots. Their reality was far from mine. In spite of all that had happened, in spite of the atrocious crimes committed against the Shia'a, most of the people rejected religious divisions. Today, Naji Abbas's family said they hope people in Iraq will be able to enjoy their life freely and Hamza Abbas hoped he could regain his job back as a professor in the university. This interview was a well-deserved vacation for this broken family, as they shared their smiles, cries and outbursts with the world. Their ultimate hope was to rid their precious Iraq from the evils of Saddam Hussein, the *cancer* of Iraq.

SATURDAY APRIL 12, 2003

Still stuck in the south, I was literally counting the days to leave back to Kuwait. The news and media wires all indicated the race had begun; Iraq's throne was now open for prestigious tribal men, Iraqi exiles, and Dr. Ahmed Chalabi, the latter, a long time exile residing in London. As the head of the Iraqi National Congress he fulfilled the hopes of many Pentagon officials to head a transitional authority. The crowd outside the 7th Brigade today was lit with questions and different complaints. Iraq's first steps towards self-governance revolved around distrust, vanity, and obstacles to pulling together the many tribes and expatriates into one cohesive authority. The infamous name on media tongues and simple people of Iraq this morning was Sheik Muzahim of the Tammimi tribe. Tapped by the British government to administer a portion of Southern Iraq, this Shia'a religious leader voiced the values and needs of the Bedouin Southern Iraqis who lived under the suffering of Saddam's regime. Only yesterday, reporters from the Sunday Telegraph and Newsweek witnessed a clash outside Muzahim's house in Az Zubayr during a mass riot organized by the residents of the neighborhood. Barbara Jones stood giving us precise directions to the man's home as she explained how tribal leaders were too close to Hussein. Iraqis who lived abroad and were back to grab a piece of the pie, like Chalabi, ridiculed such local leaders for their wide misconception of the word *democracy.*

Outside the Sheikh's home in Az Zubayr close to Basra, I could feel the tension. An armed heavy bearded man governed the roof with a shiny Klashnikov rifle. The tribe's lawyer and head advisor Mansour Tammimi wore his old-fashioned sunglasses, the Ray-Bans worn in the eighties, as he waived us into their reception room. Following the crew, I locked the car, and tied a *kuffiyah* (head wrap) over my uncombed dusty hair. In the room, dozens of tribal men who sat on the sofas and the ground stood up to greet us, but Muzahim was no where to be seen. Don discreetly sat on the carpet beside two of the men and went on capturing the deepest details of these men's wrinkled faces and surroundings. In a rush, Mark put his tea aside and moved right to the interview because we could hear a restless crowd gathering outside the house.

I sat on the only space on a red sofa, across from Mansour Tammimi. Quickly, I relayed Mark's questions, practising my newly acquired Iraqi accent.

"What do you think of Dr. Ahmed Chalabi arriving to Iraq with his Freedom Fighters from Britain?" Mark asked.

The man adjusted the black *ugal* supporting his Bedouin head wrap and then responded with a well-prepared sarcastic remark, "We call Chalabi the opposition of the five-star hotels."

The man spoke for the dozens of Shia'a men surrounding him as he expressed his desire to see Iraq holding real elections, maybe a in a year when the water and electricity had been fully restored.

At this moment, Don crawled across the carpet and whispered in my ear, "Which one is Muzahim?"

More Tamimmis entered the room, interrupting the interview. We had to stand up and greet every single one of these elderly men. I had a feeling the Sheikh was not going to show up after the demonstration outside his home yesterday. In his Latino hat, Don still photographed the men, hoping he was one of them. The men seemed like warriors, meat eaters, nomads whose prestige and self confidence had emerged almost entirely from years of fulfilling the intricate set of requirements of a real *Arabawy* (Man of real Bedouin origin.) Around fifty leaders, religious scholars, and elders of the Tammimis sat staring at me, trying to join our conversation, but their official articulate lawyer continued to slam and mock Chalabi and his likes.

"Iraq is weak right now and needs support. It's like someone who is dead and everyone's fighting over the inheritance," Mansour Tammimi added.

That must have been the best metaphorical expression I had encountered during the last days. I knew Chalabi was an outsider; haunted with criminal allegations across the world. The perplexing games of fortune had just surfaced days after the fall of Saddam. The diplomatic race and dollar bills associated with it, had now started among the tribes and the exiles.

"What do you think of Chalabi's suggestion to ban any former Ba'athi from returning back to new government post-war jobs?" Mark asked.

I relayed the question quickly to the man knowing very well that such inquiry would bother Mansour.

"*Austaz* (Mr.) Chalabi believes in a "de-Ba'athification" theory which leaves no room for many good people, as I understand from the media, with his zero tolerance out look."

"Yes, since I have been in Iraq I understand very well that many people had to join the Ba'ath Party just to secure their lives and maintain good jobs. It will be confusing," I commented.

Instantly, I asked the big question:

"Do you see in the future any bloodletting or score settling between the Shia'a and Suni Muslims?"

"There are no problems between us Muslims here, no chance for *fitna* (sedition) *Inshallah (*In God's will). Chalabi is Shia'a like us too," Mansour replied, confirming what I already knew.

My mood dimmed with the set-up of this interview. The man's aura was sleazy, a front for Sheikh Muzahim. The men of the tribe were now murmuring, triggered by their spokesman's words. On old wooden chairs and carpets, they sat modestly beneath framed calligraphy of phrases and prayers from the Koran. A couple tried to interrupt the interview to remind the clan that the afternoon prayer was minutes away. They were restless to catch up with the call for prayer at the mosque, or maybe a way to avoid Mark's heated questions. Others still interested in the subject mumbled in Bedouin dialect about their unhappiness with outside leaders. I overheard an old man possibly in his eighties squeal his opinion to his buddy with slight aggravation, "We don't want men who go to bars in England."

Austaz (Mr.) Mansour Tammimi stood up politely and ended the conversation with another derogatory comment adding, "We need for someone to figure out who is going to pay for the funeral."

Walking outside towards the entrance I tensed at the sight of Sheikh Muzahim's weird guards standing alert around the house and on the rooftops with rifles. The men of the tribe escorted us outside and rained us with compliments and invitations to come eat with them. My crew practiced the little Arabic they had acquired with some of the more friendly ones. A younger Tamimmi wearing Ray-Ban sunglasses approached me and grabbed my hand. His was face was heavily bearded and his head wrap covered his hair. Smoking his Marlboro, he offered me a "Tammimi tour." Alert to his rowdy enthusiasm the man whispered in my ear, "I can take your crew on a real tour of Iraq, whatever you want, mass graves, weapons of mass-destruction, even Saddam himself!"

Mark laughed at the man's delusional offer, a sort of "offer you can't refuse." The residents of the neighborhood watched us closely with their furious eyes.

"We have our own vehicles and we will send armed men with you," the sleazy over confident man offered. The whole vibe was that of Mafia movies. An egotistical need for power. Truly, seconds later Mansour Tammimi approached us, pulled the hyper man away and ordered him to *"Forget about it,"* in a heavy Arabic Bedouin accent.

The residents despised them with passion. The locals typically showered us with viscous comments. One guy pointed to Mark's notebook and complained, "Sheikh Muzahim advised Saddam Hussein, resulting in the killing of lots of people. Another passing mechanic slammed the brakes of his bike, and whispered:

"These people, the Tammimis are not good."

Mark got caught up with some of the men in the crowd who spoke broken English. Walking towards the jeep, a man grabbed my arm peacefully as he whispered quickly, "You are an Arab...I advise you to leave from here now... there will be trouble, they will fire now."

Yesterday, it was a riot governed by stones. Today I was not sure what could happen. I glanced at the guards on the rooftop, scanning their evil murderous look. They were not bluffing. Immediately, I shouted to Mark and Don and urged them that we should leave right away. I got nothing but a nod from Mark who was once again busy drilling into the minds of the angry civilians. I hustled towards the crowd around him, but he grabbed my shoulder and said, "Tell me what this man is saying."

"Can we leave man? It's not safe here at all," I replied, ignoring his request momentarily.

"Ok. He is saying, 'How can Muzahim say he is representing the people if he's hiding behind guns? Just like Saddam did."

A different man again whispered in my ear with news that there will be trouble now and we could get hurt. I watched Mark continue his questions expecting me to follow as usual. Another short man, who must have been in his late 80's stopped me and aggressively waived papers in my face, asked me to read them, and print them. Weak to the aged man's pleading, I scanned the first lines. It was a hand-written five page warning letter to the coalition, outlining the evils of Sheikh Muzahim Tammimi. These were times when I wished I did not speak Arabic. I ignored the ambitious man then impatiently informed him I was not in the military. This is when I lost my temper, raised my voice, and scolded Mark as I split from the ring of Iraqis.

"I am heading to the car right now. Don is there and I have told you three times, the men are cursing and warning me in Arabic. You do not understand them. I don't want to get hurt."

That was the first time I had slipped out of line since we met in Kuwait. More than any other morning, today I wokeup craving my home, my woman, and cleanliness. I had stopped brushing my teeth, combing my hair, or even eating right. Subconsciously, I praised my good luck and God's protection, which had me alive until today. Words like 9mm bullets, bomb shrapnel, and incoming artillery now translated into phobia, bloody civilian deaths, and precious human body parts. My war in the south was over, yet a look into this Dr. Ahmed Chalabi's infamous (FIF) Freedom Iraqi Forces about a 100-miles north in Nasiriyah was about to inspire me for more raw truth.

Sunday April 13, 2003

I welcomed this morning with excitement, two boiled eggs, orange juice, crackers, and coffee, our first solid breakfast in weeks. Half way through my feast, my phone rang bringing the soothing voice of my Iraqi girlfriend calling from Dubai.

"*Ishlonak?* (How are you in the Iraqi dialect which also literally means: What is your color? in most Arabic dialects)"

"I'm coming soon. By the way, we are advancing to Nasiriyah today to meet Ahmed Chalabi in his camp."

"Ok. Please take care. I want to see you soon. Give me a call when you get there. I want to know everything about this crook. You know he owned a bank in Jordan when he got involved with fraud and was smuggled out in the trunk of a car," she added, with scrutiny.

"The Pentagon issued a deck of cards with the photos of the 55 most wanted Iraqi Baathi officials. Could you get me one? It must be all over the place there," she asked, surprising me with this dazzling news.

During our three-hour drive up north towards Nasiriyah, I wove in and out of sleep several times. My eyes scanned the road for signs of battle. Along the road on either side of the strategic bridges, Iraqi sniper towers were partially destroyed. Trenches dug by U.S. soldiers were deserted just like the many Iraqi tanks and army personnel carriers. The word Nasiriyah means victorious in Arabic. Ironically, there was no sign of any damaged or destroyed coalition military vehicles in sight. However, Nasiriyah is where that first U.S. Apache was shot down weeks ago by a farmer's rifle according to the reports broadcasted on TV. The peasants then received the 25,000 *dinars* reward advertised by Saddam for any Iraqi who succeeds in bringing down a coalition aircraft. Days later, the farmer's furniture bought with the prize got robbed during a looting spree.

Saddam Hussein neglected many of Iraq's vital needs, but not the highways. I enjoyed the well asphalted roads and rings of bridges on the way. Some of the highways were actually wide enough to land a Boeing 747, yet we still got lost. Under the pale semi-sandy sky we scanned our maps for a lead back on the right road. I still had no complaints as I watched Don signal a U.S. military fueling convoy and ask for directions. At first, the driver was not too cooperative, but I could see him ease down gradually. It turned out that Don Bartletti is from the man's hometown; Orange County, California. For the first time since we entered Iraq, our media credentials proved useful as the U.S. officer checked them with precision and wrote our names down on a small paper. Apparently, the officer was planning to lead us straight to his top-secret base miles away, and also minutes away from Chalabi's headquarters. The officer stared at my CFLCC credential then leaned over to the window and asked, "You're Mohamed?"

"Yes I am," I answered, as I looked away at the horizon of desert.

The soldier glanced at Mark looking for some sort of subtle confirmation, and he got it as Mark nodded and thanked the man. Once again, I could feel the sensitivity of carrying the name *Mohamed* during these dark decades. I wondered what kind of reactions I would get about my name when I went back to North America or Europe.

Slowly, we followed the tail of their convoy trailing behind clouds of sand emerging from their big wheels. Off-road, past muddy hills, the off-limits U.S. headquarters appeared well fenced, surrounded by cement blockades at the entrance. The convoy went through as we parked meters away on the sand with another five European and Japanese TV crews. The base seemed busy with military planes flying in and out. Saddam had called it Al Talil Air Base when he used to own an air force. Its location was ideal and strategically enclosed by miniature hills.

"Sir, you have to move your cars further back right away. You're blocking our view. If any enemy vehicles approach us, you would get hurt," a sergeant Simon ordered, as he pointed to a high caliber machine gun mounted on a Hummer at the entrance of the secret base.

Just as he finished talking, a bus proceeded by two cars and surrounded by an entourage of security vehicles rushed past us into the base. I spotted Dr. Ahmed Chalabi's face in the bus, surrounded by his guards and accompanied with just one female. All the TV crews of course tried hopelessly to enter behind them. Like us, other media were not just interested in chatting with Chalabi. It was publicly proclaimed that the first meeting with representatives from Iraq and external diplomats was scheduled on Tuesday the 15th. This news flooded the world with hope. It was to be the first official meeting to discuss the formation of a new interim government. The mid-size southern city of Nasiriyah remained the venue, yet security was set as the number one concern on the coalition's agenda. Al Talil Air Base also hosted the ziggurat of Ur city, the birthplace of Abraham, and we were now haggling with the U.S. guards to enter just to see it. Chalabi's camp was miles away and we had bigger plans for him. I could see Chalabi and his followers walking up the stairs of the ziggurat from a far distance, followed by the ancient city's curator. Don jumped on the roof of our truck armed with his Cannon and its long fish lens then went on shooting the sculpture through the dusty horizon. The officer explained that the ziggurat was off-limits for the soldiers too, but not for Chalabi; the Pentagon's dearest son.

I retreated away from the noise and dived into a can of baked beans and watched a Euro crew argue and complain in French and English. One delicate French journalist backed up by eight more men, yelled at the U.S. guard as he adjusted his silk scarf and shouted, " You Americans destroyed the image of journalism in this war with your ill-treatment....I will not accept this... *shit*... Give me your name... now...."

"Sir, I have orders. You can't spend the night out here in front of the base," the soldier responded firmly.

"We are self sustained... oooffff!... You don't know who I am...... Tomorrow morning your name will be in Washington!!... You don't know who I sit with... *merde*!" the French man threatened, as he wrote down the soldier's name, unit number, and location.

Mark, Don, and I laughed at the silly French reporter and cherished the beginning of the sunset waiting for Chalabi to finish his tour of this sacred historical city. I refused Mark's idea about renting a room at a family's house for the night. The war did end, but the after shocks were definite; by now I trusted my personal instincts.

6:30 pm. Chalabi's bus swept past us at high speed but not fast enough to lose our Mitsubishi Pajero 2003. We followed him along the Nasiriyah highway, ten minutes off-road, then back onto another short stretch of asphalt straight to the gates of his camp, which was clearly marked Freedom Iraq Fighters (FIF). Early darkness had conquered the camp as I spoke to the main guard Hussein. I explained what LA Times was then requested to spend the night inside. The English speaking guard waived his flashlight through our car as his guards searched thoroughly. A few moments later, Zaab Sethna's (an advisor to Iraqi National Congress head Ahmed Chalabi) voice screamed through the radio; okayed our entrance, but rejected three of the other media crews behind us. Chalabi had been bitten hard by many controversial reports from various media; especially those outlining his shady background without any credit for his positive whiff of power promoting a *free* Iraq

The setting was dim, with shadows of soldiers dispersed all over the bombed out air base. The only intact building was a sandy flea-infested warehouse that had no running water, windows, or bathrooms. I parked the car quickly by neglected military vehicles that had no wheels, doors, or seats and rusted by years of harsh weather. I ran behind Don and Mark who were already outside the warehouse chatting with the guards under the only floodlight in the camp, powered by a noisy generator. Dozens of mosquitoes surrounded the light as Hussein, his main guard, patted us down for a quick security clearance. Followed by his closest guards and his daughter who was also dressed in a military outfit, Chalabi appeared quietly and sat on an army cot ordering his people to offer us tea. Before the avalanche of questions, I whispered in his ear for a quick pose as Don snapped the photo. Waving the bugs away from his face, Chalabi sat comfortable in his shirt and jeans as he started the press release with a clear statement:

"I am not a candidate of any sort. We are all working for the sake of Iraq's future." My linguistic skills were not important now, as I comfortably weighed the media questions and his cautious replies.

On his "de-Ba'athification" zero tolerance views, Chalabi elaborated,

"That's the same argument in Germany after the fall of the Nazis," he said, trying to shout over the generator's annoying rattle.

Speaking into the microphone of a radio journalist, Chalabi added, "The idea that Ba'athists can make the trains run on time doesn't hold water."

"What do you tell people who mock you as 'opposition of the five-star hotels,' an outsider?" Mark asked gracefully.

"Look around you. Does this look like a five-star hotel?" the fifty-eight year old Shia'a exile replied.

I observed the man's calm features wondering what he went through during the last quarter century positioning himself as a leading opponent of Saddam, his meetings with the CIA, or his last phone call with the Pentagon minutes ago maybe. His guards were hyper and alert as one of them followed Don to snap a rear view image of Chalabi surrounded by journalists. These loyal guards along with some 700 fighters and advisors were also airlifted last week into the heart of liberated Iraq.

"It's what the Iraqis want that I think is more important."

I don't know if it was planned, but the interview died short when dozens of Free Iraqi Forces barged in on foot chanting, followed by more fighters in pickup trucks. Almost immediately, Chalabi ran towards the chanting mass:

"My home Iraq! Long live Chalabi... My Home Iraq!"

His guards and daughter trotted around him for security, as he melted into his fighters who still continued to chant louder raising their rifles high. We all followed him through the mass celebration, trying to identify the men's facial features under the dim light of the moon. Suddenly, a few of his happy guards fired shots in the air, the Arab way of expressing utmost respect. His guards raised their hand guns right away, and I split the circle of newly recruited fighters and listened to his American advisor order the soldiers to stop and refrain from shooting, "Calm down now, none of this...

boys.... *Yalla,* (let's go) take him in." A tall white American wearing glasses and a baseball cap; a graduate of George Town University and a previous advisor in the White House for years accompanied Chalabi into his warehouse, quickly ordering the journalists away.

"I saw you checking his daughter out. This is your chance Mohamed," Mark teased, as he assembled his tent.

The camp remained quiet as I watched the soldiers patrol in the dark. I dialed my girl's number using our sat-phone as I paced around the camp checking out the facilities, ammunition, and the poor sleeping quarters. Don had borrowed a foldable army cot and slept peacefully behind our car.

"Hello sweetie. I am in the FIF camp now, its unbelievable. He is so backed up by the U.S. in every way," I whispered to the imaginary ears of my sleepy woman.

"Oh. I wish I were there. I saw him on TV a while ago."

"When are you coming back? It's been too long."

"I have a slight temperature and my bones ache. *Inshallah* (In God's will) a day or two," I answered.

"Listen, I think this man is set-up to be the next president of Iraq," I added.

"Are you crazy Moody? You have no idea about my people or my country's history. There is no way we will let him be president. Listen. You've really pissed me off and I don't want to talk to you! Good night," she exploded, hanging up the line.

Instantly, the skies scattered spits of rain, invisible rays of water signaling me to retreat away into the backseat of the Pajero avoiding a worse fever. The rain drove the hyper mosquitoes away and left me to my home sick dreams.

MONDAY APRIL 14, 2003

"Free Iraq….Free Iraq!" were the loud chants that interrupted my dreams. Numb from my fever medicine, I watched Chalabi's forces marching following their commander's orders. My eyes followed them through, watching their wavy line formation and their mismatched uniforms. Most of them wore "chocolate chip" army uniforms as Mark described them last night, but under today's sun the whole camp seemed bigger and busier. Chalabi was pacing back and forth talking on his sat-phone. I could see he had established a measured path, a sort of simultaneous aerobic exercise to fit his schedule. A partially destroyed brick mural displayed Arabic paint portraying the name of this Iraqi base: "Air Base 71, Imam Ali Camp."

My knees were weak, I swallowed two Panadol pills and watched Don prancing around the camp with his camera, sleeping on a cot must have rejuvenated his back. Waiting for the pills to kick in, I walked over to a destroyed building where the forces stored boxes of uniforms, duffel bags, and hats. Each box labeled "Property of the U.S. Government", also had a squared black stamp displaying the FIF letters. The Kurdish soldier in charge smiled at my request for an army hat then handed it to me saying, "*Sank* you."

"How are you feeling now?" Mark asked me by the car

"Better, after the pills. Did you speak to Mary Braswell, your editor?" I asked, hoping he heard news about our return.

"Three or four days more."

"Let's go talk to Chalabi's men."

Mark approached an older recruit who seemed busy looking for water.

"Excuse me, we are with the LA Times and would like to ask you a question or two. This is Mohamed," Mark said, as he opened his notebook.

"Did you get training after joining?" I asked.

"There was training, but I couldn't spare the time from my business," said Salman, a taxi driver who joined in Phoenix, Arizona.

"Do you have any military background?" I asked slowly, when I realized his English was weak.

"*Plus*, yes, I was in the Iraqi army from 1970 to 1972," Salman replied.

"Good luck. Did you pick up any Spanish in Arizona?" I asked, extending my arm for a quick handshake. "*Sie, Un pouquito* (Yes, a little)."

Following Mark towards another group of soldiers, I smiled happily at the positive vibe surrounding me. They were normal butchers, taxi drivers, bakers, or fast food waiters who left their jobs back home for a chance to taste real freedom in their home land, Iraq. A U.S. Special Forces soldier was watching over some Iraqis line up from an all-terrain Hummer. I watched Mark note down his comments, "The problem is; they really don't have platoon commanders." Under the Iraq Liberation Act passed by Congress in 1998; these fighters are overseen by 200 U.S. Special Forces and other troops who drive them around, cloth them, train them, and guide them on patrolling routes. This soldier stood relaxed as he added, "There are a few officers, but they are only giving orders over very big groups." The soldier then clarified why the men had some winter coats, wool gloves, and forest green pants that stand out in the desert; they were shipped with them from Hungary, where some of the Iraqi exiles underwent training right before the war.

Like many rumors that originated in the confusion of the war, the word around this camp was that a shipment of new semi-automatic guns and rocket-propelled grenades had arrived from the United States. The FIF commanders were not excited like their soldiers as one Abdul Hamid Salman clarified, "We're all familiar with Klashnikovs." Salman who joined from Syria months ago showed off his rifle adding, "Every Iraqi knows how to use the Klashnikov. They're simple, reliable and all over Iraq. Anything else could make people confused."

"You arrived on a U.S. C-17 aircraft only last week. Don't you think if you came in earlier you would have actually fought and defended your goal against Saddam?" Mark asked the commander.

"We tried to get involved earlier but the U.S. ignored us. Then when they find they need us, they let us come. That's the American policy."

"What is the nature of your role now?" I asked.

A former Iraqi soldier joined the conversation and answered on behalf of his commander as he clarified how the FIF met with tribal leaders and farmers guiding them to keep their weapons well hidden and to cooperate with the coalition. The language barrier remains a serious obstacle between the army and the civilians. The soldiers also instructed civilians how to proceed through checkpoints, where there have been several civilian deaths when Americans fired after residents failed to stop. "If we'd been involved in the war from the beginning, we could have avoided more casualties," the soldier said. "We could talk to people, even the militia Fedayeen, and say don't be stupid by playing a losing card."

Almost half the soldiers are Iraqis returning home while others were recruited locally. Recent arrivals poured in from Iraq, United States of America, Jordan, Syria, Britain, Norway, and Canada, among other countries. Each one had a different story. Abu Zaman, a 38 year old Shia'a Muslim who just arrived from St.Louis, where he owned a small business, joined the conversation with his own tragic history. He had been forced to flee Iraq after his involvement in the Shia'a uprising of '91. He had just been married when Saddam's troops stormed into Basra to crush the rebellion and arrested him. Three years after his escape, he received a letter from his sister saying that Saddam's Ba'ath Party had forced his wife to remarry a soldier.

"The government divorced her from me, raped her and forced her to remarry someone else," Abu Zaman complained, bringing a rush to my body with the cruelty of his story.

12:30 pm. The temperature well over 36 degrees Celsius, shirtless I relaxed by the car admiring Chalabi for his ability to wear a full suit in this weather. Surrounded by his entourage of guards Chalabi rushed over to a BBC crew for a live broadcast feed. The world including my girlfriend were probably eager to hear what he was going to say but no one was going to see the white sneakers he was wearing since the camera shot his formal demeanor above the waist only. The camp was bustling with action and Don and Mark were too busy as usual documenting. I spotted his daughter, Tamara Chalabi standing alone by the warehouse, so I quickly put on a shirt and my media credentials for a quick chat. After introducing myself, I learned she had a PhD in History from Harvard. Supporting her dad in every way, Tamara stood relaxed in a white shirt and black pants.

"We came in to Nasiriyah through the north of Iraq, which is much cooler and full of green mountains, beautiful. The south is beaten down and poor," she complained, brushing her long hair away from her face.

"What about your mom? Where is she?" I asked curiously.

"My mother is Lebanese. She does not get involved with this."

"Are you worried? You seem restless," I asked.

"Yes. There are too many *men* here," she replied, with a smile.

Trying to keep the conversation light, away from politics, I added, "My girl friend is Iraqi. We met in Montreal. Her brother is a rapper and his lyrics are genuinely political. He has a group called Euphrates. Anyway, he's been on CBC and in many paper reviews."

"That's great. We need people like him in the near future to raise money and support our cause. Stay in touch!" she yelled, as she handed me her email address and excused herself.

"His latest track is called *Iraqnophobia*," I shouted, as she waived and gave me the thumbs-up.

Preparing the jeep for our day trip, I swallowed two more pills and drank our last bit of bottled water. Coincidentally, a huge flat bed six-wheeler truck hauled into the camp, with a huge bag of water supported on its stern.

The bag, which seemed like a huge waterbed was marked clearly with big black letters: **WATER.** I had never imagined such an invention, and I shared my reaction with the soldiers too, as we all waited in line to fill up. Like me, the soldiers were astonished at the superior technology of the U.S. army, to be able to facilitate such a flexible three-day water supply in the desert, for a whole army.

In the car, Mark stopped outside the gate of the camp to chat to a man hoping to join the FIF. Abdul Hamid Hasona claimed he represented 50,000 villagers who wanted to join. Most of them were motivated by freedom, patriotism, and a desire to eliminate Saddam's regime. The free clothes, U.S. packaged meals, and the precious $150 monthly wage definitely represented valuable perks in a destroyed economy. Outside the gates we encountered a Sheikh Lami Abbas who came complaining about his past, looking for any retribution. By now, I was so familiar with such tragedies, yet hearing them over and over from different people moved me each time. Sheik Lami reminisced about his imprisonment for being a Shia'a leader. He explained how he was hit, prodded, eyelids pulled back, and electrocuted on the head and genitals. He demonstrated how his hands were cuffed behind him then raised until he was off the ground. He recalled how jailers forced ten suspects into an 8-by-6-foot room so only two could lie down and sleep at a time while the other eight were forced to stand. We promised the man to write his story then left him to try his luck with Chalabi.

At the city of Nasiriyah, we stopped briefly at a horrendous sight. Hundreds of civilians gathered outside Nasiriyah's former police station yelling and protesting. The men clawed and pushed one another to get into a modest-sized hole. Few did actually manage to squeeze into it as rumors racked the crowds that prisoners were trapped in underground cells. This was another rare moment when I wished I did not speak a word of Arabic. Men of all ages grabbed my shirt and pulled my hands asking for help. U.S. helicopters patrolled over the crowd in case of trouble. Mark and Don were also worried at the looks in the local's eyes. Several people then threatened to topple a statue of a vase in the center of the roundabout as a weirder rumor spread that political prisoners released in 1991 had been seen exiting from a secret trapdoor under that statue. Two members of the 15th Marine Expeditionary Unit moved in to check the hole, but the investigation only found dirty sewer pipes. We headed for the car quickly, as soldiers yelled and pushed the crowds back violently. One solider mistook me for one of the locals and yelled, "Get away from the car, step back into the crowds now!" I immediately waived my credentials and unlocked the vehicle for

Don who jumped in and continued to tease me about this incident for the duration of our drive back to the Al Talil top-secret U.S. base.

Outside the base we met with the same U.S. commander who had promised us a tour of Ur city ruins. The officer was optimistic as he waited for his orders to let us in. Waiting for the decision, the officer showed us a stray puppy he had adopted last month. The officer was ordered to let the pet go although most of the soldiers were attached to it by now. He explained how this puppy reminded him of home and his own dog. I did not know how such a puppy could disturb their operation, but military orders were final.

We got the ok to enter the base for a tour of the ziggurat. I locked our car then jumped into the back of the U.S. Hummer assigned to escort us inside. Sharing the back with us was a lieutenant from Ohio and an African-American soldier from Brooklyn. The latter was quiet while his buddy went on talking about his service in Germany, then switched to his wishes of heading back home to see his family and daughters. I was shocked to hear him say he had been in the Gulf for six months as he showed us his daughter's photos. Like most of the soldiers, he entered through Kuwait, but trained in the deserts of Saudi Arabia and Qatar before entering Iraq.

In front of the ziggurat, we all stood amazed and happy. The soldiers prepared their personal digital cameras as we all waited for the curator to walk us through this historical city. Their commander looked at me and said, "My wife bought me this camera when we found out I was going to Iraq." I felt happy about this unexpected tour. A long staircase of maybe seventy steps led to the top of the temple. We all posed for photos then suddenly I looked at the stairs, gathered my strength, and ran up without a stop. At the summit, I jumped, waiving everyone up then I just breathed a load of the fresh air. For seconds, I owned the place. My soul was sore. I was now closer to God away from the horrors of this war. The sight was magical; different shades of the desert sand were clear from this view, the greenery was amazing too. Seconds later, the soldiers, Don, and Mark accompanied by the Iraqi curator of the city joined me. Everyone was proud as we listened to the guide relay his treasure of knowledge. Ur-Nammu had built this ziggurat in the 21st century BC to the city's patron deity Nanna the Moon God. The curator spoke good English and went on sharing his wealth pointing at his own mud house meters away from the ruins. Ur was excavated by a joint expedition of the British Museum and the University of Pennsylvania under Sir Leonard Woolley between 1922 and 1934. The man explained how Saddam never visited Ur but ordered its renovation. We all followed the curator down the long steps and like everyone else I was touching its ancient precious stones just like I did when I entered the Giza Pyramids in Egypt. I tried to visualize the kings and queens of the Early Dynastic Period walking down these steps followed by their slaves under the lights of torches at night. The keeper shocked me again with news that the sculpture was older than the Pyramids. Indeed, Iraq is the cradle of civilization. The curator showed off examples of the first writings engraved on some of the ancient bricks in the ziggurat. One of the most important cities of Sumer, Ur lay west of the Euphrates River. Its walls enclose circa 60 hectares. I had forgotten my fever with this unexpected vacation and stood posing with Mark and the soldiers. I listened carefully to the curator now leading us through sand dunes towards the ruins of the city. The city continued to thrive in the Old Babylonian Period and the Bible claims Ur as the home of Abraham before he left for the west. At the city, only minutes away, we entered the king's tomb first. I was stunned at the cool air inside, more like an air-conditioned room. Across from the king's tomb was another smaller room. It was his servant's tombs. The curator explained that there was evidence of human sacrifice, just like the Pharaohs in Egypt. Three Jewish American female soldiers joined us minutes later as they posed for the camera. Everyone, Christians, Muslims, and Jews were honored and blessed with this short holy vacation from the war. Walking through the rooms of Abraham's home, our guide pointed at the center where a drainage hole was geometrically positioned to absorb the rain's water. I touched the walls and lost the group for a quiet tour alone, trying to get a sense of the place, its design, its past, and today, its destiny without Saddam. Back in time for more history, I heard the curator say, "The city was finally abandoned in the 4th century BC."

On our short walk back to the cars, I handed the tour guide five dollars. Everyone else gave him extra cash for being a keeper of God's history. The joke circulating among us and the soldiers was that we were luckier than the Pope since Saddam Hussein had banned him from visiting Ur in the millennium of 2000.

I took more photos with Don and Mark by the ziggurat. Suddenly, a military Hummer rolled in close to us then two U.S. officers approached us with cold pop. It was perfect timing especially that these guys were actually military historians coming to see Ur for the first time too. Chatting with them, I checked all the goodies in their trunk and what a surprise they had. Not too far from this base, they had actually found an RPG training camp. They had confiscated actual targets in addition to a prototype of an RPG with Arabic labels marking its parts and usage. They threw around some of the books they found, with no clue what they are. Coincidentally, I realized one of the books was an old Koran.

"I speak Arabic. Let me see these books," I said, grabbing the ripped holy book.

"This is a Koran and that one is just a tank driving manual," I commented.

"Oh. We thought you were kidding? What are you doing here?" asked one of the historians

"He's our *Enforcer*," Mark joked, as he pulled me towards our jeep.

5:00 pm. The Enforcer was out of service. My fever got worse, accompanied by stomachaches, probably from the unwashed vegetables I ate with a Bedouin yesterday. I got a lift back to the south with a Russian crew reporting on Basra. Upon my arrival at Basra, I hitched back with a convoy of water aid trucks heading back to Kuwait, another sign of Kuwait's vast support to the Iraqi people. Indeed, Kuwait remains the gateway to Iraq. On the drive back I recognized many farmers and kids in Safwan. Youth of the new Iraq, their eyes are the soul of the future, even if Saddam is not captured or killed. I felt peace upon crossing the border into Kuwait with the sight of buildings, streetlights, well fed people; security. My crew was to follow me the next day after covering the new government meeting in Nasiriyah. I knew I would be back for Baghdad *blues*. Just the resonance of the city's name brings tears to the eyes of most Iraqi exiles I have met. A vacation away, Baghdad remains a city that has changed the history of the 21st century.

VI

BAGHDAD BLUES: FRAGMENTED

Chapter 6: A wall-size mural in Saddam's conference hall at the Jumhuri Palace in Baghdad. The Iraqi flag marked with Allahu Akbar (God is the greatest) is stamped on the rocket heading to space. Photo by Mohamed Fahmy.

Sunday April 20, 2003

My short vacation in Dubai or the New York of the Gulf as many label it, left me rejuvenated, grateful to be alive, and in awe. I was shocked at the shallowness of the masses that had already grown indifferent to the daily Iraq news, as if they knew the outcome of the war from day one. One taxi driver in the modern Gulf city left me disgusted and speechless with his ridiculous remarks: "Bin Laden and Saddam are the new pillars of Islam."

7:00 am. I drove the same SUV across the Kuwait border into Safwan-Iraq with my new partner, Mark Fineman. A veteran of the Gulf war, Mark had reported in Iraq during the early eighties. He was also one of the first journalists to enter Kuwait right after the Iraqi invasion in 1990. Laid back, Mark carried on with his chain smoking as he explained his connection with Iraq: "Iraq is all about anarchy, and I love anarchy." I did most of the listening and noticed how his plastic rimmed shades would move up his nose as it wrinkled whenever he made a joke (often not a very funny one). Finally, I had to confess to Mark that he reminded me of the musician Willie Nelson, with his grayish ponytail hanging out of his cap, the loud Hawaiian shirts and a carefree passion for life. Mark was a warrior journalist known for his years covering the Tamil fighters in Sri Lanka. Just as he got into his colorful storytelling mode, I coincidentally played a new Indian-trance tape I had prepared for the trip.

Images of the war and the people I had left behind haunted my dreams throughout my vacation. I promised myself to hold my composure; trying to block out any negative thoughts. Socializing with my peers during my vacation reminded me that I was a witness to history and that invoked a special excitement within me, to be in this position: It cast a light of wisdom on my life.

Passing through the all too familiar roads of Safwan, Umm Qasr, and Nasiriyah, I reminisced about our first tour of duty. Most of the beaten Iraqi tanks were removed and the once scary bridges stood peaceful over the magical Euphrates River. In attempts to beat the clock to Baghdad, we only stopped twice to refuel, using the gasoline we had brought along from Kuwait. We were also worried about the thirty thousand dollars Mark was carrying for the LA Times bureau in Baghdad. He raved on and on about the convoys of industrial goods and products conquering the trail from Kuwait to Baghdad. Assigned as an investigative reporter he was following the war's money. Mark excitedly noted down the names of companies imprinted on the trucks, the type of goods, and bombarded me with loads of information on the contracts signed by American companies like Bechtel and Kellogg Brown & Root. I had fallen asleep half way through the ride only to find him waking me up pointing at two shiny brand new Mercedes Benz hauled on a flat bed truck on route to Baghdad. "I wonder who these babies are for?" he said, lighting another red Marlboro.

3:00 pm. Mark drove right through the heart of the city after I asked strangers on the street for directions. The crowds lined the streets, bustling into the normality of their new life. The tranquil beauty of Baghdad was shadowed by a violent reality as U.S. military vehicles roared by, patrolling the shady streets. Mark called the Times bureau in Baghdad for clearer directions, then minutes later we finally reached our designated hotel.

Al Hamra Hotel is situated in the Al Karada neighborhood and harbored dozens of journalists. As I watched Mark clinging to the Marlboro cartons he had brought with him from London, I wondered how we were going to share a suite for three weeks. Regardless, I had no real complaints: There was room service, a hot shower, a piano bar, and a swimming pool to top it all off. This four star hotel held a low profile compared to the mess at the Ishtar Sheraton or Palestine Hotel several blocks down the road.

I watched Baghdad from the balcony with its magical horizon of palm tree groves, surrounded by houses and well-asphalted streets. I could see Uday's palace at a distance. A melancholy and disconcerting sadness hung over the ancient city with its usual military backbone, now gone. I overheard Mark inform the bureau that we were on our way to check in with them and prepared my digital camera.

As I tried to figure out the way to the bureau, I realized that I was driving in the area close to Saddam's palace where "Shock and Awe" first started. As one crosses the *Jumhuriya* (Republican) Bridge over the Tigris River, one's eye is caught by the massive gates of the *Jumhuri* palace-the site that the CIA expected Saddam would be sleeping during the first air raids on Baghdad. A few minutes later, I finally drove through Al Masbah square, only a street away from our bureau. Mark pointed at a crowd surrounding a U.S. Bradley tank and asked me to park close to it. We walked through the crowds towards the officer in charge who welcomed us as the only media on the scene. As soon as I walked into the entrance of the building, my jaw literally dropped at the sight of two sports cars well hidden behind what used to be a concrete wall in the foyer. A burgundy 740-BMW parked adjacent to a red 500-SL Mercedes shined behind the remains of the brick wall. I let my eyes tour the white leather interior of the BMW, customized with full options, a TV set, and a VCR in the back seat. Parts of the tinted glass were smashed, revealing stickers of Saddam's face stamped across the dash board of the car. A couple of soldiers tried their luck but failed to turn the ignition on. Mark chatted with the soldiers who surprisingly revealed that they got a tip from the residents that two of Uday Hussein's automobiles were hidden behind the walls of the building. Apparently, cars were like Uday's babies. He had an employee whose job was to surf the Internet and fill three-ring binders for him with pictures of new and rare European sports models, along with Arabic translations of their specifications.

I chatted with some of the building's residents who were shocked to see the soldiers break down the walls with sledgehammers, as they had no idea these treasures were tucked away behind the concrete. The crowds cheered as a Bradley dragged the gorgeous Beemer out of the building. Mark switched our car's ignition on impatiently then we split the scene during the loud fiasco.

At the bureau, I was impressed with the beautiful villa LA Times had rented for the next year. Two floors with a whole crew of cooks, maids, drivers, and security guards mechanized the paper's impressive reporting. I met reporters like Michael Slackman, Carolyn Cole, and the famous John Daniszewski who had endured tough reporting throughout the war. Mark sipped on a cold beer while I checked my email. We were both still dazzled by the scene with the cars and I could hear Mark tell the story to everyone in the bureau. I was glad to be working with him on investigative reports away from the trouble of dailys. However, Mark insisted that we go back with Times photographer Wali Skalij for a quick snap shots of Uday's toys.

We got there too late and Wali returned to the bureau when we realized the cars were gone. Mark smoked his cigarette as I translated his simple questions to the residents of the building. Just as we were ready to leave, a white Mercedes approached the entrance at high speed, stopped suddenly with a loud screech, then a tall dark man with a thick mustache stepped out of the back seat yelling, "Where is that rat? Where is the building keeper?" I then spotted the middle-aged keeper speed across the road to another building. In a split second, I watched the angry man lean back into his car. Like many residents of Iraq, I had established a sixth sense during the war, one that warns and foresees danger. I pulled Mark away as we walked slowly with our eyes focused on the car. Just as I finished saying "I think he will pull a gun," the man pulled out a shiny Klashnikov and rained the neighborhood with bullets. We ducked and ran the opposite way. As I sprinted I could see with the corner of my eye the wild man leaning from his moving Mercedes as he continued to pound the street with bullets trying to track down and kill the building's keeper.

We caught our breath a street away. Mark lit a cigarette: "Did you see the size of that machine gun? You picked it up right away, that's good," he commented. Three hours into Baghdad and we were already dodging Klashnikov bullets, a scene that had become normal in Iraq now.

8:00 pm. Three hours before the strict curfew enforced by the army, I stood in the balcony admiring the magical night hovering over Baghdad's placid horizon. The city looked haunted: There was no electricity in the neighborhood except for the Hamra hotel and a few houses lit by generators. Without warning, sporadic rattling of gunfire echoed across the night. Louder pounds from U.S. tank machine guns responded. I tried to spot the source of the shots but failed. Louder continuous rattling of automatic weapons broke the silence again, but from a different direction this time. I turned off the lights in the balcony and listened for clues. It was like a gun show. Handgun shots came from a corner followed by the well known chained rattles of Klashnikovs coming from the other end. I could see and hear units of U.S. tanks maneuvering around the hotels and across the highways throughout the night. Just when I thought the shots were over, more threatening blasts of gunfire interrupted the calmness.

11:00 pm. I sat with Mark in the hotel's restaurant waiting for our food and listened to him complain over the relaxing tunes of the piano. The whole scene was bizarre as the restaurant bustled with journalists and military officials. Mark went on about his memories in Iraq as the electricity cut off twice. "I still don't understand why a hotel like this doesn't have a bigger generator," he complained.

I observed the other tables and watched Mark greet most of the journalists. I drank my beer and listened to the French journalists across from our table while he said his hellos to his Russian friends on another table. There was a sense of privilege between everyone sharing the impossible fragments of Baghdad's history with so many professional dedicated people. I dipped into the *tabouli* and *hummus*, then for a second trembled at the sounds of three consecutive gunshots just outside our hotel.

"What the hell is that? These shots are too close Mark!" I insisted.

"Yeah, that's another thing we need to figure out tomorrow," Mark said.

Back in our suite, 706, with no electricity I smoked with Mark and listened to him compare Iraq to Cuba. He saw the same anarchy in both countries. "So what's the game plan for tomorrow?" I wondered. "We have breakfast at seven. Maybe check in with the bureau first then go hang around the palace. I need to track down some of these American contractors. That's what I'm here for; to figure out where all this money is going," Mark answered, with total persistence in his tone. I surrendered to the small bed in my room listening to the nonstop gunshots, trying to guess what they could be.

MONDAY APRIL 21, 2003

8:30 am. On the front steps of Al Hamra Hotel, Mark and I stood puzzled trying to choose a driver for the day. Baghdad was a big city, not to mention the dangerous streets we were advised to avoid like the famous Al Rashid Street. The air remained motionless and everything seemed to radiate heat. I mingled with four drivers while Mark watched with amusement. Haidar, our driver, appealed to Mark right away and he nicknamed him Curly. "*Yalla*, (Let's go)" Mark yelled, guiding Haidar to our 4x4. In Iraq highly ranked late model cars like our SUV earned honorable nicknames. Curly got out of his old 82 model Toyota and jumped into the front seat of our jeep as he expressed his honor to be driving the "Lion of Babel", our Mitsubishi. His eyes sparked when I informed him we were headed to Saddam's *Jumhuri* (Republican) Palace.

Outside the gates we by passed by a set of well-arranged barbed wires then slowly stopped for ID inspections. "LA Times!" Mark yelled. (Like "Open Sesame" it worked every time) The second barricade consisted of three soldiers who inspected the car for bombs, specifically the engine. Patted down by the African American guard, I wondered how many times I would have to go through this security clearance in my stay in Iraq this time. Once cleared, Haidar drove us into the palace grounds, a road he did not dare approach a month ago. A mile later, we stopped at the east gate of the palace, where a U.S. Hummer parked on duty marked the security of the gate. Officials from the Office of Reconstruction and Humanitarian Assistance (ORHA) and U.S. Agency for International Development (USAID) resided in the palace among the other six hundred U.S. civilian contractors and military personnel. I waited in the shade with Haidar while Mark introduced himself to the public affairs officer in charge (PAO), then minutes later we followed him into the palace. I walked slowly behind Mark trying to record every detail with my eyes: The garden, Saddam's outdoor pool, and a huge statue of his head mounted on the palace's dome. There were no signs of battle, maybe not on this side of the palace. I smiled at Haidar who walked slower behind me, trying to maintain his cool.

I flipped the lens of my digital camera then quickly instructed Haidar to press the button to photograph me by the gold door framed with maroon wood. I held on to the gold handle and smiled at Haidar who had never seen a digital camera before but successfully caught my pose. Mark disappeared with the PAO. Haidar and I wandered quietly around the hallways of the palace walking on white marble, which kept the place cool. The ceilings of the walkways shined, decorated with golden chandeliers and lined with tiny finely engraved verses from the Koran. I watched the awe on Haidar's dumbstruck face as we entered the guest's bathroom, consisting of five stalls. As expected; gold plated faucets, door handles, and vanity mirrors. The detailed perfection of the palace's hideously decadent luxury rendered us speechless.

Still waiting for Mark, a Major Anderson from the Marines approached us with a friendly proposal: A tour of the ballroom. Again, we walked astonished into Saddam's ballroom, another display of architectural beauty. I stopped, tilted my head inspecting the dangling lights in addition to a tremendous amount of interspersed star like spotlights in the far ceiling. Louvered wood divided the glassy lights with a symmetrical pattern. Along the walls of the huge room, U.S. personnel had set up their single beds along with separate wooden cabinets for each person. On top of the beds, well-engraved huge verses from the Koran conquered the majority of the conditioning walls. The posh palace had no running water or air-condition; government officials residing there tried to cope with electric fans and military MREs (Meals Ready to Eat). In the center of the ballroom, employees of the U.S. government sat busy around a simple network of computer screens also surrounded by electric fans. Still amazed at the geometry of the décor, I paused with a long stare at the long marble balcony, visible to only those facing the entrance of the ballroom. Behind a series of glassed-in booths, an American employee sat trying to figure out the network of electrical switches.

"Man, I' m going to cry. That dog… this is my people's money!" Haidar moaned, with the least of curse words possible. I had visited the Versailles Palace including many pillars of architecture in Europe, but something felt different about the authenticity of this palace. *Affluent, tacky, fake, undeserved richness…* were just some of the adjectives roaming in my mind. "Take a photo of me please. I want to show them at home how this bastard lived, while we struggled for bread!" Haidar said, with an insistent gesture drawn on his face.

After the photos, a journalist from the New York Times joined us for the tour as Major Anderson pointed to the statues hanging on the high walls of the room: "These eighteen sculptures represent the eighteen districts of Iraq." I tried to figure out which one stood for Baghdad. Najaf's statue was obviously identified with its perfectly carved figure of the Imam Ali mosque. Haidar then pointed out the Basra statue represented by a combined sculpture of the marshes, a palmtree, along with the usual dinghy. Before I could contemplate some more, a Major Vernon identified by the stitched name on the pocket of his uniform approached us and added, "George Bush doesn't live that lavishly. We'll show you more of the palace next time. A Mark Fineman is waiting for you outside."

11:00 am. "You won't believe these contractors. Ooofff! They've signed contracts for millions of dollars. How about *900* million dollars!!" Mark vented, as he puffed out his Marlboro smoke.

"Whom are you talking about exactly?" I asked curiously.

"Aw man… Kellogg Brown & Root. Anyway, I have to go write. This story'll take a day or two" Mark replied. "There's a clause in the reconstruction contracts that states: [only if the vicinity is permissible] No wonder it's taking forever to start fixing this place, if it's ever possible!"

Along the riverside back to the Hamra, we could hear some sporadic loud gunshots from a distance. Haidar pinpointed the location of the shots pointing towards Saddam City, a poor ghetto piled with Saddam loyalists. "Mohamed, why don't you go to that Shia'a mosque down the road and find out more information on all the shooting going on at night. Just mingle with them, be yourself. I'm thinking of writing a feature soon," Mark added, before heading to the hotel's lobby.

"Leave Curly here, I might go meet a friend of mine from the Wall Street Journal at the Sheraton. Explain this to him in Arabic before you go."

Abu Shuja'a Shia'a mosque dominated inner Karada with its domes and arches. I cherished the ten-minute walk to the mosque away from the suspicious looks I got sitting secured in the "Lion of Babel", our Pajero. I wore a heavy beard just like most of the young Shia'a men seated on the floor of the carpeted mosque. I felt safe as I placed my boots in the hallway before setting foot into the carpeted shrine. Inside, I scanned the faces of some of the guys looking at me. Regardless of my brown color, beard, or anything I could have done to fit in, I was a stranger to them. As soon as I crossed my legs and sat on the cushions lining the floor, a short heavy bearded man knelt towards me with a cup of tea. "Welcome to Iraq. I am Ali," he said.

"I am Mohamed. I'm an Egyptian journalist."

Ali disappeared for a while. I sipped on the tea quietly and observed the modest richness of the huge walls blessed with banners glorifying Islam along with many framed verses from the Koran. A framed photo of the late Ayatollah Mohamed Sadiq Al-Sadr occupied a corner of the shrine, discreetly framed by black curtains. Still sizing up the place, a young man approached me, handed me a flyer, and then continued with his task of distributing leaflets. I had spotted him in the entrance with a group of peers, all assigned to distribute this same flyer. The title of the document was "The Occupier's View on Democracy". Not too offending until I scanned it well. The bullet points outlining the flyer were blatantly anti- Zionist. I didn't finish the document, but was sure to check the signatory at the end, which was clearly marked by the name Sheik Fateh Kashef Al Ghuta.

Shortly after, Ali returned with a leading Shia'a Sheikh crowned from the mosque with a white *Imama* (turban) wrapped around his head. The mentor who later identified himself as Kazem also sat calm beside me reading the flyer distributed all over his mosque and to similar mosques in the Baghdad area.

"Did you read it?" Sheikh Kazem asked me, in a low well-toned kind voice.

"Yes. It could cause trouble. Who is Sheik Ghuta?" I asked.

"This is the enduring of freedom Bush advertised. Ghuta is of a fearless Shia'a family," Kazem added, running his fingers through his long grayish beard.

I had figured out the Shia'a mentality but their inner conflicts were still unclear to me. I knew that Mohamed Baqir Al-Hakim's followers struggled against the Sadr Brigade also called the "Army of the Mahdi," a radical Shia'a organization led by Muqtada Al-Sadr. Sadr's followers repeatedly denounced Al-Hakim for collaborating with the Americans.

"In Iraq you have to learn to read between the lines. Ayatollah *Sayed* (Sir) Mohamed Sadiq Al-Sadr was assassinated by the Ba'ath on a highway on route from Najaf to Baghdad in 1999. He left many pure Shia'a seeds behind him," the Sheikh clarified in his toned Iraqi accent

"What is the reason behind all that gun firing at night, even before the curfew?" I wondered.

"This is the guerrilla generation of thugs Saddam left behind. They are settling scores. Also, many guys test the guns they buy at night. Don't forget Saddam freed more than forty-thousand criminals," Ali added, as he offered me more tea.

Sheik Kazem's youngest son, Hussein, joined us as he stretched his hand towards me for peace. I listened to the three of them exchange comments concerning the sensitive contents of the flyer now circulating across the city. I gazed at the deep lines in Kazem's face, the cracks of wrinkles, probably due to the many physical and psychological scars that Saddam had inflicted on such Shia'a believers

"You are a Muslim Mohamed. You know where this war is going. We are just waiting to see what the Americans will do," Kazem added, as he stood carefully folding the edges of his black robe, then excused himself.

His son Hussein, a less aloof character, leaned closer then added, "There are meetings held at night. We can't trust anyone. I am with the Sadr Brigade.

If *Sayed* Hakim agrees to disarm his brigade to the request of the Americans then we are obliged to do the same. This is weakness. We want a religious rule in Iraq. We paid the price."

"So you are saying there is a chance for a civil war?" I asked.

"Listen. The Najaf devout Shia'a leaders will never let the Americans reach that ultimate goal. If Saddam failed in breeding a *fitna* (sedition) then Bush won't succeed. I heard a silly comment by a British journalist the other day, 'When the cat is away the mice will play.' Do you see the Shia'a as mice? Read the flyer my Arab friend! Publish it in your paper! The Egyptians are men of honor!" Hussein yelled, with a tone of anger, a violent one.

I gathered my energy and walked through the entrance. Crowds of men stood talking about the provoking content of the flyer. I slipped back into Baghdad's streets, walking like an anthropologist staring into every detail of the ancient city's buildings, trees, people, and vehicles. The streets seemed like they were bleeding without actual blood. The citizens eyed me for answers *-another stranger in their home*, albeit I was a harmless one. I felt helpless at the failure of civilization. Iraq's population emerged immobilized without electricity, water, or even the freedom of leaving; the basic necessities. I glanced at the Shia'a flyer while walking, and only when I flipped the paper did I realize the severity of the information it contained. I read the Arabic accusations simultaneously translating it to English in my mind, trying to imagine the public's reaction let alone the response of the Coalition Forces on the ground, who are struggling to build any sort of stability.

9:00 pm. On my bed I sat cross-legged staring at "The Occupier's Views on Democracy," trying to translate its well-arranged information. In true propaganda style, the document appeals to the emotions, then jumps right into the facts with a little flashback of insulting history, to whoever reads it. I got stuck on some of the more complicated Arabic terms so I paced around the living room, and then switched on the TV for some news. Fortunately the one channel broadcasted on our television was the BBC. A segment about the SARS epidemic filled with imagery of mass panic in China depressed me. Back to the lap-top, I continued translating the piece, then emailed it to my closest friends, family, and girlfriend for a taste of the reality boiling in Baghdad. The subject of my email read: *Read the attached document, but try not to weep. Are we just pawns on a chessboard?*

The Occupier's Views on Democracy

1. Zionist organizations associated with Israel purchase houses with high prices to build settlements in Iraq.

2. Opening internet channels and center is a way of spreading liberal awareness in Iraq although they know there are approximately a million two hundred pornographic websites including gay sites for both sexes in addition to sites that display paternal sex; father and daughter, mother and son, or between father and son, mother and daughter.

3. Ensure the increase of private night clubs; open to members only so they can spread liberal ideologies that encourage total freedom without any religious restrain in social values.

4. Feeding Iraqis with news about looting, prowling, and the kidnapping of women so that they seek protection from the occupying authorities. They also provoke a violent reaction in the Iraqi people by selling alcohol in the streets or printing pornographic photos in the daily paper or displaying pornographic movies in the cinema halls. Such issues contradict with the Iraqi social taste and religious association so the reaction will be violent and could be labeled "terrorism" and a breach of civil rights under the definition of "terrorism" in America.

5. Continuity of the occupation for a period of two years at least which could be extended to six years; where the occupying forces will be responsible for the following:

   a) **Social front:** Prepare the society to implement liberalism and the western values in the areas of media, education, and culture. Enforce these values and ideas even if it requires the use of sedition or nationalism as a weapon.

   b) **Economical front:** Total control over Iraq's natural resources especially oil; exporting it through politically profitable channels like that of the Zionist establishment in specific or through granting opportunities in Iraq to companies associated directly with the Zionist lobby.

c) **Political front:** Dividing Iraq into four or more states to split the Iraq political decision.

d) **Regional front:** Set Iraq as the center of America's police station to fight what they call "terrorism" against the Palestinian militants in Syria and some of the Islamic movements in Jordan and Hezboallah in Lebanon. They also aim to control or cut the aid that reaches the Palestinian groups in the West Bank and Gaza Strip through the east or the south or through Egypt and Morocco.

6. Other missions of the bloody occupation remain to create a wedge between the Islamic flow in Iraq and its base on the Iraqi streets by deepening the differences between the Islamic groups and parties which may affect their role on the Iraqi street and lead to their failure in providing civil needs. Eventually, the threads of civil administration will be in the hands of America which will stop the Islamic groups or parties with a hand of steel from playing any role in the reconstruction of Iraq.

7. Increasing the number of parties associated with America and with America's liberal plans. Decreasing the number of Islamic parties or even dissolving them by force; arresting its followers so that the arena remains under the parliamentary system of the liberal parties.

8. America and Saddam have a long time relationship but more evident is Saddam's personal relationship with his republican friend, Donald Rumsfeld, who holds the position of U.S. Secretary of Defense. The relationship started in 1983 when Saddam asked Rumsfeld for a security system to help monitor the marshes, the Shia'a movements in Iraq, and the Kurdish movements in the north of Iraq. He knew that this security system would involve satellite monitoring. In 1984 Rumsfeld visited Baghdad and asked Saddam for his secrets in chemical weapons manufacturing. Rumsfeld returned to Washington and got the acceptance. Rumsfeld returned back in the same year and was present in Iraq when Saddam used the chemical weapons for the first time against the Iranian army. He confirmed the potency of the weapon on the battlefield before heading back to America. In a special visit to Iraq in 1985-1986 Rumsfeld agreed to help Saddam spy on the Iranian army using American OX planes located in Saudi Arabia.

After the end of the war in 1989, Rumsfeld visited Baghdad and granted Saddam five million dollars as a gift for what Saddam did for America and for destroying the gist of Islam as they claimed back then.

9. In 1986-1987 Iraq received development in the manufacture of biological weapons in Britain through PhD Rihab Al Tikriti. In 1994, during the damning economical sanctions, Britain exported twenty thousand tons of Anthrax as the Minister of Trade in Britain at the time confessed to the Al Jazeera correspondent, Yousri Fouda. We wonder how much this deal cost and where did Saddam use this dangerous weapon.

10. In 1993 the manager of a leading oil company signed a contract with Iraq binding on the development and renovation of the industrial refineries in Iraq that had been destroyed during the second Gulf War. The manger received a commission of twenty three million dollars at the time. We are not surprised to learn that the name of this manager is Dick Cheney, the U.S. Secretary of Defense after the second Gulf War against Saddam, and the Vice President to Bush the son in 2003.

11. One of the most important investment projects in the world and America is an investment fund called Carlyle, which outlays huge amounts of cash for the manufacture of arms and specifically Bradley tanks used in the attacks on Iraq. The Carlyle fund is not restricted to Bradleys only, but also invests money in the manufacture of Cruz missiles also. The Bush family and the Bin Ladens are two of the most important investors in this fund. The Ladens started their relationships with the Bush family in 1976 through the arms manufacturing business, through the Laden's eldest brother, Salem Bin Laden with the aid of a Saudi-American lawyer called Bin Mafouz. Just for the record, the President of this investment fund is James Baker.

12. The Ruling of Iraq will follow this scenario:

a) Forming a local municipality to serve as a mediator between the occupying forces and the population. The formation of a local municipalities leads to controlling the population and calming them down with terms of the occupying forces similar to what the Zionist accomplished in the West Bank and the Gaza Strip.

b) During the occupation period all the national and Islamic movements will be crushed under the excuse that they interfere with the civil rights handed to the local authority; a form of " terrorism" as another justification.

c) Forming a temporary interim government commissioned to organize a number of handpicked persons included in a committee of new parliament candidates.

d) Testing a parliament of a liberal and tribal minority, without including a majority of Islamists, religious, or advocates

e) Dissolving all the political parties, shutting down and confiscating all new papers and radio broadcasts to prepare for the setting of a new parliament. Some of the parties will submit new applications to the government to form new parties under new names and committees different to the ones used before, in which nationalism and patriotism will be considered and therefore religious parties will be destroyed completely.

f) The country's constitution will be similar to that of the Zionist establishment, comprised of a liberal mix of scientific and religious nature. Small Islamic movements could emerge similar to the religious Zionist movements based on expressing the opinions of the different religious sects who follow the same foundation. These movements must contribute to the permanent government and can never form their own government, but may fall under the umbrella of big parties and can not exceed a mere number of four political parties only.

g) The role of the permanent government is to create good ties and peace treaties with the neighboring countries and we mean the Zionist establishment by that.

Sheikh

Fateh Kashef Al Ghuta

Tuesday April 22, 2003

Haidar was now our official driver for the duration of our reporting in Baghdad. He had survived Mark's mood swings and demanding tests of driving under pressure. His nickname Curly suited him especially after he approached me today with a loyal morning greeting "I want you to trust me… I see nothing…hear nothing…and know nothing." I had established a solid relationship with the parking lot guard outside the Hamra Hotel too. Known as Mohamed the Egyptian, working with the American media, the guard, Haidar, and his driver friends practiced their Egyptian accent with me. They had acquired it from watching Egyptian movies broadcasted on Iraqi television for decades. Over three million Egyptian workers had migrated to Iraq in the 80's due to the strength of the Iraqi dinar back then; one dinar was equivalent to two and a half dollars. The bond remained mutual as I practiced my new Iraqi terminology with Mustafa, the skinny guard outside the hotel, armed with his Klashnikov, day and night.

On the Qadsiyah highway going towards the convention center to catch a press briefing revolving around the general security of Iraq, Mark continued to share his research on the Halliburton story. I had overheard him talking at dawn with his editor in Los Angeles, trying to figure out his angle on the story. "You won't believe this Mohamed. Kellogg Brown & Root is signing a 7-billion dollar contract to get the Iraqi oil up and going!" Mark shouted, sitting in the passenger seat.

"This story is driving you mad, huh? Didn't this Kellogg Brown company build the Guantanamo jails in Cuba, bases in Afghanistan, and Djibouti?" I asked.

"Yeah, how do you know that?" Mark asked.

"I read it in your notes on the table upstairs."

"Don't read my stuff. This is private," Mark answered, with a gawk in his eye, shaking his head in distress.

"I couldn't help it. Your papers are all over the place. It's not like I' m a stranger!"

"What you don't know is that KBR signed an open end contract to build infrastructure for the army for ten years, only two months after the 9/11 attacks."

"Ask Haidar… Are we almost there? I'm only going to this briefing to see how they are going to clean up this mess. I need to come back and write." Mark added, as he lit another Marlboro.

At the convention center the security was tight, yet it only took us a couple of minutes for the usual security pat down and media credential check. A public affairs officer with USAID urged journalists to add their email addresses to a mailing list, a new approach for announcing press briefings and military press releases. I squeezed my name and address in too when Mark asked me to sign his name. He went on greeting his veteran journalist friends inside the auditorium. Another lavish Ba'athist setting, the convention center resembled more Saddam tyranny with its expensive carpeting, marble stairs, and state of the art sound equipment. Cameramen for stations like CNN, BBC, and Aljazeera had set-up their camera stands in the back end of the auditorium waiting for General Jared Bates to appear. The cameraman from Aljazeera was easily identifiable with his dark Arab complexion and unshaved beard. Amused at the many Iraqi nationals working for Aljazeera, it was now clearer why they got such an edge during the first stages of the war. Who would have thought that CNN and other American media tycoons would have to buy broadcasting rights from such relatively new (not to mention rival) stations like Aljazeera?

Complete silence marked the arrival of General Jared Bates, and then the live broadcasting of his militant words began. I listened carefully to every word. Like every print media journalist in the hall, Mark noted down his exact words with the chicken scratch handwriting journalists are famous for. I watched his face listening to his positive assertions identifying law enforcement as the priority of the coalition. Bates continued to measure his words linking the importance of restoring electricity to the overall security of Iraq. As he announced his statistics on looting and crime, my mind wandered away. I lost his speech, gazing at the wooden sculptured verses from the Koran, hung high behind the General on the walls of the auditorium. The wooden blocks spelled: "Consult God upon hearing the advice of others."

I wondered for a second who Saddam had employed for such tasks. What manipulative imagination they must have. Back in focus, I clicked on to General Bate's words on the police force as he said, " They' re coming on Sunday and will wear part of old uniforms, but with white shirts and insignia of their hats."

For a good ten minutes more, Bates talked about the coalitions' round the clock efforts on restoring peace, then a quick question period followed. I took notes for Mark, who left the auditorium following a civilian contractor he spotted leaving the room.

A Sunday Times reporter introduced himself then asked: "What is the process of moving toward interim authority?"

"It has to be representative in terms of region, ethnic background, tribal groups, and towards the totality of the country," General Bates replied.

In broken English, a French correspondent from Le Monde proceeded with another critical question: "How long will it take to restore electricity to its normal power?"

"Only about 40 percent of the power is back (it's fluctuating). Hope to get it eventually back to pre-conflict levels." (Typical, he didn't even answer the question).

Last but still important, ABC's question: "Anything set about the currency?"

"A team of 'treasury rangers' is here working on that. We'll be paying people in dollars initially," Bates replied, as he ended his brief.

Back at the LA Times bureau, we enjoyed home made *timman bagela* a typical Iraqi dish made of rice, broad beans, and dill as Mark went rambling on about his disappointment in the U.S. civil administration in Baghdad. I also got acquainted with Mohamed Arrawi, the Iraqi technical supervisor behind the network of internet satellite connection extended through the two-floor villa. He also had perfected the Egyptian accent including the slang. The Iraqi crew supporting the Times reporters showed much bravery because the increasing propaganda about Saddam's loyalists was beginning to target and kill any Iraqis collaborating with the foreigners. I was not too sure where I stood in this equation. As the tongue of the reporter with the looks of an Iraqi, I left it all to destiny, just like I did a month ago when I stormed into Basra during the climax of the war.

2:00 pm. I dropped Mark at the hotel so he could continue writing his KBR story.

Outside in the parking lot, Mustafa the guard hustled towards me, grabbed my arm, then whispered in my ears, "I have a piece for you, a clean gun." I had asked him to keep an eye out for a small firearm when I first arrived, but I was not too serious. Haidar followed us with his eyes, but immediately stared away when I looked at him. He knew something was up when I strolled with Mustafa farther into the lot for a quick peek at the gun. Mustafa finally discreetly pulled the piece out of his pocket, a shiny black 9mm. I looked into the chamber and checked the trigger on the Beretta. Mustafa held the magazine of bullets in his hand as I weighed the gun on my palm.

"How much?" I asked, with the gun still in my hand.

"Three green bills," Mustafa answered, in a leveled tone.

"$300! Too much, I am not buying the Klashnikov on your shoulder man," I replied, handing him the piece back.

"This is a barely used *Tarek*. Two hundred fifty is the least I can go," he added firmly.

Iraqis had *honored* the 9mm Beretta with the name Tarek, as in Tarek Ibn Ziad, the leader who led the Islamic troops into Spain in the early 8th century.

On the short walk back to entrance of the hotel, I convinced Mustafa to introduce me to his arms dealer after I slipped him a fifty-dollar bill. Mustafa warned that I could not bring Americans with me, but ensured my safety since he knew these bandits very well. "Mohamed, come back in an hour. We'll go together but in a cab, we don't want to go to Al Rashid area in your flashy car."

An hour later, I waited for Mustafa across the street of the Hamra in a taxi, a Passat model 84, a *Brazili* as Iraqis call it. Mustafa showed up without his machine gun and sat beside me in the back seat of the old beaten up cab. I had left my watch, my expensive sunglasses, and my sat-phone in the room, and only brought along little money just like I would have done if I were entering Compton New York or Batnya in Egypt as a foreigner. My intentions were far from buying a gun; I just had to see the underworld of weapons in Iraq, pure curiosity. The coalition's occupation gun policy in Iraq banned small firearms but allowed each family to own an AK-47.

The irony also lies in the U.S. "assault weapon" debate where senators are arguing that American citizens are not fit to own similar versions of the same weapon. It sounded extremely crazy, but families needed to defend themselves from the thousands of Ba'athi rejects and criminals roaming the streets. Women in Iraq were voluntarily subjected to being imprisoned in their homes, a sort of house arrest as fathers feared for their daughters out in the streets.

Passing through *Bab Al Sharg* (gate of the east) towards Al Rashid district, my thoughts drained away into the haunted streets of outer Karada. Rows of shops remained closed, surrounded with scattered debris of rubbish. Some signs were damaged while new graffiti covered the walls: "No America No Saddam" another spray painted slogan read, "Yes to democracy, Yes to Ahmed Chalabi." Dr. Ahmed Chalabi with his FIF army resided in the hunting club in the Al Mansour upper-class neighborhood. Approaching Al Rashid, I stared at the ruins of the National Olympic Building. My imagination worked on the semi-toppled building, wondering about the various stages of its collapse. After all the blasts and tragedy, the fire had died, leaving many buildings burned, looted; like a cosmic stink.

When you enter Al Rashid Street, you feel like you have gone back in time, to the days of Sinbad, Ali Baba, and the Arabian Nights. I only spotted U.S. soldiers mounted on Bradleys outside the Al Rashid bank, other than that, the *souk* (market) bustled with trade and action. The sidewalks were occupied by merchants selling everything from women's stockings to cigarette lighters and fake sunglasses, remained dusty with years of negligence. Mustafa instructed the cab driver to stop across the street from a shoe store called *Baytukum* (your house.) I followed the thin man into a side street occupied by a number of *kebab* restaurants then he asked me to sit outside a café and ordered tea for me before he disappeared. The alley, like the side-street was seedy and well shaded by a tall building. The floorboards of the café were warped from years of spilled beverages, the simple wooden chairs dented from careless use and maybe even through occasional brawls. Many of the Iraqis passing by looked at me innocently, except for one man who sat to the far right of the café, drinking tea alone, eyeing me subtly. A few minutes later, Mustafa returned with his usual confident smile, sat down, and said, "Ok. Follow me into this house on the corner of the street. It's the first flat on the ground floor. I told them you are an Egyptian businessman, and you needed the gun for protection."

Following Mustafa into the building, I realized the man from the café was following me too. As soon as I walked into the apartment an older man with white hair patted me on the shoulder then shut the door behind me quickly. The room was dark, with only filtered sunlight from a small window high up in the corner. The man was still leaning as he sat on the chair looking at me. "I only agreed to deal with you, because Mustafa says you are a good friend of his. You are Mohamed, right?"

"Yes. I am not too good with weapons. I did not think it would be that dangerous in Baghdad," I replied, with a poker face

"I have light weapons only; hand grenades, 9mm Berettas, Belgium 16mm, Klashnikovs, RPGs and mines!"

I smiled and sighed at his words then asked him to show me the arsenal of the so- called light weapons. I followed him and Mustafa into the smaller room in the flat as he expressed his happiness with 'The New Iraq.' Under the light emitting from the one light bulb hanging from a wire in the middle of the room, his samples of weapons shined.

"After the fall of the regime many of the normal citizens and thugs raided all the police stations and cleaned out its weapons. Even the official Ba'athi camps had been stripped of it ammunitions and rooms of weapons," the man explained, handing me a loaded 9mm.

I thumbed the weapon's safety up, then for a few seconds aimed at the wall.

"How much?" I asked, as I placed the gun back.

"For a Tarek, I ask $135. If you want a 16-Belgian piece like the one over there, then it will be more, $165."

"I have just been extremely worried after hearing all these gun shots at night. Even before curfew. When will it end?" I asked him.

"It's simple. These are all expected retaliatory massacres. Murder after murder, I get richer. The Americans just opened a new can of worms," the man responded, with a new flare of insights, he wanted to talk.

"Every family has a variety of weapons. Mines are abundant too in every district in Iraq. Two weeks ago my boys were selling weapons on the sidewalks so they can eat and feed their families. The U.S. crackdown won't work even if they offer money for the weapons."

"How much do you sell the heavy stuff? Klashnikovs or RPGs?" I wondered.

"The *Klashin* goes for $75. An RPG like that one in the corner with the grenade goes for $45. You want one?"

"So you are saying the bigger the weapon, the cheaper it is?"

The man walked to the only wooden cabinet in the room and pulled out a card board carton of *rumanas* (hand grenades) then picked one and handed it to me for a quick inspection.

"One of these is for a dollar. I sell this box of ten grenades for six dollars," the man sighed, as he tucked his valuable bombs away.

"What about that vehicle mine? I have seen them in Basra," I asked, pointing at the beige mine, which easily blended in with the beige shade of the desert's sand.

"I only have a few heavy load land mines. It goes for $100 a piece."

Back to the other room, I sat shocked at the prices and the arsenal I just saw. I handed the man $150 for a 9mm Beretta and two boxes of bullets. I never expected such a scary reality. In Iraq you could arm a small army for a mere five hundred dollars.

The man wrapped the piece in a newspaper and handed me the bullets, then added, "If the Americans want to disarm the populace then they have to take responsibility for them."

"You are an educated business man. What is the U.S. stance on the cluster bombs?"

"They wanted to reach Saddam in his bunkers," I replied, with no mood or answers to start such a debate.

"I will tell you. U.S. forces are using artillery projectiles containing large numbers of cluster munitions. The unexploded cluster munitions from the ground launches are dispersed all over Iraq as we speak now. The Brits have more humanity; they at least released a known limited number of cluster bombs they have launched. The U.S. can't even recall how many they used. The children of Iraq have been paying for this brutality since 1991 with their lives and limbs," the man vented, as he revealed his previous post in the Iraqi army as a detonation expert.

I hid the gun with Mustafa in the cab ride back to the hotel. From a distance, I could see masses of men crowding outside the Baghdad mosque. As we got closer, I realized it was the beginning of a Shia'a strike against the arrest of Sheikh Fateh Kashef Al Ghuta, the author of the document I had just translated last night. The young men held several English white banners painted with red slogans stating: *Where is freedom Mr. Bush?* Another one written in Arabic read: *Free Sheikh Ghuta today. Where is U.S. democracy?* Avoiding the hundreds of protestors, the cab driver reversed then swerved into a back street towards Al Hamra.

Wednesday April 23, 2003

9:00 am. Mark finally shared the contents of his story with me, well-written but held by the editor for simple corrections. His front page masterpiece exposed every aspect of KBR's reconstruction administrational plans and secret bids. On the subject but not mentioned in the story was an email I found lying on the room's table under the phone. Waiting for Mark to end his morning shower, I read the email sent from Contessa L. Kellogg, Press Secretary and Floor Assistant to Republican Maxine Waters. I read it like a classified document to myself with admiration for Maxine Water's stance on the conflict of interest lingering all over KBR's contracts. Finally, a voice from within the U.S. House of Representatives not necessarily employed but at least vocalized. The lady's attitude left it all for the objective U.S. citizen and those subconsciously auditing the administration's global decisions:

SUBJECT: Congresswoman Waters Proposes to Eliminate Conflicts Of Interest in the Iraq War

Washington, D.C. ——Today, Rep. Maxine Waters is urging her colleagues in the House of Representative to support her amendment to eliminate potential conflicts of interest from affecting U.S. policies in Iraq. The amendment would ensure that Administration officials could not use the war with Iraq to obtain financial benefits for companies with which they have been affiliated. The amendment is expected to be offered to H.R. 1280, the Defense Production Act Authorization of 2003, during a Financial Services Committee markup.

"There has been a considerable amount of suspicion about the motives of this Administration in pursuing a war with Iraq," said Congresswoman Waters. "My amendment protects the individuals who are advising the President on matters of war and peace from conflicts of interests."

Prior to the 2000 elections, Vice President Dick Cheney spent five years as the chief executive of the Houston-based energy services Halliburton. On March 6, the Pentagon announced that it intended to use a plan by Kellogg Brown & Root, a Halliburton subsidiary, to control Iraq's oil well fires that might accompany military action. Prior to the onset hostilities, Halliburton was invited to bid on up to $900 million in contracts to rebuild roads, bridges, and other facilities in Iraq.

Halliburton is also expected to be well-positioned to obtain contracts to repair and redevelop Iraq's oil industry.

"Halliburton contracts in Iraq would create the appearance that the Vice President maybe using this position to increase his former company's profits in a time of war," said the Congresswoman.

"Many people have expressed concerns that our country is initiating military action in order to secure control of Iraqi oil fields," said Congresswoman Water. "My amendment would eliminate the appearance of conflicts of interest at a time when the Administration's decisions are affecting millions of lives around the world."

2:00 pm Haidar sped through Al Rusafa neighborhood heading towards the Ministry of Health so we could witness a conference on the proposed plans for energizing the health system with its new requirements of doctors, equipment and eventually a minister. The USAID budget for this system remained unannounced officially as it was still under development. As the journalists and NGO employees filed into the considerably small hall, officers handed out an outline of the proceeding speech. Mark and I grabbed seats closer to the podium as the conference started shortly with the arrival of the speakers. Their highly incompetent translator stood by the podium translating their words. I noted the appalling statistics about the health system under the Ba'athi regime with sadness. Hospitals all over Iraq had suffered majorly with the lack of bare medical essentials like defibrillators. The fact that 50 to 70 percent of the equipment and generators were not working shocked me too as Mark and I exchanged gestures of dismay:

"Any company that wanted to sell drugs to the Ministry of Health had to pay 10% service which went to the Ba'athist treasury into bank accounts in Jordan," Dr. Ali revealed, with confidence, as his translator relayed the sad truth.

The tragic facts continued to rain on us. Vital regulators in the intensive care of most hospitals across Iraq dated back to 1980. Physicians were hungry for more knowledge, a natural right for doctors holding such a humanitarian profession. The newest medical journals available to them revolved around the dates of 1970-1997. The thirty-six years of Ba'athi oppression left no space for a normal healthy life. One Iraqi medical student sitting beside me leaned over when he saw the distress on my face and said, "Doctors received a $20 monthly salary; pharmacists got a $1 monthly salary, everything else is siphoned to the lunatic's palaces."

During the briefing, a Joanne B. Giordano, Deputy Assistant Administrator of Public Affairs for USAID walked around the hall distributing two sets of forms to the former Iraqi doctors and employees interested in joining the Ministry of Health's administration under the supervision of the coalition. As journalists, we did not get the forms, but Mark asked me to pick up a set since he was busy taking notes. The briefing suddenly took a totally different course. Any Iraqi interested in rejoining the ministry's body had to sign one of two forms, a procedure required across most sectors of the new Iraqi governmental structure. When I got the forms and handed them to Mark we realized they were all about the "de-Ba'athification" of the system. Yes, the Office of Reconstruction and Humanitarian Assistance backed up by USAID and the provisional authority of the coalition wanted a fresh new start for those involved in the running of such a vital program like the health system. A brief five-minute intermission was granted to the attendees so that they could read and sign the forms.

We stood aside watching the loud confusion of the highly merited doctors and nurses trying to grasp the contents of the forms, their implications, and the consequences of signing them. Mark read the forms, handed them to me shaking his head, commenting, "McCarthyism, de-Nazification." I had been aware of the debates about "de-Ba'athification" only during my short experience at Ahmed Chalabi's camp in the dusty town of Shatra in Nasiriyah. Iraqis had requested the inscription of "de-Ba'athification" in the 13-point statement signed in the political organization meeting in Ur on April 15, the one meeting I missed when I left back to Kuwait. The two forms circulating the hall causing serious hesitation read:

AGREEMENT TO DISAVOW PARTY AFFILIATION

I,________________ (name), hereby disavow and renounce my membership in the Arab Socialist Renaissance Party of Iraq (Ba'ath Party). I understand that the Ba'ath Party is disestablished and abolished. I express reject and denounce the Ba'ath Party and Saddam Hussein and his regime, as well as my previous association with it.

I acknowledge that any continued association with, or involvement in, the Ba'ath Party or its activities constitutes a violation of an order by the Coalition Provisional Authority. I pledge to cooperate fully with the Coalition Provisional Authority in serving the people of Iraq and building a new Iraqi government. I will obey the laws of Iraq and all proclamations, orders, and instructions of the Coalition Provisional Authority. As God is my witness:

Form 2:

DENUNCIATION

I,____________________ (name), am not, nor have I ever been, a member of the Arab Socialist Renaissance Party of Iraq (Ba'ath Party). I understand that the Ba'ath Party is disestablished and abolished. I express reject and denounce the Ba'ath Party and Saddam Hussein and his regime, as well as my previous association with it.

DATE:____________________, 2003

____________________	____________________
(name of signatory)	(signature)
____________________	____________________
(name of witness)	(signature)
____________________	____________________
(name of witness)	(signature)

I totally understood the need for the "de-Ba'athification" of Iraq. The suffering the Iraqis witnessed during the thirty-six years under the Ba'ath left them crippled. It should be removed by the roots therefore breaking the emotional wall of fear and paralysis that has imprisoned most Iraqis for decades, that depressing dark green color symbolizing the Ba'ath. The State Department supported this idea but showed some leniency; prompting mid and low-level party members the chance to rehabilitate as the previous first form conveys; rejection.

"Mohamed 'de- Nazification' after 1945 was accepted by the Eisenhower administration, but there was never any agreement on its actual implementation. Besides, the Ba'athists ruled for a longer period than the Nazis. But I'm with Chalabi on the 'up rooting' of the Ba'athis all in all," Mark commented, putting out his cigarette as we walked back into the auditorium.

My mind still pondering on the long-term implications of these forms, I exited the auditorium for a chat with some of the people who had signed the affidavits. A highly qualified doctor who refused to give his name welcomed my questions:

"I signed this form because I want to build the health system. I was honest, but I assure you most of the men who signed lied."

"Are you saying this 'de-Ba'athification' will not work?" I asked, putting my pen away.

"Sir, you have been in Iraq for months as you say. You know very well that many people just joined the Ba'ath to reach the top, to prevail in their careers. Many people who signed did not know the witnesses who attested their signatures, including me. Did you see the confusion inside minutes ago?"

"Yes, I did. I don't know if it will work. I have been positive about the situation," I added, shaking his hand.

Truth is, I had my doubts that this "de-Ba'athification" would work. The idea of rehabilitating ex-Ba'athists seemed shaky considering their malignant views of democracy. It was a joke to them. Years of Saddam's brainwashing propagated anti-Americanism, thus anti-capitalist beliefs, which went against the whole idealistic goals of Operation Iraqi Freedom. Chalabi's "up rooting" of the Ba'athis could also work considering the abundance of professionals in Iraq that never even recognized the party. I had personally met scores of Iraqi exiles abroad that dream of returning back home for a chance at rebuilding their country.

9:00 pm. Mark waited for me in the restaurant for a tasty dinner and beer. The usual gunshots conquered the night in Baghdad's haunted streets. Standing in the balcony, I chatted with my folks, then my woman using the satellite phone, making sure its antenna faced south for clear satellite reception. Still mesmerized at the echoing intervals of gunshots, I smoked a cigarette nervously. I don't know if it was extreme paranoia or just a culmination of the day's stress, but one chain of loud machine gunshots shook me like never before I ducked tripping on my own boots, finding myself flat on my back in the balcony. I lay down laughing at myself for a bit, glad that no one saw my silly cowardly reflex.

Saturday April 26, 2003

During my war coverage in Basra, the dinar had fallen to as low as 4,000 per dollar. A week ago when I set foot in Baghdad I had exchanged $20 at a new rate of 2,000 dinars per dollar, a wad of 40,000 dinars, too big for my pocket. Today, just as the U.S. administrators began handing out the $20 emergency payment to Baghdad's one million government workers, the rate has slumped to a mere 950 dinars per dollar.

10:00 am. Inside the Baghdad zoo with Mark, we waited among scores of journalists and zoo employees for the American civil administrator's arrival with the money. Mark and I had taken the long way in, through the zoo's center passing by the animal cages. What we found was pathetic: Most of the empty animal cages were riddled with mortar and gunfire holes. Iraqi anti-air assault guns were left abandoned pointing to the sky. Mortar holes dotted the asphalt ground along with littered of metal ordinance. Saddam must have chosen this position for its cover of trees and its close proximity to the many palaces. With the zoo manager, Mark pulled out his notepad noting the details of the battle between the Iraqi Republican Guard and the U.S. 3rd Infantry Division that left the place in such a mess. A zookeeper joined us shortly as they both showed off the few animals left alive due to the hostilities. The animals were left to starve without food or water. At the lion's cage, the keeper pointed to a 20-foot mortar hole that led to the escape of a number of lions. One lion was shot by American soldiers after he attacked a horse and charged at them, while others were forced back into their cages only when U.S. soldiers used Bradley tanks to surround them. I looked deep into the seemingly sad eyes of a lion behind bars when the zoo keeper explained how they found him sitting lonely by his dead lioness outside their destroyed cage. Strolling with the Reuters, ABC, and CNN journalists, the zookeeper revealed that a starving bear roaming the city had killed three Iraqi civilians before it was captured.

"The two giraffes were eaten and many of the exotic animals were stolen for pet trade. We also have a couple of Tigers alive and well," the zookeeper commented, as we returned back to the masses of people waiting for their $20 payment.

Waiting under the hot sun with the twenty-four employees expecting their emergency payments, Mark approached a Stephan Bognar who works for WildAid, a wildlife conservation organization based in San Francisco.

"When I walked in, the animals were starving, there were feces on the wall, everywhere; the place was filthy; it was really disgusting," said Bognar, "and looters had just stripped the place."

"Do you see a positive change in the moral of the returning zookeepers, with this new $20 payment maybe?" Mark asked.

"The biggest challenge was to provide immediate relief to these guys. In a place where teachers earn $3 a month, $10 makes a difference," said Bognar, "Within four days, 95 percent of the zookeepers had returned. We also started providing meals everyday because we weren't sure they were getting enough to eat at home."

WildAid had a long way to go with this job. They had paid $10 to the zookeepers as a first move to begin the clean up. A circle of journalists with their cameramen cramped around Mr. Adel the manager for a brief statement. Without consulting with me Mark had offered my translating services for the whole lot, a live briefing in front of television. Here I was in the spotlight with the manager of the Baghdad zoo trying to translate his Iraqi accent into comprehensive English words suitable for the public ear.

Mr. Adel began with a thank you to the coalition and WildAid for their efforts. He repeated the list of animals still alive in the zoo then left me struggling with the translation of the word baboon when he shared the news about one that was found wandering in the desert and rescued by the U.S. army. I maintained my composure as I translated his last bit of shocking news that the zoo once filled with over six-hundred animals was now struggling to sustain the lives of thirty animals that were left. Mr. Adel then urged journalists and people to help the zoo with their donations as he announced that until now the zoo had received a mere donation of $400. The workers confessed discreetly their life-long dislike of the zoo's manger who had inherited the Ba'athi style of tyranny until only days before.

The spotlight shifted to a tall American soldier with the U.S. administrators assigned to distribute the money as the ABC and CNN crew followed him through to a small office near the entrance of the zoo's gate. The bulky man in full uniform and helmet seemed awkward carrying a small tin box, the size of a piggy bank containing the whole sum of the greenback emergency payment. The twenty four employees lined up one after the other to receive their money in small bills; a ten, five, and five one-dollar bills.

Mark was too busy mingling with a Timothy Carney, retired U.S. ambassador to Haiti and Sudan, working as a Senior Ministerial Advisor with the Office of Reconstruction and Humanitarian Assistance. He talked about the problems of forecasting the economic changes in Iraq: "Over 400 million dollars stolen from Baghdad's banks after April 9 are pouring into circulation now."

People are living off their savings. The Ministry of Finance had been burned and looted while the Central bank remains closed, partially damaged. Today, the $20 handed to these poor Iraqi civil servants is worth half its value than on the streets.

12:30 pm. Our next coverage of the $20 emergency payment took place at the *American* Girls School, reputed as one of the best secondary schools in Baghdad. Outside the brick walls of the three-story building parents waited for their daughters patiently until they finished their full day of schooling. The city's unpredictable situation left no chance for peace or security. Inside the principle's office I sat on the only sofa with Mark and Wali, our Times photographer. The lady principle sat behind her wooden desk complaining about the twenty dollars: "It barely covers transportation costs," she said, in English. Her assistant supported her words with a nod then added in weaker English "I swear there is no security, water, and the electricity returns for an hour or two a day. We were happy but this is not a life to live."

The tall American Major in charge of his unit walked into the room holding a plastic see through bag with the green money. Without his helmet, he stood modestly in the center of the room addressing the principle with careful passion. The eyes in the room transfixed on the big soldier who must have been over 6'4 feet standing groomed in his clean American uniform well sewn with slots for all kinds of pens, food, knives, or guns.

I was unusually quiet knowing very well the Arab prejudice involved in this situation. These mothers and daughters of Iraqi soldiers and commanders in the army were carrying the sole responsibility of bringing back the bread to their defeated men at home.

"What is $20 going to do? My son is an injured soldier and I have to pay for his cigarettes and help his wife too!" the principle complained, not expecting an instant solution.

"This is just the beginning Mam. Education in Iraq is right next to the priorities of health care and security problems," answered the Major, in a calm manner as he handed her the money for a quick count before the distribution he had to witness.

Her assistant got a little rowdy with a rather philosophical comment: "I want you to know that I forced my son to stay home! Our soldiers did not fight! You did not win the war! Iraqis are proud people!" she yelled, in a loud condescending voice.

"Mam, could you please start the payment in an orderly fashion according to your list of teachers?"

I observed the Major's coolness, his pure belief in goodness: That naively optimistic military belief that one can set out to make the world a better (more American) place.

The first English teacher that walked into the room seemed aggressive, with her black scarf demurely wrapped around her head and knotted under her chin. "Get the photographer out of here! You want to advertise our humiliation to your people? *Your Bush*?" she yelled, pointing at Wali who had taken his position for a photo.

Outside the room, Mark and I smoked a cigarette as the other teachers observed our every move. The sight of Mark's shoulder length hair was peculiar, to say the least. They whispered trying to guess my land of origin, knowing I was not a westerner. A more concerned teacher approached us with her complaints, which amused Mark who was getting restless with the whole scene.

"I want say that gun shooting in *za* night could make bomb. Because some bullets fall on Benzene car tank or generators and make big bomb," the math teacher said to Mark, who listened with concern to her broken English.

"Yes. Big *mushkela* (problem)," Mark answered, using some of his Arabic vocabulary, in respect to her attitude.

With the ice broken, the middle-aged teacher's attitude changed as she smiled pointing at another colleague, "See that lady? Stay away from her. She is an original Tikriti (Saddam's hometown), very Ba'athi woman." Indeed, the woman she pointed out had extremely manly features sitting isolated away from the others eyeing us like a time-bomb ready to explode.

Mark lit up another cigarette and puffed more smoke in my face as we waited with the soldiers surrounded by the students who were now on their recess. The girls were filled with anticipation and excitement at the sight of the armed white men, 'the friendly liberators. I must say seeing girls back at school in their gray and white uniforms uplifted my spirits. The supervisor expressed her relief in Arabic as she explained to me the status of the school with its high-class students. I could hear the curious girls gossiping, eyeing down the soldiers. One hyper girl called her friend over in a lowered voice saying, "Look! All the soldiers have blue eyes!" When the supervisor started hauling the girls away that same girl ran back toward us with her friend asking to meet the principle, probably an excuse to watch more of the foreigners. The trouble maker smiled as she talked to her buddy in a hushed tone; "That man has hair longer than yours! But his friend looks Arab…"

Outside the school parents waited for their daughters patiently. With the incidence of rape that had increased during the anarchy that prevailed after the war, the fathers left no chances for lawlessness. In Iraq and the

Arab world the stigma of rape is particularly humiliating to the father of the rape victim. In more close minded families, more of the tribal nature, rape victims could face death at the hands of their family members, aiming to "cleanse the honor" of the family.

In the car, Haidar who had been sleeping in the driver's seat looked at me with a glare in his eye saying, "I want to tell you that I am proud to work with you. I have not seen humans until I have worked with Americans." I was sure Curly was not saying this due to the good salary he earned, but he actually lived every moment with us, exposed to our kindness and the decency of every LA Times reporter in the bureau who treated everyone equally. The school's keeper was also busy painting over the pro-Saddam slogans outside the school's gate, another sign of victory.

"You know, maybe someone should tell them that sixty three million dollars have been allocated to the education contract in Iraq," Mark complained, as he recalled the pressure the teachers laid on the American soldiers earlier.

"Who won this bid, KBR?" I asked jokingly.

"RTI based in North Carolina has secured a hundred and sixty seven million dollar local governance contract. A Creative Associates International among seven other organizations will fix the schools here..."

3:00 pm Mark Fineman was an Iraqi veteran; with many memories in the Al Rashid hotel located only minutes away from the *Jumhuri* presidential palace. Our mission there was far from reporting, just a spiritual break as Mark called it. I had my doubts until we actually approached the gates of the hotel, which was closed to the public. I only linked Al Rashid hotel to the famous tile mosaic of George Bush Sr. on the foyer floor of its entrance after the Gulf War. For Mark it was a totally different experience as I learned when I watched him plead the soldier on post at the hotel's gate to let us in for a quick tour. When the soldier refused with persistence, Mark gave him a piece of his mind appealing to his patriotism:

"You have no idea what this place means to me. Here is my business card, radio in to your battalion commander and tell him my name. Please, we won't stay long," Mark pleaded.

The soldier returned quickly with news that we were welcome, but for a short time since they were renovating the partially damaged hotel, a landmark of Baghdad. I took a photo of Mark posing in front of the beautifully carved statue of a young boy looking up to a woman, another fountain that was out of order. Mark snapped a photo of me standing by a row of five U.S. military humvees parked in the lot outside the entrance.

One of the first things the Americans did was destroy the Bush mosaic with hammers, leaving no signs of his face or the caption under it which used to read "Bush is a criminal," a state sponsored insult. Saddam had chosen to place this doormat mosaic at the Al Rashid since it was the base of operations for foreign journalists and delegates. The workers had also agreed to his decision after a Tomahawk missile slammed into the hotel in January 1993. The battalion commander walked us through the lobby as Mark shared his memories of the 80's, telling us about how the *Mukhabarat* (Iraqi intelligence) used to follow him around Baghdad: "They used to bug the rooms and they had cameras every where. Oh God! I hated them," Mark commented. He then stopped at the reception desk and mentioned the name of an Amira Mekho, a twenty one year old receptionist, his Iraqi friend that died in the hotel during an attack. Smoking his cigarette Mark led us through to the bar and pointed to the stools adding, "It still looks exactly the same. I used drink in this bar back in '84. I met Mohamed Ali, the boxer at this restaurant when he visited Iraq."

The hotel was uninhabitable, but the workers walked around assessing the damage for future renovations. The battalion commander showed us through to the hallway of shops, which were in good shape including the oriental restaurant in the lobby. Some of the soldiers were actually sleeping in the rooms, a sign that the hotel could be back in action soon. Outside by the empty pool, the officer showed us some gunshot holes in the walls since some Iraqi snipers had used the hotel for cover during the siege of Baghdad.

"Jesse Jackson invited me onto his jet during the Gulf War right there," Mark said, pointing to a leather sofa in the reception. As we walked out, I looked down on the floor at the remnants of the Bush mosaic and remembered part of the Conan O' Brian late night show where he opened with an anecdote saying, "Don't you ever insult the president's father again. Look what happened to Iraq!"

MONDAY APRIL 28, 2003

Only in Iraq does the word "Hello" actually mean goodbye. Pronounced with a twist: "Hallaw Hallaw" is used to greet your exit in a tone implying that you are welcome back. In cases of sincere care the noun *Aini* meaning "my eyes" follows it for extra adoration; "Hallaw Aini." For days, Mark and I have not stopped using these expressions wherever we went.

1:00 pm. 40 degrees Celsius does not help when you work out doors; trying to track down a story. The sidewalks are lined with ice dealers selling big blocks of ice at 1000 dinars for a quarter kilo; a very lucrative trade in a country where electric generators are treasure boxes. I barely made it out of bed, way later than usual, around noon. Haidar had brought an icebox so we were prepared with freezing water and sachets of orange juice I had purchased in Kuwait. Still unexcited about the heat, I sat in the backseat of our air-conditioned car silent behind the yellow lenses of my shades. We approached the security checkpoint outside the *Jumhuri* Palace for the usual pat down, a chance to briefly interact with the isolated soldiers. One solider asked about NBA sports news, without any answers from me. The scene remained cynically the same with lines of Iraqi civilians waiting outside for news on jobs, electricity, compensation; their vague future.

Inside the palace grounds, Haidar drove slowly towards the east gate, past new cement barricades. At the gate Mark learned that the USAID administrator he wanted to interview had gone out for the day on some field assignments. We drove farther into the palace ground exploring its various aspects. Very discreetly, away from the eyes of the military, I snapped photos of Saddam's mosque fitting in its rich blue dome, the monument of the 'unknown soldier', and his wife Sajda's smaller quarters which looked like the palaces of Aladdin, crowned with white marble domes and arched balconies facing a beautiful garden. Further down the clean roads inside the palace grounds, side buildings like the auditorium and staff bunkers were demolished to the ground with a few cement columns left standing. It was impossible to perceive the size of the palace's vicinity. During the controversial search for the weapons of mass destruction months before the war, I ran across an article in Time magazine that displayed a drawing of the Radwanyah Palace located in Baghdad. Apparently, its vast grounds compared to a distance similar to that running from Hyde Park to Bermondsey and from King's Cross to Elephant and Castle in England.

"Tell Haidar to park here. I want to go say hello to these guys. They are from the 2nd Infantry Division, their commander is my friend," Mark said, pointing at a huge building across the street from Saddam's mosque.

"Mohamed, these guys won the war. They fought their way to the palace."

I rolled down the car windows and lay down in the backseat for a quick nap.

"Haidar, wake me up when Mark comes back," I said, yawning away from this slow day, not aware of the madness that was to come.

3:00 pm. The Iraqi music Haidar was playing in the background relaxed me and I woke up feeling refreshed after a short nap. Still waiting for Mark, I walked around the vehicle stretching my limbs. I flipped my camera's lens for a discreet photo of a tower clock mounting high amidst the forests of green trees in the palace grounds. Suddenly, a speeding Hummer stopped right by our Pajero with a loud brake. A bald officer stepped out of the front seat then asked to see my credentials.

"You are not supposed to be taking photos here. Who are you with?"

"I am with the media as you see on my ID. I had no idea this was a no photo zone," I replied, in a leveled tone.

"Alright, refrain from doing that," he ordered, as he jumped back into his svelte olive green vehicle.

As soon as he rushed away, a convoy of three loud Bradley tanks roared by with their usual disturbing noise caused by the friction with the hot asphalt. Just as their cloud of dust simmered down, a small Vitara jeep rolled in and parked behind ours. Two chubby guys with Iraqi features walked towards the soldier guarding the 2nd Infantry Division's building. I could see them haggling with him helplessly without a word of English. Haidar and I observed the suspicious looking guys, both wondering how they entered the palace area without a military escort. After failing to by pass the guard, the two men headed back to their vehicle, following the orders of the angry soldier.

"Maybe you can help us. You speak English, right?" The bigger man hollered at me.

I waited till they were both standing right in front of my face before I started my quick interrogation. My first question was "How did you get in here?"

Both men reacted fast, flipping out well laminated plastic IDs that displayed their recently taken photos with a heading portraying emblems of the United States Government. I first made it clear to them that I was media and not some undercover officer or anything of that sort. I read the name of the large Iraqi man with the green short-sleeved suit. Sabah: *Associate of the United States government. The Cardholder agrees to abide by all laws and regulations at palace sites. Misuse of this card constitutes a violation. This card is the property of United States Government. If found please return to the CPA Public Affairs Office.*

Sgt. XXXX In.

"Mohamed, we need you. We have helped these American *snakes*, and now we want our money," Sabah complained, as his friend stood nodding with supporting facial gestures.

"We have cassettes, original documents, video tapes, but we need money right away. Everything we have is top-secret."

"Who gave you these cards? Who is that officer on the card?" I asked, trying to grasp the magnitude of the information blasted to my ears.

"Look, Sgt. XXXX told us to come see him anytime. Now, they owe us money. Look at the bullet holes in our jeep…" he replied, pointing at the triangle of holes on the right flank of his car.

Now very excited, I lit a cigarette then listened to Sabah spill more information as he hesitated to show me the well-folded paper in his pocket. "They put us on the front line, we could have died. We want our money. You have to help us talk with them," he complained, as he handed me a document he was instructed to hide away. I read it quickly as the paranoid man held on to its edges, as if it was going to fly. It went something like this:

Date: April 23, 2003

Subject: Thank you— Reward to Mr. Sabah

The above-mentioned person has assisted directly in the arrest of Muzahim Sa'b Hassan al-Tikriti, Number 12 on the Black List.

We acknowledge your efforts and may use your help in the near future. You're entitled to the following reward.

Reward: $10,000 U.S. Dollars

Sgt. XXXXX. In

His buddy Ali had the same paper as he asked Sabah to hide the document back in his pocket. I was impressed, excited, and ready to help these guys who went on describing the scenario of their bust. These tough informants had led the U.S. forces to the house of the previous fugitive, and entered his house first ahead of the soldiers. During the raid Sabah's knee got injured leaving him bruised. Ali's stitches above his right eyebrow were still fresh from the recent bust only five days ago. Their vehicle also took a rain of bullets amidst the seizure of Muzahuim al-Tikriti, head of Iraq's air defense. The month of April witnessed the arrest of fifteen of the fifty-five most wanted Iraqis.

"Where are the tapes?" I asked.

The men led me to their car right away, to a box of audiocassettes all labeled top-secret with insignias of the Iraqi government. I flipped through the titles which all revolved around the Iranian war, dating back to the 1980's.

"What about the video tapes?" I asked, from the backseat of their blue vehicle.

"Here is one. We have *boxes* at home."

The sample tape they had was also stamped [**TOP SECRET**] in red, with the title 'RADAR INSTALLATIONS 2001.'

"So what are you guys? *Mukhabarat* out for some extra dollars or what?" I asked, standing outside the vehicle in awe.

"Mohamed, we used to work with Saddam's secretary. You can make very good use of us. We don't trust the Americans anymore. We have been spending money from our own pockets," Ali replied, with calm confidence.

At this point, Mark showed up apologizing for his long delay inside. Now, the situation took a very different turn with Mark's temper and the men's pushy attitude. Stuck in the middle, I introduced the men to Mark who was already suspicious and like me his first big question was, "How did these *Mutt* and *Jeff* get in here?"

I explained to Mark the sensitivity of their situation as they presented him with their shady IDs. Like me he was baffled, especially after seeing the tapes, which were only a sample of what they claimed they had. Trying to formulate a plan, Mark and I agreed to follow them home for a credibility check, a peek at their elements, and most importantly those top secret tapes.

In the car following their blue jeep, Mark asked me to explain the whole story all over again with every detail.

"I can't believe this. We don't even know who they are. These guys could be very dangerous," Mark added, lighting a Marlboro.

"It's an amazing story. It fell right onto our laps. Did you see the document from the U.S. Government?"

"Mohamed, if these guys want money from us. They won't get it. LA Times doesn't work this way."

"All they want is money, but I did not promise them anything. Why won't the Times pay for the tapes or documents?"

"I have to teach you that. Ethics of journalism forbid paying money for a story or an interview, regardless. TV will pay them... Tell them to go the military! The CIA could use these guys. Maybe they have recruited to them already!" Mark shouted, with impatience at my persistence.

"They are pissed off at the military for not paying them. They don't trust them with the tapes or anything else for that matter. Let's at least take a look at what they have, listen to their story."

"This could be a treasure. I agree..." Mark added, as we parked our vehicle outside the gates of their house in the *Al Khadra* (the green) district.

Inside the homes of 'the frontline agents' as Mark labeled them, a young boy, Sabah's son, brought cold lemonade to us. Ali then dragged a big cardboard box filled with the stolen video tapes. I scanned through them translating some of the more sensitive titles to Mark. Of the more striking titles also labeled top-secret were Republican Guard Meeting 2001 and Satellite Clips 2002. The tapes were all VHS while Sabah and Ali only had a Beta video player, leaving us puzzled at the actual footage on the pile of unlabeled tapes.

"Could you just explain to them in front of me that we cannot pay them money for anything?" Mark insisted.

Translating to them his words, I added more lip, giving them hope that I was going to get them money for these tapes no matter what. When Mark went to use the bathroom the men urged me to help them, portraying distrust to the American man with the ponytail as they labeled him. I was stuck between the ethics of my job and my own curiosity for truth; maybe a breakthrough about any vital information on chemical weapons, executions, or info on the whereabouts of the Kuwaiti POWs or their remains. Before Mark returned I grabbed Sabah's arm firmly and added, "Just be patient. Mark is a good guy, but he can't pay you cash. We'll meet tomorrow after six outside the Hamra."

"Ok. So let's hear what you have to say," Mark said, in English looking at me to mediate his words to Mutt and Jeff.

Both men seemed more relaxed after my promise. Sabah dropped his pants to show us the purple bruise on his knee. Ali, supporting his round belly, started spilling out his stories, which left Mark and I shocked as I tried to translate every word. Reading between the lines, trying to separate the lies form the truth, Mark just listened without taking any notes.

"Saddam is still in Iraq. I can find him or any of the wanted guys," Ali spoke confidently, with a low voice.

"Where are the documents you promised?" I asked Ali in Arabic.

"We have a third partner. I will bring them to you to tomorrow. I also have fifteen computer disks with Ba'athi private bank accounts, all stolen from his personal secretary's office."

"Computer disks?" Mark repeated after me, listening with total concern.

"Do you know anything about the Kuwaiti POWs?" I asked.

"Saddam killed them all. I was imprisoned with some of them. They were so ill-treated, fed only a loaf of bread a day," Ali answered, with sad honesty in his eyes.

"Saddam killed his own people. Do you think he would hesitate to kill the Kuwaitis?" Sabah commented.

"Saddam destroyed me. I have been imprisoned sixteen times. Sabah and I have trading licenses; he closed our company down and took my land," Ali complained, as he handed me his trading license, of the first degree as it stated.

"What about chemical weapons?" Mark asked, in English waiting for my translation.

Ali began to chuckle, "He has nothing. But I know sites with millions of dollars and gold well dug and hidden underground."

Sabah then interrupted the casual interrogation with another surprising piece of news. "We have a document written in Saddam Hussein's hand writing on official presidential stationary stating: If our Republican Guards surround the invading American infidels in Baghdad, do not kill them and even assist them indirectly if possible."

Mark rolled his eyes at my literal translation of Sabah's alarming words.

"When can we see this document?" I asked, with skepticism.

"What are you telling them?" Mark interjected.

"Nothing, I just asked to see this document."

"I also have another confession," Ali added.

"I saw Osama Bin Laden here in 1999. I assisted a friend in painting the room he was staying in."

"How long did he stay?" Mark asked.

"He stayed for a one month only and I got a chance to greet him. He was very modest," Ali replied, in a low voice.

With this amount of staggering information, Mark invited the men to our 706-suite at the Hamra first thing in the morning, tomorrow at 9:00 am. "Bring the documents and keep the video tapes for later. We do not have a VCR there," Mark added, as he stood up heading to the door.

"We ask one thing of you. We want you to help us get our reward," Sabah said, standing at the door.

"Ok. Tell him I will try my best to talk to the guys from the 2nd Infantry Division about their situation, but no money involved."

I relayed Mark's words then confirmed our meeting at 9:00 am. Mark had perfected the use of the word "Hallaw" as he waived them goodbye outside the gate of their house.

"Mohamed, you are our brother. If you need anything in Iraq we are here. We just need you to help us communicate with these sleazy Americans," Sabah told me, in a hush-hush tone away from Mark's ears, who was still looking suspiciously at the chubby Iraqi man.

As I rolled up the car's rear window both men greeted me yelling loudly, "*Hallaw Aini, Hallaw* Mohamed!" as I rolled up the car's rear window.

Tuesday April 29, 2003

8:30 am. Mr. Mark Fineman and I started our day at low gear, our heads weighing heavy after the Johnny Walker we had drank last night in the room. I prepared myself for Sabah and Ali who were a handful to say the least, not very invigorating at such an early time of the day.

Right on time 9:00 am, the phone rang bringing the voice of the receptionist who confirmed that Sabah and Ali where here to visit our room. Usually, the front desk would not question our visitor's destination, but their gangster like attitude must have alarmed him. In their same outfits from the prior day, the two men walked in quietly holding two plastic bags. Upon offering them orange juice, the men were ready to talk as Ali handed me a black two-ringed binder full of paper.

I flipped through the documents one by one carefully reading their headings in Arabic then out loud in English, scanning the details of the more juicy ones. What a perfect way to start the day: Shocking Ba'athi scandals along with secret documents revealing the hidden agendas of the former sadistic regime. We struggled to memorize the details of the more sensitive documents, since we were not allowed to keep them. It sure beat the usual caffeine high of coffee that early in the morning.

One official Central Bank document consisting of five pages revealed the account sheet of a $22,000,000 dollar loan obtained by the Vietnamese Government. Stapled to an Arabic typed letter waiving the debt, the document was signed by the Minister of Trade, Saddam Hussein's representative. The date: 2003.

A more light-hearted document titled "Accepted Gifts," presented an official bribe of a $50,000 Rolex watch to Foreign Minister Tarek Aziz (a key figure from the regime who had surrendered on April 25, 2003) for his *efforts* on finalizing an oil deal with the Yugoslavian Government.

On a more personal level, a Soviet senior political figure sent Saddam Hussein a set of gold swords enclosed in real leather pouches as a thank you for facilitating the smuggling of an oil liner to Moscow, after the bid had fallen on the Turkish Government.

Dozens of documents filled the file, all labeled top-secret with signatories of senior Ba'athi officials. The papers all revolved around illegitimate business deals and lavish bribes for the illegal facilitation of mostly oil contracts, wheat, and financial scams.

"Where is that crazy document you mentioned yesterday? The one where Saddam urges his soldiers to avoid fighting the Americans around Baghdad?" I asked Ali.

"Here is it is..." Ali said as he pulled out a folded piece of paper from his shirt pocket.

Dated March 21, 2003, it was a photocopy of the hand written document, which indeed did contain a line ordering the Iraqi troops to avoid fighting the Americans if they surrounded them. Although the men claimed it was sent from Saddam Hussein to the head of the Republican Guard and the *Mukhabarat*, the document was not even stamped or presented on presidential stationary or even typed. I had my doubts about its authenticity and so did Mark who handed it back with one quick glance.

"Ok. Tell them I want to know more about them, their own personal story," Mark said, as he prepared his notebook for the information.

"He wants you to talk about your own personal struggle with Saddam," I explained to them in Arabic.

"Honestly, Saddam is a dirty dictator, and like I told you, he took my land away..." Ali commented, with a tone of despair

"Why?"

"It was a legitimate business deal at first. Saddam's advisors approached me with a proposal to use my land; to build training camps for Arafat's PLO troops. The location was suitable and the area was big enough for the training site including sleeping quarters and minor facilities too."

"Ask him what year that was," Mark wondered.

"1996... The deal was that they would use the camp for two years then leave for me all the buildings and furniture they had compiled during this time. After three years, not two, the PLO fighters finally left. Just like we agreed I went to claim my ownership of the property, yet found nothing but open sarcasm and humiliation."

"A week later, Uday Hussein imprisoned Ali and the land was confiscated. They also took away a shop he owned and revoked his trading license temporarily," Sabah added, with a tone of consolation for his partner Ali.

An hour later, Mark wrapped up his interview with the two thugs, who obviously refused to pose for my digital camera. Their next destination: Saddam's palace for another attempt on locating their Sgt. in hopes for claiming their reward. I discreetly arranged for a six o'clock appointment outside the Hamra without Mark's knowledge.

Anyone in Baghdad who saw the long gas lines outside major gas stations felt sorry for the population of Iraq. In a car culture similar to America, in a country with decent roads and multi-pump filling stations, gas shortages meant a crisis. Mark finally insisted on uncovering the truth behind the snake-like lines provoking any person out to fill their car's tank.

Inside the office of the Baghdad station, we both sat waiting for the manager who was breaking up a loud argument escalating among his employees and the angry customers. The heat was unbearable but still customers waited outside patiently for the gas tankers to arrive. When the man finally returned to his office, he walked in complaining about his job, brushing the obvious sweat off his forehead.

"We have the second largest oil reserve after Saudi Arabia, but we can't supply our people with gas. It's out of my hands, they don't understand that…" the manager complained, as he leaned over to shake my hand.

"So, what is the major problem?" I asked, after introducing myself cordially.

"*Habibi* (my dear) there are many problems. Distributors are not delivering the refinery's production on time, for example," he said, waiting for me to translate his words back to Mark

"What else?"

"Many of the tankers used to transport the fuel had been stolen or hit by American bombs during the attack. You'll see them charred across the city."

"Did you see signs of such a crisis right before the war?" Mark asked.

"I knew this would happen. U.N. sanctions restricting oil exports led to a low production level only limited to domestic needs. We could not reserve anything for the war."

"Tell him I read that the Daura refinery which produced 110,000 barrels of oil a day is at half its output…" Mark said, trying to get his facts straight.

"You saw the looting. The Kirkuk oil field in northern Iraq from which Daura receives most of its crude oil had been looted, including sensitive parts of the pumps," the manager clarified to me.

Suddenly a man walked in with tea for us, placed his tray on the gray metal desk then looked at me saying, "Why are you sitting like this? Don't you see that the bottom of your shoes is facing my boss's face?"

Without a second to think, I stood up and reacted with an equally insulting reply, "What, you think a man like you is going to teach me how to sit or deal with people? We are not in a mosque here!" I yelled, refusing to continue the interview.

"Mohamed, I can't deal with your attitude right now. Now translate for me this last statement so we can leave," Mark complained, not too sure why I was standing fuming in the middle of the room.

"He is just saying that he would like to see a tank outside the station to control the crowds. He also just said that there was an explosion at a gas station in Rahmanya due to the chaos, where 35 people got injured with life threatening burns. " I wasn't smiling anymore.

In any culture sitting with your feet facing someone else is not a compliment, but not a crime. In the Arab world it's a particular slam. Pointing the soles of one's feet at someone is a serious insult, maybe when it's your elderly grandfather or in a diplomatic community maybe, but I didn't think it would be a big deal at an informal setting like that of a gas station. I was wrong.

With the arrival of the tanker we oozed outside through the impatient crowds. A fist fight broke out between two men who had been waiting since dawn to fill their tanks. Some people had given up reverting to black market dealers who lined the sidewalks of Baghdad with their jerry cans and hoses selling the gas at outrageous prices, almost fifteen times the official price on the market. One taxi driver we chatted with confessed that he had to work less since he dedicated a whole day just to fill his cab's tank. Another angrier man pushed his old truck closer to the pump as he blamed America for this problem. Meanwhile, U.S. soldiers across the city had established new tactics to fight profiteering from the black market by confiscating jerry cans from kids selling the gas. Untrained for such civil duties, the soldiers handed the cans back to hospitals and schools.

3:00 pm. Listening to Mark relay the details of his gas story to Tyler Marshall, our new Baghdad bureau chief, all I could think about was Sabah and Ali. The contents of the tapes or the disks remained my goal for the night. Full from the homemade food, I watched the bluish glow of the television screen, flipping through the channels for updates in the political arena. No matter what happened in the world, America was still able to reduce it to virtually meaningless snippets of news updates.

6:00 pm. I spotted the top of the informant's blue jeep from the balcony of my hotel room. Mark had planned a dinner with Jane Arraf from CNN at the Palestine hotel, so I was free, as I expected. I forgot my sat-phone as I rushed down the seven floors of stairs.

On the street, I looked behind me before I jumped into the backseat of their jeep.

"Head to the Sheraton, Sabah," I said, as I inspected the suitcase of tapes.

"Why there?"

"I will take you guys to Abu-Dhabi T.V. They will pay…" I answered.

"We went back to the palace today. They yelled at us and their translator asked us to come back tomorrow. These Americans will not pay, but I won't leave them alone," Ali warned.

Chapter6—Baghdad Blues: Fragmented

Inside the busy lobby of the Ishtar Sheraton, I left the two odd looking informants alone in the coffee shop. I first approached a young Jordanian journalist wearing a beige vest with the blue falcon insignia of the famous Abu-Dhabi station. A quick synopsis about my treasure of tapes fired up the man who hustled us up to the 17th floor of the hotel to his boss. Abu-Dhabi TV had reserved private floors in the hotel including the roof which they turned into a stage arena for a live talk show, the rage in the Middle East now. Synchronized with the aftermath of the war, they hosted a mix of politically aware Iraqi, Kuwaiti, and Western guests. They broadcasted to a live audience on the open terrace, I guessed that music was a part of the show as I watched their crew assemble a drum set on the stage.

Up at the lavish suite, I walked in with Mutt and Jeff to a room full of video cameras, editing equipment, boxes of tapes, and of course an army of female presenters, cameramen, sound engineers, technical supervisors, and the most valuable; Mr. Mohamed Dourrachad, the Deputy Television Director of the station based in the United Arab Emirates. The man led us into a more private room as I sat beside him on a couch explaining the whole story, showing him the documents and tapes. After a quick scan through the titles of the tapes, the polite man started a long bargaining debate with Sabah that led to nothing. Finally, Mr. Mohamed agreed to pay them two thousand dollars for everything they had including the computer disks. "You have to understand I am buying air. I am taking a risk here..." he concluded.

"I want fifty green papers," Sabah said, as he started packing the tapes back into his brief case.

I sat silent trying to alleviate the tension.

"It's like I am buying fish, before I catch them. I can't pay you more than that," Mr. Mohamed added, as we exited the room.

Our next stop was at the Al Arabiya Arabic news station, behind my hotel at the Karma hotel. As soon as we walked in to meet their manager we realized that we were wasting our time. The station did no even have a VCR, let alone the professionalism to deal with such a situation. The manager tried to convince us to leave the tapes with him overnight, but reached a dead end with the egotistical tensed attitude reflected on Sabah and Ali

On the short drive back through the dark streets of Baghdad I could still hear the crackling of machine guns. I was able to convince the two men to lend me the computer disks for the night. I had understood their one-track mentality which only revolved around money.

"Your best bet is western channels, tomorrow when you pick up the disks I will have some names and people for you to meet," I told them, as I left their car with the valuable computer disks.

10:00 pm. Mark Fineman walks into the room with a bottle of whiskey then slams the door shut.

"Where have you been? I was worried sick about you!" he yelled, waiting for an answer

"I was visiting friends at the Sheraton."

"Mohamed, you were with them, weren't you?"

"Yes I was. I was just curious, I got the computer disks!" I said in a positive voice.

"Do you realize what you are doing? These guys are gangsters. These men can kill you! I'm not letting this one go. You disappear for hours, you leave your phone behind, and you are not telling me the whole truth!" he yelled, throwing his cap across the room. I know Iraq... I have been a journalist for years. I think I'll have to fire you," Mark threatened.

"Fire me? Why?"

"Because I need to know who you work for, are you CIA?" Mark demanded. His blue eyes were bulging now.

"What? Look I'm sorry man. I was just curious. Why do you think I am CIA?"

"Your have the only sat-phone number that starts with 844 and you're always looking into my papers."

"Mark. I said I was sorry. I do not work for any organization and I honestly forgot my phone. It won't happen again, and these guys were just too paranoid to deal with you!" I replied in a firm loud voice, as I sat down on the couch watching him pour another drink.

"What's on the disks?" he asked calmly.

"They are encrypted."

"Listen. I hate the CIA. I just hope you are not working for them. Just remember that you are in this position only because you work for the Times and me," Mark added, as he retreated to his room.

Thursday May 1, 2003

Baghdad felt like home with my favorite restaurants established and the safest routes discovered. By now, I had saved over two hundred photos of the city's architecture, war torn buildings, and the many faces of its dear people. In quieter more romantic moments I had even orchestrated a future plan of moving to Iraq with my girlfriend for a deep spiritual trip; an inspirational journey to suit both our creative minds.

1:00 pm. Away from any peace, Mark and I asked Haidar to stop at the site of a ten-floor government building burning heavily, enclosed by fuming columns of horizontal black smoke. We joined dozens of civilians watching the damaged building flare up the sky blocking the sun's light, forming a gray shadow over our heads. Just like everyone else we were only curious to find out how this massive fire started, waiting for answers. No sign of looters yet, but the masses suspected it was the work of a thief, maybe trying to divert attention. The only other journalist on site was a Japanese photographer who happened to be passing by too.

"Ask this shop owner what he saw before the fire!" Mark shouted, referring me to a barbershop right across the entrance of the building's two-floor garage.

Half way through my query, the man advised me to leave right away shutting the door of his shop without a second thought. Right at this instant, I shuddered then froze for a split second at the crackling sound of gunshots intensified by its own echoes. Like startled chickens, masses of people, Mark, and I ran in different directions as the rattling of gunfire continued. I could see Mark was way ahead of me running fast towards our car as my mind got caught up with the loud screams of a man shot in the knee, the speeding black BMW that stormed out of the building's parking lot, and the Japanese photographer who had fallen flat on his face from fear. Like a trance my eyes recorded everything in slow motion, still running away from the invisible gun rounds with my eyes fixed only on Mark. I've never been so scared in my life. All I aimed for was the car, with the bullets still raining on the street. I could hear the *whoosh* of the bullets fired accompanied by repressed sounds of their bangs into various metal or stone surfaces along the road. Haidar had opened the back door of the car, so as soon as I reached it, I jumped into the backseat of our moving vehicle. Catching my breath, I laughed out loud with intervals of jovial lunacy at the thought of my girlfriend, my muse, seeing all this. She had warned me about going back to Iraq. Mark was in no shape to talk after this long scary run. His heart condition endured the chain smoking, but dodging bullets at any age was no fun. He yelled at Haidar to drive faster then lit another Marlboro.

6:00 pm. Sabah and Ali showed up with good news that they had sold their lot of tapes and documents to a leading American TV station based at the Palestine hotel. When I returned the computer disks with news that they were encrypted, they showed me the four thousand dollars they collected from selling their valuable stolen tapes. Sabah informed me that he saw some brief footage of mass executions. Still, they waited for their reward with no result, but maintained their loyalty to the U.S. army.

7:00 pm. I gradually started giving into the crowd around the poolside of the Hamra hotel. Many journalists cherished the swimming pool, adapting to their daily laps before their work or at night for a cool down after the heat. I had been amazed at the diversity of professionals Iraq attracted during this war. A social getaway well secured behind the concrete walls of the hotel, the poolside bustled with journalists, military officials, freelance writers, photographers, and various representative of reputed NGOs.

I had met a Victoria Fontan, assistant to the famous Robert Fisk, and also a freelance writer. Under the dim lights at the outdoor pool, we sat enjoying cold Turkish beers; as I listened to her complain about how demanding Fisk remained during this war. She almost burst in tears at the workload he had laid on her. When Robert Fisk joined us at the corner table by the pool with his laptop and sat-phone, I was excited to finally put a face to the name I had heard for years among the scholars of the Middle East. I had not read much of the British writer, but my girlfriend spoke positively about the man who resided in Beirut-Lebanon for over twenty years. An expert on the Middle East, Fisk revealed the deepest political issues of the region including the "sick" of the Palestinian-Israeli conflict. When I complimented him with my woman's admiration for his work he said arrogantly, "Women at this age glorify me all the time, I don't know why!"

Back in February of this year, my girlfriend had read an article written by Fisk in the Independent, titled "How the news will be censored in this war". In his article, Fisk questioned the credibility of CNN and forecasts their deliberate censorship in the Iraq war. My dear girlfriend, who is a big fan of conspiracy theories, asked me about the truth. Concerned, I contacted a CNN producer in Kuwait for an official statement. The next day I received a fax with the following reply from Eason Jordan, the Chief News Executive of **CNN: March 5, 2003**

LETTER: FAIR REPORTING

Sir: Robert **Fisk's** column "How the news will be censored in this war" (February 25) is not the first time he has singled **CNN** out for misjudged and misleading criticism. As a global news leader, we are happy to take all the legitimate complaints that come our way. But once again he is way off mark and the record needs setting straight.

His main complaint is about a **CNN** script approval unit called "The Row"- named after where they sit-which for some reason he claims is new and finds deeply sinister. The fact is that like most other professional news organizations we have a process that reviews and approves reports before they are recorded for transmission. It is not new, **CNN** has had this policy for 23 years, it is designed to ensure that our reporting is all that is should be—fair, impartial, and accurate, we make no apologies for that.

Our editors, far from being "anonymous" as **Fisk** states, are well known to all **CNN** journalists. **Fisk** even identifies one by name. These talk to correspondents on an hourly basis to discuss scripts and reports and story developments. A healthy news organization does that.

He states that reports can not be edited until scripts are approved. This system is no different to the job sub-editors do on newspapers before publication; there is no mystery, conspiracy, or censorship involved.

Fisk also refers to new technology to justify his claims that **CNN** distorts the news; sadly the truth is less colorful than his claim. He is referring to an electronic template that helps us manage the enormous volume of news copy and retrieve library archive.

CNN reporters will not wear military uniform if war happens in Iraq as **Fisk** claims. They will wear protective clothing, helmets, and flak jackets, provided by **CNN**. We hope to save them from serious injury or worse. Finally he claims- and has claimed before – that Pentagon officials worked in the **CNN** newsroom during the 1991 Gulf War. Not true. During the 1999 Kosovo conflict an over- zealous human resources manager arranged for a small military internship at **CNN.** Interns have no editorial function and are there to observe. When editors at **CNN** discovered the program it was immediately ended.

Robert **Fisk** is a gifted commentator who enjoys the luxury of giving his opinion based on his views of the world. Journalists at **CNN** have a different mission, which is to report the world truthfully, impartially, and with fairness. **Fisk's** article would not have passed fact checking at "The Row."

On a more personal level, I met an Ann Rachel Marlow, a Harvard educated Jewish writer from New York. The beauty of this story lies behind that fact that almost a year ago I had randomly picked up and bought her only book off the dusty shelves of a second hand bookstore in Montreal-Canada. Today, by some weird twist of fate, we sat conversing on her views of this war, so far from politics. She was fascinated by the Iraqi culture, the sexual ambiguity of the Arab masses. Days later she emailed me an article with the subject title: Baghdad Nostalgia. And here's some of what she wrote:

At the Al-Hamra Pool I am a Babe Once More, And I Wanna Iraqi! by Ann Marlowe

I spent many evenings in Baghdad sitting around the pool of the Al-Hamra Hotel in a bikini. It was one of the Western oases in Baghdad, and at the white plastic tables foreign reporters drank cheap beer, gossiping and creating the viewpoint that magically becomes the consensus press stance in each war zone here, it was that the Americans were failing...I was not terribly interested. I was there because all I had to do was sit in my bikini, copying Arabic verb tables in the dim light, to feel again, thanks to the skewed gender ratio, the sexual power I had at 25. I had not expected this. The sex I had been thinking about when I arrived in Baghdad was between Iraqis. I was fascinated with an article that claimed as many as half of Iraqi marriages were between first or second cousins, and that this made democracy difficult.............................. At the Al-Hamra pool, I let cousin marriage alone and set about enjoying the flirtation in the air. The journos weren't the most intellectual bunch Anyways trying to trade books, I was offered John Grisham. But I was only looking for pleasure and consolation, and I had come to the right place. Most of the reporters were men who had been in Iraq for months, ever since they were embedded, and they missed female company. Mainly, they were a decent-looking lot, tan and slimmed down by the heat and Baghdad's indifferent restaurant food. Partly due to the strict 11 p.m. curfew, there was little social mingling between journalists and Iraqis......... Another was the chance to see the surprising contrast between what middle-class women wore inside and outside the home. The same university student who wears a long-sleeved tunic and long skirt in somber colors when she goes out changes to a low-cut blouse and short skirt as soon as she comes home. Matrons will walk around wearing shorts. And the young men of the house see nothing like this in the outside world. In Baghdad, I was more covered up than my hostesses, it felt odd. On the street, we foreign women wore long-sleeved shirts over pants or Ankle length skirts on the street. Just outside the Al-Hamra, most women wore headscarves and many wore abayas. Before I arrived, I had thought I might find the abaya suggestive of a secret eroticism............In the Shia'a shrine cities of Najaf and Kerbala. Aside from an obsession with plaid shirts, urban Iraqi men dressed pretty much like Americans. The journalists around the pool looked at me as if I were insane when I asked if they had dated Iraqis. And when I said I would like to, the prejudices came spilling out, a tribute to one of the last acceptable bigotries in American life: "Fat Arab men," "sexist Arab men" and so on. "Arab" may be a code for "Muslim"; when I mentioned that in New York I had dated two Muslim men, one young woman journalist from a grand American family blurted out that "Arab" men couldn't possibly have been fun in bed. If only she knew. Neither Muslim was an Arab. Each was astonishing in his own way; one I had adored. This prejudice suggests something tragically askew in the American understanding of Iraqis, for it is those you cannot imagine making love with that you won't admit to full humanity. Yet I had to admit that, until now, I had traveled in the Muslim world for decades without looking at the romantic possibilities.........But I began to think it more likely that veiling eroticizes the uncovered women you see in your home and leads to the desire to marry close relatives. As it turned out, I never did date an Iraqi. At the pool, I met a Californian tall, handsome, who lent me good books I read on the way back to New York. Ahmed Chalabi, for his part, has turned out to be more relevant than the journos guessed, with a spot on the governing council................Here in New York, I am working on my Arabic and planning to go back to Iraq in the fall. When I do, I suspect that the reporters at the Al-Hamra pool still Won't be socializing with Iraqis, much less finding romance with them.

11:00 pm. Understandably, my Iraqi girl friend's reaction to Ann Marlow's goals in Iraq was simply: "How can this woman think about sex when my people are dying all over Iraq?"

Saturday May 3, 2003

11:00 am. I finally got on a whim to conduct my own reporting on a story from Al Aathmya, Baghdad. My first freelance article for Aljazeera.net:

Tears of Survival

BAGHDAD— —Al Najat orphanage in Baghdad survived the famous looting spree in Iraq due to the wit of its director as she orchestrated a play pleading the armed looters for mercy. Aniba Jabar sat in her office explaining how she rounded up her precious orphans and instructed them to cry in front of the armed looters who were threatening to kill her. The plan did work since her orphanage remains untouched with its forty orphans running around with hopes of a better future without Saddam. However, now that Saddam is gone with his annual subsidy to the orphanage, Aniba asks, "Who is going to pay the annual one million dinars he donated to each orphan?" The ages of kids living in this two-floor orphanage range from one year olds to teenagers. Like many concerned Iraqis, Aniba is angry about the security issue and worries about sending her older orphans to school.

Most of the orphans harbored here were either abandoned or victims of the oppressive Baathi Regime, as their parents were executed by Saddam Hussein. The determined director reveals how she is willing to work all her life without pay just for the sake of these innocent kids. When asked to name two cases that touched her the most, Aniba asked not to open their scars with questions about their past. However, she recommended two sisters whom their parents were actually executed then later found not guilty for the charges brought against them. The two sisters were dropped at the orphanage by the Police.

Another heartbreaking story belongs to Areeg Abdullah, a crippled seventeen year old girl that was abandoned at a hospital entrance when she was only a year old. With no signs of her aunts or uncles, Areeg fought her agony alone escorted between hospitals trying to find a solution to her crippled body. Standing at a mere height of 133 cm, the strong orphan revealed how the Iraqi Red Crescent served their duty as she added, " They have operated once on my hands and feet back in 1995." Dr. Saad Hussein from the Red Crescent later informed Areeg that she would need one more operation, but when her bones grow more developed, about the time she graduates from high school. The truth remains that this one operation costs a bundle and that is the only reason why Areeg still suffers from a birth defect that holds her prisoner to her reality.

The kids were filled with joy as they enjoyed the toys given to them by the U.S. Agency for International Development. Joanne B. Giordano, deputy assistant administrator of public affairs at USAID explained how dozens of toys confiscated from Uday's (Saddam's eldest son) palace were now distributed to these beautiful kids. The kids loved Joanne and played with her long blonde hair. USAID also granted the orphanage suitable amounts of rice, soap, gas, and diapers.

Singling out the two sisters, Sanaa and Samia was an easy task, yet only four year old Sanaa was willing to talk since her wilder sister was too busy playing with her new remote controlled car. Sanaa smiled as she stated how she would like to be a doctor when she grows up. When asked if she was happy the Americans were here, she sighed and blushed as she squirted the word "Yes."

Young Areeg then joined the interview and added, "Are you going to ask me questions too?" Areeg wants to be a lawyer when she grows up because she likes articulate people. She also added that she is happy the Americans are here but would like to see more stability in her country. Not interested in the free toys, the romantic girl displayed her love for music; specifically Iraq's exiled musician, Kazem El Saher. With her crippled feet tucked under her chair, Areeg waived her twisted deformed hand and pleaded, "I have a wish; I want to do an operation to fix my hands and feet." Following the soldiers and reporters for their autographs and photos, young Areeg Abdullah limped towards one reporter and whispered, "Could you help me with my operation please?"

Monday May 19, 2003

In my last tour of duty in Iraq I was privileged to work with journalist Warren Vieth. Calm and cool to his surroundings, you could hardly piss him off if you tried. A drummer back in his college days, Warren appreciated my new set of tapes for this trip. Mark Fineman handed me over to Warren days after our arrival to Kuwait. On our drive back to Kuwait, we took back embedded journalists Eric Slater and Rick Loomis. At the border check, our Iraqi money was confiscated, but not the bills we hid in our shoes for souvenirs.

Warren's style of reporting was totally different than anyone I worked with. He made a list of prospect stories, those revolving around banks, airlines, farms, currency, oil production, or education for example. As his writing progressed, he would bless me with parts of his story then continue on with his day working on something completely different. A previous editor at the *Times*, he tailored his stories with caution, before landing them on the front pages of the paper.

I escorted Warren to Saddam's Republican palace on our first day in Baghdad. At the palace Joanne B. Giordano with USAID greeted us with her usual smile, before giving us another longer tour of the palace. By now I was getting deeper into photography as I snapped some photos of Saddam's living room. The spacious room had been reorganized hosting a cafeteria for the Americans living in the palace. Its artistic ceiling remained the same portraying a painting of the Al Aqsa mosque of Palestine, surrounded by four Arabian horses and inscriptions of Islamic verses; all framed with a set of golden chandeliers.

We both posed for a photo with a wilder wall size mural, portraying seven huge rockets covered with the words *Allah'ukbar* (God is the greatest), penetrating the cloudy blue sky, heading towards space. Once again, Saddam's tacky style let alone his understanding of God shocked me. In another hall, 99 blue cubes hung from the high ceiling bearing the 99 names of *Allah*, artistically inscribed in the wavy Arabic text typical of Islamic calligraphy. On the way out, Joanne showed us her trailer, among dozens more parked across the huge garden, equipped with beds, closets, and split unit air-conditions. Officials now living in the palace also enjoyed Saddam's outdoor pool along with the freedom of jogging around the premises of the base.

After setting appointments for a number of interviews regarding Warren's stories, we learned that the Coalition Provisional Authority (CPA) formerly known as ORHA was now getting their laundry done in Kuwait and delivered back to Iraq.

Researching his economy story, we went shopping at a local supermarket. After we bought bags of various products like tuna, crackers, juice, pop, and soap the owner refused to take American dollars, due to the unpredictable fluctuation of the exchange rate. On the drive back, I spotted a black and white poster of Arnold Schawarzenegger hung outside the entrance of an old building in the Karada area. This gym had gone noticed until the owner actually hung Arnold's photo outside. "To Americans the membership is $5 to Iraqis they have to pay $10," replied the gym owner about the membership fees. Inside his office the owner complained about Saddam of course. He was accused by the Ba'ath of conducting business with the enemy. His only crime was a subscription to Joe Weider's Muscle & Fitness magazine. Staff photographer Carolyn Cole, joined us after we called her. She went around the gym documenting the old beaten dumbbells. "Tell him Arnold is running for governor," Warren said, as we left the man's office.

"He will win!" the bulky man shouted, using the little English he picked up from muscle magazines.

Back at the Hamra, I shared suite 706 with Times writer John Hendren. A dedicated writer with a 'no fear' attitude, John was upset he had to cover the war from the private rooms of the Pentagon rather than living it on the ground in Iraq. He arrived from Jordan with a box of cigars. "They make good gifts, if you know what I mean," he replied, when I asked why he had boxes of Cubans.

ANOTHER DAY IN BAGHDAD: MAY 2003

Today, I met staff writer Bob Drogin. His mission in Iraq is to report on the weapons of mass destruction; the announced motive behind this war. He had been following the U.N. search for the weapons months before the war. On the ground in Iraq, Mr. Bob Drogin followed every thread of clues on the subject, including the CIA's involvement in the matter. After a five-day desert trip with the military, he stormed into my room drunk in the middle of the night yelling, "They have nothing! They don't even know what they're looking for!!"

My favorite groups of professionals in Iraq are those enlisted with humanitarian organizations fighting global poverty. Dealing with employees of organizations like *Save The Children* or *CARE*, I realized the extent of the whole purpose of these kinds of organizations and it moved me. On a brief encounter with Margret Hassan, CARE director who has lived in Iraq for thirty years, I was shocked to learn that locals who were previously hired on a monthly basis to run the operation had not been paid in months. Yet, they still worked hard to reach their ultimate goal: To benefit Iraqis. Her updates were straight:

"In a situation like this, everything is priority. Electricity is sporadic. The security situation is unstable. Prices of goods are going up. Diarrhoea is on the rise. Food is running out. Water is not safe to drink. Repairs to generators are being repeated over and over again."

"What about the hospitals?" I asked her quickly in the lobby of the Hamra.

"You cannot run a hospital, or a country, on backup generators because they are just that; backup."

Indeed, word in Baghdad is that doctors are reporting deaths due to lack of oxygen in hospitals.

On a lighter note, I had met a literally funny NGO, outside an orphanage days ago. *Clowns Without Borders* were the topic of my second freelance article to Aljazeera.net:

CLOWNS WITHOUT BORDERS: HUMANITARIAN AID FROM THE ARTS

Baghdad———Clowns without borders are now roaming around Baghdad's hospitals, orphanages, schools, and refugee camps, trying to calm society and improve the psychological situation of the population. It's an NGO born on the 26th of February 1993, as the consequence of need was expressed at the refugee camp of Veli Joze (Savudrija) in Croatia. The five clowns blessing Baghdad with their sense of humor identified themselves as Maxmilliano Stia, Jose Asako, Walter Garibotto, Pepe Vivuela, and Negro Casali. On May 1st of this year they were busy performing at Circus Cric in Barcelona, trying to raise money for their short expedition in Iraq. Busy all year round, CWB perform regularly at Guatemala, Nicaragua, and Salvador. Their objective is to raise the morale of kids in living situations of post-conflict, social exclusion, or those affected by natural disasters. Their efforts were highly appreciated in Salvador in February 2001; right after the earthquake shook the country apart. After spending twelve days, earlier this year in the Palestinian cities of Jenin, Ram Allah, and Gaza, they have appreciated the Arabian hospitality.

Negro Casali, who is been a clown for five years, enjoys using laughter and humor as therapeutic resources for healing displaced kids. Off-duty without his red nose, he added, "In Europe, kids have a lot of toys, I saw a bigger smile on the faces of kids in Palestine, Iraq, and Africa." Almost two weeks in Iraq, they have already performed in Al Kathmiyah Teaching Hospital, Al Karkh Hospital, Al Najat Orphanage, and Al Mansour Teaching Hospital. Their live show usually lasts for a good hour, yet here in Iraq they have gone performing for three and half hours at hospitals; in the rooms, hallways, and outside in the street. Their performance usually revolves around juggling, acrobats, puppets, and cheerful facial expressions. Their preferential beneficiaries are aimed at kids between 4 and 12 years of age. Unlike Europe, performing in the streets of Iraq proved strenuous as Negro clarified: "When we try to work in the streets of Iraq, it's difficult because the kids jump on us and we have no space to perform."

With his broken English and a Spanish-English dictionary in his hand, clown Pepe Vivuela drew a smile on his face and added, *"Laughing is international language, it is shorter road."* With straight faces, the clowns explained how doctors are usually skeptical about their work until they actually see the reaction of the kids. Dr. Hussein Turkey from Al Mansour Teaching Hospital in Baghdad paid the clowns a visit at their hotel and invited them to perform in his hospital after he heard of their success at Al Kathmiyah Teaching Hospital. CWB aspire to merge with other organizations in the near future. They have already worked along side with Doctors Without Borders in several projects.

"Not only food is necessary to treat malnutrition, jokes and plays are important too, so we are working hard," said Negro, as he literally drew a smile with his finger across his face. CWB have also worked briefly this year in Angola, and last year in Mali as they collaborated with the French aid agency, Action Contra Famine.

In Spain, their homeland, CWB have performed at centers for the mentally impeded patients. With an army of 70 clowns, actors, and puppeteers performing across the globe, CWB employ only artists and educators who serve as examples of hope, positivism, and with a sense of humor. They must be willing to work for a fairer and more solid society.

In San Francisco, clown Moshe Cohen organized another CWB branch. "The world is big; it's not possible to perform everywhere," Negro added as he prepared his clown outfit.

On the reconstruction of Iraq, Negro responded, "I think it will take a long time, reconstruction of cities is possible, but people are more difficult." Clowns Without Borders makes its resources available by providing live arts for social education. "We would like to provide workshops for talented Iraqi people, to reproduce here, and teach them to be clowns," Negro said.

ANOTHER DAY IN BAGHDAD: JUNE 2003

With the rise of U.S. causalities on the hands of unknown resistance, the mood in Iraq remained somber. My positivism had also diminished with the news that a U.S. helicopter had been shot down in the town of Heat. With the toll of attacks rising in the town of Fallujah, I was glad to be reporting away from dailies. My days of Kevlar bulletproof vests were over.

That night, the Times crew relaxed at a Chinese restaurant. The farewell party for Tyler Marshall and John Hendren entailed all the norms of any party elsewhere, with drinks, chicken noodles, and even a chocolate cake. Amidst the dining and wine, our driver Ziad called with news that he just saw an American humvee explode at the Mansour upper-class district. In a flash, I joined writer John Daniszewski and photographer Carolyn Cole for a speedy night ride towards the scene of the attack. The humvee had been already removed, yet the soldier's blood tainted the black asphalt. The army had closed up the perimeter searching for the man who threw the hand grenade at the moving convoy. There were no victims due to the soldier's quick reaction. He had noticed that a grenade had bounced into his humvee and was able to jump out, ejecting away from the loud explosion. As we interviewed the bystanders, John and I realized they were all saying the same thing. Their main concern was the lack of security, and they were all hinting that the future would be grim; full of such sporadic attacks. With U.S. soldiers dying daily, is this war over?

The question is; will apprehending or killing Saddam Hussein stop these attacks? The crystal ball remains in the hand of Georges Bush's Presidential Envoy, L. Paul Bremer III. He had served as an Ambassador at Large for Counter- Terrorism under the Regan administration along with an eleven-year stint with Kissinger & Associates. When he replaced the "cowboy" Lt. General Jay Garner in Iraq everyone welcomed this "can-do-type of person." Bremer (Jerry) has consistently advocated a 'get-tough' stance towards terrorists. In an August 5, 1996, Wall Street Journal opinion piece titled "Terrorists' Friends Must Pay a Price" Bremer called on the Clinton administration to "get serious about the fight against terrorism."

Bremer advised Clinton to deliver ultimatums to Libya, Syria, Iran, and Sudan telling them to close down terrorist bases or they will "receive the full weight of American might." Ironically, Iraq was not mentioned in the piece. After the September attacks on the World Trade Center and the Pentagon, Bremer wrote: "Our retribution must move beyond the limp-wristed attacks of the past decade, actions that seemed designed to "signal" our seriousness to the terrorists without inflicting real damage. Naturally, their feebleness demonstrated the opposite. This time, the terrorists and their supporters must be crushed. But," he added, "We must avoid a mindless search for an international 'consensus' for our actions. Tomorrow, we will know who our true friends are."

As an interpreter in this war I know that people in Iraq want to live by each other's happiness and not misery. The country is so big. There is room for everyone in its rich land.

To the religious men of this country, I beg them to remember that the kingdom of God is in man, all men, a pathway to "universal brother hood." The power Saddam took from the people will return.

To the insurgents killing soldiers, I warn you of giving yourselves to brutes, men who despise you and slave you, tell you what to do, what to think and what to feel. You are men; do not follow that unnatural man; Saddam. He fears the way of human progress. The natural way of life can be a beautiful adventure.

To the American people, I say don't let speed and machinery shut you in. Don't let knowledge turn into cynical views. Spread kindness and gentleness with your clever minds. In the name of democracy, let the world share your power.

To the twenty-one journalists who died in this war, I salute them for their humble voice, that of the voiceless people of Iraq. To Mr. Mark Fineman, May Your Soul Rest In Peace.

Saddam Photo Album

Acknowledgements

My thanks are due, first and foremost, to Hala, for her love and support and frontline editing. Then to Dooly and Narcy for their real help and Hussein and Ghada, for being there. If it was not for Khaled Al-Khuder, this book would not be here. Thanks also to Mohamed Arrawi for all his help in Iraq. Also, to Mark Sykes for his inspiration. Thanks to the late Mark Fineman for saving my life. Adele Smout saved the day.

My sincere gratitude to Mark Magnier. Thanks too, to Brian Walski and Don Bartletti for letting me use their extraordinary photos.

This book could never have been completed as fast as it was without the hospitality and support of Wafaa Bassiouni and Fadel Fahmy.

About the Author

"Mohamed Fahmy was born in Kuwait and holds a dual Egyptian-Canadian citizenship. He graduated with a B.A. in Marketing from City University in Vancouver, Canada. Since then he has worked between Canada and the Gulf and writes poetry and short stories in his free time. After obtaining a TESOL certificate, he sometimes teaches English to beginners. He currently resides in the Gulf and fulfills his passion for traveling and adventure by working on a film about the IRAQ WAR."

He maintains a website at baghdadbound.com
or www.trafford.com/robots/03-2289.html

CPSIA information can be obtained
at www.ICGtesting.com
Printed in the USA
JSHW012244301122
34152JS00001B/70